Discovering Musicals

Discovering Musicals

A Liberal Arts Guide
to Stage and Screen

Marc Raymond Strauss

Foreword by Christine Pedi

McFarland & Company, Inc., Publishers
Jefferson, North Carolina

ISBN (print) 978-1-4766-7450-6 ∞
ISBN (ebook) 978-1-4766-3632-0

Library of Congress and British Library
Cataloguing data are available

Library of Congress Control Number: 2019942894

Front cover image: Gene Kelly in *Singin' in the Rain*,
1952 (MGM/Photofest)

Printed in the United States of America

*McFarland & Company, Inc., Publishers
Box 611, Jefferson, North Carolina 28640
www.mcfarlandpub.com*

To all lovers of musicals who haven't made
it to live shows yet … but are saving up.

Acknowledgments

To my parents—Ann Louise Dalmas Strauss Berk (March 24, 1933–April 2, 2000) and Guy Armand Jacques Strauss (October 2, 1930–February 18, 2014)—for taking my brother and me along in the back seat of their fifties Ford to see the film version of *South Pacific* at the Wellfleet Drive-In when I was not yet five years old. Little did they know...

Table of Contents

Introduction

If a book, or an article, or a college course, or a YouTube video has the word "history" in it, such as, say, "The History of the Great Depression," or "World War II History," or even "A History of the Musical," how might many of us react, do you think? I would venture to say that most of us would give a little shudder and say, "Ugh, history. Lots of dead people we can't possibly care about." I hate to say it but, in our 21st-century world of micro-second Tweets, Facebook, and Instagram posts, that answer is, sadly, accurate. To bring past times to life, even the relatively recent, requires active and conscious and continuous concentration and imagination on our parts because, let's face it, most of what matters to us right now is *right now*: tonight's rehearsal, our shortly planned (or spontaneous) lunch or dinner, what we're going to wear at the party after dinner with that cute guy or girl—that sort of thing.

And you would be right: Most of the shows discussed in this book, pulled from out of a past dating from the mid–19th century, are in fact nearly incomprehensible to us, particularly when viewed through our contemporary eyes and perception skills. In today's world, we have been trained to look for and expect many things that those early shows couldn't possibly have achieved—three-dimensional light projections or rhythmically dense tap dancing, to name just two—and so we automatically contrast the sophistication of *what we know now* against what those (generally simpler) worlds might have been like.

Still, even with our current jaded eyes and ears, we must be able to admit that the circumstances surrounding the making of those earlier shows in that particular time and place in American, even world, history, were most assuredly fascinating *for those people in their particular time and place.* In other words, if we were alive back then, those events would have been *our* events, that time would have been *our* time, and whatever happened then would have interested *us* then. Ergo, if we can today in our time at least *approximate* what those experiences were like back then, when those musical

5

shows and films first occurred, our imaginings should help us better understand *today's* achievements in the genre and provide a richer and more meaningful context for our *current* shows and films.

In this book, I have determined to provide just that. One way I've tried to facilitate our current understanding of the past contexts of these musicals is by presenting most discussions *in the present tense*, as if those shows were just opening this week—which they were, of course, back then—sort of an as-if-you-were-there experience. Wouldn't that be fun, actually, to time travel to all the openings of these shows?

In fact, in addition to speaking about these musicals, both onscreen and onstage, as if they were arriving into our world now, I've chosen to always note the exact date of the musical opening on Broadway or in Hollywood. Why? Those musicals that do in fact make it to Broadway and onto film often take years, sometimes *decades*, to reach that point—if they ever do—and by identifying the specific day of the year when a musical actually opens, it may help give the reader a better sense of just how special that event must have been. The dates are also important historical markers, and I believe we owe the living memory of these musicals that kind of acknowledgment—nay, recognition. Besides, a good liberal arts education should include a proper, accurate sense of chronology, I think.

In today's culture, one of the best ways to present such material is through video and audio examples, often via YouTube, digital video disc (DVD), or compact disc (CD), with accompanying description and interpretation of a particular song and/or dance from that show or film during its first, and subsequent, runs (and revivals). Even a song or dance from a show or film that is performed by a crooner or dancer on his or her own—such as a famous celebrity like Frank Sinatra or Ella Fitzgerald or Bob Fosse, who bring their own connective relationships, perhaps years later, to the value of a particular number from a show or film—can provide the reader with useful insights into the original. You will find Sinatra's and Fitzgerald's and Fosse's "takes" on myriad show tunes and numbers throughout these pages—and many other performers' interpretations, both from within the show and outside of the show's immediate cultural and historical context. Again, such an approach is intended to broaden the liberal arts reader's knowledge, understanding *and* interest.

Quite rightly, many of the research specifics that support this book's approach originate in a variety of expert books on the subject:

New York–based theatre historian Ken Bloom and theatre-television actor Frank Vlastnik's exhaustive 2004 hardcover edition (and their 2008 revised paperback edition) *Broadway Musicals: The 101 Greatest Shows of All Time* is one such tome. The authors literally fill their pages with endlessly fascinating details about performers, hit shows, scenic designers, directors, choreographers, and even flops. Likewise, 2004's *Broadway: The American Musical*, and accompanying six-part PBS television series and six-CD supplement, authored by director/producer/writer Michael Kantor and Tisch School of the Arts professor Laurence Maslon, are equally invaluable.

The 2014 eighth edition (and counting) of musical theatre and film historian Stanley Green's seminal 1985 *Broadway Musicals, Show by Show* (the 8th edition is revised and updated by music historian Cary Ginell) has also proved essential and remains a concise, fact-packed, and genuinely fun read. *Musicals: The Definitive Illustrated Story* (2015), *The Book of Broadway: The 150 Definitive Plays and Musicals* (2015) by arts and theatre journalist Eric Grode, and especially musical historian Ted Sennett's 2001 *Song and Dance: The Musicals of Broadway*, which has an accompanying three-CD supplement of seminal songs, are other must-have books.

There are literally dozens more similarly titled books that intelligently and insightfully sing the art form's praises. Ken Bloom's 2005 *The American Songbook: The Singers, the Songwriters, and the Songs* focuses on many tunes and their interpretations that started life in musicals, and *New York Times* theatre critic Ben Brantley's 2012 *Broadway Musicals from the Pages of the New York Times* is straight from the newspaper's own reviews.

On the film musical side, cinema researcher Richard Barrios's 1995 *A Song in the Dark: The Birth of the Musical Film* has many riches to recommend it, as do professor of cinema and comparative literature Rick Altman's 1987 *The American Film Musical*, producer and president of DRG Records Hugh Fordin's 1996 *MGM's Greatest Musicals: The Arthur Freed Unit*, and MGM executive Darcie Denkert's 2005 *A Fine Romance: Hollywood/Broadway*, the latter a fascinating investigation into what happens when transferring a Broadway show to Hollywood. Over the years, each of the major movie studios has compiled detailed information and basic descriptions, with one photo per film, on all of their musicals into book formats. These include RKO, Warner Brothers, MGM, 20th Century–Fox, Universal, and Columbia, alongside film and theatre critic Clive Hirschhorn's excellent 1981 overview of all of the studios in *The Hollywood Musical*.

Still, for the average film or Broadway musical aficionado—someone who knows *some* songs or dances or directors or choreographers or performers but can't quite place them, and someone who wants not an exhaustive analysis but a bit more insight and clarification of some particulars, someone very much a *liberal arts student*—this book is for you.

Three main approaches are used to help us achieve such comprehension:

We begin by exploring a few of the ancient dramatic forms of theatre, some pre- and post-Renaissance influences, and a full 20 of the most important 19th- and early 20th-century precursors to today's musicals. Not surprisingly, contemporary versions of these distant productions exist—everything old is new again—and we look at many of them. For example, did you know that composer-lyricist Stephen Sondheim's (b. 1930) first big hit with both his music *and* lyrics—the 1962 Broadway show *A Funny Thing Happened on the Way to the Forum*—was adapted directly from a number of farcical plays written nearly 2000 years ago by the Roman playwright Titus Maccius Plautus (c. 254–184 BCE)? Similarly, we will look at what is happening now, in the 21st century, at what is onstage and in film today that will undoubtedly contribute to musicals next season, the rest of this decade, and into the 2020s.

Through the use of the extensive CD and DVD and YouTube audio and video references liberally sprinkled throughout this book—with the title of the video noted immediately after an asterisk (*) for quick and easy reference—we can look at, listen to, and analyze as many excerpts of these musical productions as possible. The numbers are from the actual shows, filmed versions of those shows (however different they might be from the originals), and examples of those early precursors as recorded on film and CD.

Finally, and obviously, we study many of the most important people and places in the musical theatre and film musical business: directors, producers, the theatres themselves, performers (actors, dancers, singers), composers, lyricists, book writers (librettists, screenwriters), choreographers, the art, costume, lighting and sound designers (a Tony Award for Sound Design was finally added in 2006), and all of these talents within the context of their time and place.

Caveats: For every musical that *is* mentioned and discussed, there are an average of four to six times as many that *are not* included. The primary reason is space restrictions. If all the musicals that came out in the world and in film were included in this book, well it wouldn't be one book, it would be several dozen. Another limitation I set was that the show had to open on Broadway—not Off Broadway, not Off Off Broadway, and not opening in another city or three but never reaching Broadway. The show had to have opened on Broadway, even if it was for just three nights before closing (see *Carrie*, 1988).

The occasional Off Broadway show discussed in this book is each a special case. *The Fantasticks* and *Nunsense*, for example, have had runs for years and years, with songs that have embedded themselves into the cultural zeitgeist. But if a show *does* make it to Broadway, that's quite an accomplishment, because for every musical that does make it, there are dozens that don't (and most people have never heard of them, regardless of their quality).

For example, 2010 is represented in the book by eight musicals of some note that opened that year on Broadway—*The Addams Family* (April 8), *Million Dollar Quartet* (April 11), *American Idiot* (April 20), *Sondheim by Sondheim* (April 22), *Everyday Rapture* (April 29), *Bloody Bloody Andrew Jackson*

(October 13), *The Scottsboro Boys* (October 31), and *Women on the Verge of a Nervous Breakdown* (November 4). These shows provide a cross section of both the "popular" and "artistic," terms that are not necessarily mutually exclusive. Nevertheless, according to the website Wikipedia and "Category: Musicals by Year," which lists musicals since the year 1855 beginning with the one "musical" reported then, *Po-ca-hon-tas, or the Gentle Savage*, a "two-act musical burlesque," the year 2010 actually included 39 musicals that opened. Why are only 8 of those 39 discussed in this book?

Again, space restrictions and the fact that most of them did not open on Broadway (or in Hollywood) remain the primary reasons. Alphabetically, after *Addams Family* and *American Idiot, Badjelly's Bad Christmas*, for example, a play based on the works of British-Irish comedian Spike Milligan (1918–2002), with interpolated songs and sign language, opened in London's Chickenshed Theatre Company. While on paper the show looks pretty interesting, it never crossed the Big Pond (the Atlantic Ocean), and so it's not included. *Beyond Eden*, a musical inspired by real-life British Columbia provincial museum curator of anthropology Wilson Duff (1925–1976), opened in Calgary, Alberta, Canada. It, too, looks fascinating but never made it south of the border. *A Christmas Memory*, based on writer Truman Capote's (1924–1984) 1956 short story, had its world premiere in Palo Alto, California, in 2010, moved to Chicago in early 2014, and then arrived on Off broadway later that year. But that's as far as it got. Again, it is only mentioned here as an example. And on through the *z*'s: *Zangoora—The Gypsy Prince*, with a cast of 110 and crew of 250, was the first Bollywood (Hindi cinema) musical. It opened on September 23, 2010, in Gurgaon, India, and was a huge hit in India.

As another example, the Wikipedia website lists eight musicals in 1921, of which this book includes five—*Tangerine, Two Little Girls in Blue, The Music Box Revue, Bombo*, and *Shuffle Along*. And so on. That list may not be *the* definitive list, but it does give the reader a feel for the numbers and range of Broadway musicals that opened in any given year.

Insufficient information on the web and in books is another reason a show or film may not have made it into this book, particularly in productions from the 1920s and earlier. For example, even though the 1923 musical comedy *Mary Jane McKane* had a libretto and lyrics by Oscar Hammerstein (among others), there just isn't that much information available to give a reader any more than a brief factual account of that show. Same with *Dew Drop Inn*, also from 1923.

But, to get to the heart of the matter: How *does* someone pick a musical from a particular year to share in a book of this size and focus? All books are written by people (so far), and so even if the writer wanted to be as objective as possible, the writing of the book by definition involves subjective preferences.

Those subjective decisions of whittling down *x* number of shows and films out of the thousands created over, say, 125 years in the history of Broadway and Hollywood musicals are perhaps slightly comparable to the decisions a director must make on his or her show when hiring *that* particular singer for her particular sound or voice quality, or using *this* particular rhythm for *that* specific dance style, or choosing *that* exact lighting design for *this* particular scene in *that* particular Broadway show or Hollywood film or its revival or sequel. It's a complex answer, certainly.

Suffice it to say that I have chosen for inclusion many if not most of the big and important shows and films over that century plus of time. (If the gods are kind, and I have a chance to expand this book with a future edition, gentle reader, do please write to me with a show or film title that you believe should be included next time and why.) I've also chosen as many shows and films as room permits that include at least one important song or dance or number that *significantly* adds or contributes to the musical art form in some intriguing way. For example, while the 1939 Rodgers and Hart Broadway musical *Too Many Girls* is hardly as familiar or famous in both song and dance innovation as their 1936 show *On Your Toes*, *Girls* does have two excellent oft-overlooked tunes in "I Like to Recognize the Tune" and "I Didn't Know What Time It Was," both rendered by Mary Jane Walsh and Barbara Cook in subsequent recordings. The numbers burnish and augment, I hope, the Rodgers and Hart canon, and the show is discussed herein.

Likewise, Hollywood's *At the Circus* (October 20, 1939) from the same year, may have been primarily another chance to watch the Marx Brothers at their zany, anarchic best, but how many people know it housed another fine Arlen and Harburg tune in the same vein as their work earlier that year for *The Wizard of Oz*? Groucho Marx and ensemble make riotous work of "Lydia the Tattooed Lady"—aficionados, I suspect, already knew I'd be mentioning that song—while later, as an extra bonus, Harpo whales away on harp to Rodgers and Hart's 1934 "Blue Moon," a surprising treat.

Anyway, I wish you as much pleasure reading this book as I had putting it together.

ONE

Ancient Greece through the Mid–19th Century

An asterisk before a title indicates a YouTube video

The art of telling stories, either through or with songs and other means, dates back at least as far as the ancient Greeks, who included music and dance in their stage comedies and tragedies as early as the fifth century BCE (before the common era). While some Athenian playwrights may have interpolated existing songs of the time, authors such as Aeschylus (c. 525–456 BCE), Sophocles (496–406 BCE), and Euripides (c. 480–406 BCE) apparently composed their own tunes for such plays as *The Oresteia* (458 BCE), *Oedipus the King* (c. 429 BCE), and *The Trojan Women* (c. 415 BCE) respectively. Staged in open air amphitheaters, these plays featured sexual humor, political and social satire, juggling, and anything else that might entertain the masses. The songs were often a means for the chorus to comment on the action, but they also took part in the plot, and musical solos were not unheard of.

As we shall see, similar unique elements continue to this day in contemporary musicals such as in the sexual farce *La Cage aux Folles* (1983), the political and social satire of *The Book of Mormon* (2011), juggling in *Barnum* (1980), and chorus-filled shows such as *A Chorus Line* (1975) and *Spider-Man: Turn Off the Dark* (2011) (John Kenrick; "Musicals 101"; http://www.musicals 101.com/musical.htm; retrieved March 23, 2015).

Aristophanes (c. 446–388 BCE) was a comic dramatist who wrote forty plays, eleven of which survive. Many satirized well-known citizens of Athens and their conduct during the Peloponnesian War (431–404 BCE) between Athens and Sparta. *Lysistrata* (411 BCE), written during that war, argues not so much for pacifism as for the idea that states ought not fight one another but combine to rule Greece as one country. In the play, this is accomplished when the women of the two states show off their bodies and deprive their husbands of sex until they stop fighting ("Aristophanes"; http://www.crys-

11

talinks.com/aristophanes.html; retrieved March 29, 2015). Contemporary director/choreographer Dan Knechtges (pronounced connect-us; birthdate unknown) worked on the 2011 Broadway adaptation, *Lysistrata Jones*, about a fictional Athens University basketball team that was denied sex until it won a game (see *Lysistrata Jones on Broadway: Trailer).

Aristophanes's *Frogs* (405 BCE) tells the story of the god Dionysus who, despairing of the state of Athens' current tragedians, travels to Hades and brings Euripides back from the dead to save theatre. To engage the audience, the first scene consists of a battle of potty humor jokes. In 1974, *The Frogs* was turned into a musical by Stephen Sondheim; in his version, George Bernard Shaw and William Shakespeare battle it out for best playwright. Originally performed in the Yale University gym pool with Meryl Streep (b. 1949), Sigourney Weaver (b. 1949) and Christopher Durang (b. 1949) in the ensemble, an expanded version opened on Broadway in 2004 starring Nathan Lane (b. 1956; *The Producers*, *The Addams Family*) and directed/choreographed by Susan Stroman (b. 1954; *Crazy for You*, *Big*); see *Sondheim at 80 The Frogs Invocation to the Audience.

Today, shows such as the animated television series *South Park* (1997–) use not only social satire but a lot of toilet humor, such as a talking poo called Mr. Hankey. Of course, in their 1999 film *South Park: Bigger, Longer & Uncut*, Trey Parker (b. 1969) and Matt Stone (b. 1971), with additional music and lyrics by Marc Shaiman (b. 1959), continued the timeless popularity of baseness in songs such as "Mountain Town" (see *Mountain Town Song, South Park), one of the film's "milder" tunes. Similar crudeness in the Old Attic Comedy tradition can be found in Parker and Stone's 2004 film *Team America: World Police*, their uber-popular Broadway hit *The Book of Mormon* (2011), and with input from Robert Lopez (b. 1975), the previous decade's *Avenue Q* (2003).

Aristophanes's plays were notable for their political and societal commentary, usually in the form of satire and parody. Old Attic Comedy was extremely conscious of the world in which it functioned, and it accurately, even bitingly, analyzed that world. Comedic theatre was, in fact, the dramatic editorial of its time—the public conscience. Three still potent 20th- and 21st-century variations of Old Attic Comedy include the following:

- *As Thousands Cheer*, a 1933 musical revue with music and lyrics by Irving Berlin (1888–1989). It boasts the scathing "Supper Time," sung by a woman waiting for a husband who never returns home for dinner because he's been lynched. The blues, jazz and gospel singer-actress Ethel Waters (1896–1977) performed it in the original production, reprising it on television during a 1969 performance at the Hollywood Palace (hosted by Diana Ross; b. 1944) at *Ethel Waters Suppertime.
- *1776*, composer/lyricist Sherman Edwards's (1919–1981) 1969 Broadway

show, was made into a film in 1972. "Cool, Cool Considerate Men," at *Cool Cool Considerate Men, was censored out of the movie version by President Richard Nixon (1913–1994) for its incisive portrayal of arch-conservative Republicans of the time. It was eventually restored.

- *Hairspray*, in the July 2007 film version, with music and lyrics by Marc Shaiman (b. 1959) and Scott Wittman (b. 1955), contrasted its generally high-spirited tone with the anti-segregationist song "I Know Where I've Been," sung by Queen Latifah (née Dana Elaine Owens; b. 1970) at *I Know Where I've Been.

The Romans copied and expanded the forms and traditions of Greek theatre, especially in the third century BCE. In the comedies of Plautus (c. 254–184 BCE), song-and-dance routines were performed with full orchestrations. To make the dance steps more audible in large open air theatres, Roman actors attached metal chips called *sabilla* to their stage footwear—clear precursors to tap shoes. A stress on spectacle and special effects, echoes in our own time with circuses like Cirque du Soleil (formed 1984), and shows such as the 2006 show *Love*, based on the Beatles' music.

Titus Maccius Plautus attained such popularity that just his name was a guarantee of theatrical success. Plautus's comedies, which are among the earliest surviving, intact works in Latin literature, are mostly adaptations of Greek models for a Roman audience. Among his 21 extant works are full-length plays such as *Pseudolus*, *Miles Gloriosus*, *Bacchides*, and *Menaechmi*.

His humor, which became known as Greek New Comedy, differed from Old Attic Comedy in that it was "devoid of any serious political, social or intellectual content" and "could be performed in any number of social and political settings without risk of giving offense" (Sutton, 1993, p. 14). The stories, too, have much more of a focus on the home and the family rather than social or political situations, and are thus less believable than the plays of Aristophanes. They were meant to entertain the audience by means of unlikely situations, disguises and mistaken identity, verbal humor that included puns and sexual innuendo, and a fast-paced plot whose speed increased as the play progressed, usually ending in an elaborate chase scene. Broad deliberately absurd physical humor was also common in the farces of Plautus.

Popular examples of farce, with their origin in Plautus's plays, include:

- William Shakespeare's (1564–1616) *The Comedy of Errors* (c. 1592);
- Molière's (né Jean-Baptiste Poquelin; 1622–1673) *Tartuffe* (1664);
- Oscar Wilde's (1854–1900) *The Importance of Being Earnest* (1895);
- Jean Poiret's (1926–1992) play *La Cage aux Folles* (1973), with its accompanying 1978 film and 1983 Broadway musical;
- Michael Frayn's (b. 1933) Broadway production of *Noises Off* (1982).

Word play was essential to Plautus's comedy. Alliteration and parono-
masia (puns) were rampant in his work, particularly with the character of a
clever slave who not only provided exposition and humor but often explained
(and drove) the plot. In the Roman theatre, actors were thrust into much
closer audience interaction than with the Greeks, recapitulated in the relative
intimacy of late 19th- and early 20th-century Vaudeville in the United States
and the Music Halls of England and France. Being closer, ancient Roman
audiences would have wanted, even required, direct attention and acknowledgment from the actors, and so the breaking of the fourth wall—the imaginary line between audience and performer—occurred with greater frequency.

There are many instances of this crossing of the imaginary line in contemporary musicals. Here are just two:

- The 1968 Broadway production of *Hair* (1979 film) had the performers
  interact at numerous times with the audience out among the theatre
  seats. During the 2009 revival, the title song performed during the
  2010 Tony Awards had the performers literally shaking their dancing
  pelvises on the arm chairs above audience members at *Hair—Tony
  Awards 2009;
- During several sections of *The 25th Annual Putnam County Spelling
  Bee* (2005), and to this day during touring productions, audience
  members were invited up on stage to compete in part of the spelling
  competition; see *Spelling Bee and Audience Participation.

Because humor, vulgarity and "incongruity" were so much a part of Plau-
tine comedies, the slave became the essential tool to connect the audience
more closely to the show through his monologues, the imperative mood, and
his use of alliteration and puns. The imperative mood was used in the role-
reversal of the normal relationship between slave and master, and "those who
enjoy authority and respect in the ordinary Roman world are unseated and
ridiculed, while the lowliest members of society mount to their pedestals. The
humble are, in fact, exalted" ("Plautus"; https://en.wikipedia.org/wiki/Plau-
tus#Farce; retrieved July 23, 2016).

A Funny Thing Happened on the Way to the Forum (1962 Broadway),
with music and lyrics by Stephen Sondheim (*West Side Story, Gypsy*), is based
on many of Plautus's farces, and tells the story of a slave named Pseudolus
and his attempts to win his freedom by encouraging a romance between his
master's son Hero and a young virgin named Philia, owned by Marcus Lycus,
a dealer in courtesans. The humor is broad, bawdy, and fast-paced, and
includes a fair amount of slapstick, not all that different from the antics of
the Three Stooges (1922–1970; see *The Three Stooges, 1936, Ants in the
Pantry). The opening number, "Comedy Tonight," from the 1966 film version,
gives one a sense of that madcap humor, particularly in the fast-cut edits of

director Richard Lester (b. 1932), clever lyrical wordplay by Sondheim, and straight-to-the-camera entreaties of comedian Zero Mostel (né Samuel Joel Mostel; 1915–1977); see *Comedy Tonight Funny Thing.

By the time of the Middle Ages (c. 476–1450), Europe's theatrical world included traveling minstrels and roving troupes of performers that offered popular songs and slapstick comedy. In the 12th and 13th centuries, there also developed a tradition of religious dramas. Some of these works have survived, such as *The Play of Herod* (see *The Play of Herod A Medieval Musical Drama) and *The Play of Daniel* (see *The Play of Daniel A Twelfth Century Musical Drama). Intended as liturgical teaching tools set to church chants, these kinds of plays were clear precursors to our more contemporary, autonomous forms of musical theatre (Hoppin, 1978, pp. 180–181).

Commedia dell'arte, an Italian tradition where raucous clown characters improvised their way through familiar stories, developed as an art form in the Renaissance (1400s—1600s). These clowns included characters like Harlequin, Pulcinella and Scaramouche, personas that became basic elements in Western stage comedy for centuries to come. *Nutcracker* (1892) ballets the world over invariably include a Harlequin variation (see *Bolshoi Ballet Nutcracker Harlequin), and composer Igor Stravinsky (1882–1971) created his own *Pulcinella Suite* in 1920 (excerpt at *Igor Stravinsky Pulcinella Suite).

Formal musical theatre was rare in the Renaissance, but dancing played a large role in productions such as English masques, elaborate dance-music-theatre works featuring masked dancers. The practice of wearing masks and other disguises to an informal ball was common, as the taking on of another persona often allowed the wearers greater freedom of expression in their merrymaking.

This use of masks as disguise carried over, of course, into the 19th-century tradition of the Minstrel Show and blackface, which persisted through the mid–20th century in some situations. For example, Larry Parks (1914–1975) impersonated Vaudevillian Al Jolson (né Asa Yoelson; 1886–1950) in the 1946 film *The Jolson Story* (see *Mammy Scene in Jolson Story), with Jolson actually singing his own vocals. In playwright William Shakespeare's (1564–1616) *Romeo and Juliet* (1597), the wearing of masques allowed the Montagues to enter the Capulet party unrecognized (see *Romeo and Juliet I Never Saw True Beauty 'Til This Night 1968 film).

Elizabethan dance and song are found throughout the period, and Shakespeare's works are full of court dances and songs accompanied by lute or theorbo. A hint of the dance style of the time can be seen in the romantic 1998 fiction film *Shakespeare in Love* at *Shakespeare in Love Dance. Later in the 1600s, particularly in France, when the court of Louis XIV (1638–1715) demanded song-and-dance entertainments, the playwright Molière (né Jean-Baptiste Poquelin; 1622–1673) turned several of his plays, such as *The Bourgeois*

Gentleman (1670), into comedies with songs and music provided by composer Jean Baptiste Lully (1632–1687). Have a listen to an excerpt at *Jean-Baptiste Lully Le Bourgeois Gentilhomme.

By the 1700s, the kind of musical theatre that was common in Britain, France and Germany were comic/romantic operas like John Gay's (1685–1732) *The Beggar's Opera* (1728). A famous tune from the opera that gives the listener a sense of its comedy of manners, and frank sexual content, can be heard during the 1968 Original London Cast Recording of "When Gold Is in Hand" at *When Gold Is in Hand.

On the 200th anniversary of that production, composer Kurt Weill (1900–1950) and lyricist Bertolt Brecht (1898–1956) created their own adaptation with almost all new music, *The Threepenny Opera* (1928), which was made into a German-and-French language film three years later. Starring Weill's actress-singer wife Lotte Lenya (1898–1981), one of the hits of the show was "Pirate Jenny," dramatically sung by Lenya in a 1966 TV performance at *Kurt Weill & Bertolt Brecht Pirate Jenny. Keeping the character of Macheath, a 1954 English translation of the show by Marc Blitzstein (1905–1964) included the song "Mack the Knife," which became popular five years later as a number one hit for pop singer Bobby Darin (1936–1973); see *Mack the Knife—Bobby Darin.

Another comic opera in the following century, Michael Balfe's (1808–1870) *The Bohemian Girl* (1843), boasts the celestial "I Dreamt I Dwelt in Marble Halls," a version of which can be heard by Irish singer-songwriter Enya (née Enya Patricia Brennan; b. 1961) at *Enya I Dreamt I Dwelt in Marble Halls.

These early works were precursors to more familiar operas that classical composers such as the French Hector Berlioz (1803–1869) and Georges Bizet (1838–1875), German Richard Wagner (1813–1883), and the Italians Giuseppe Verdi (1813–1901) and Giacomo Puccini (1858–1924) wrote. Set in Egypt during the Old Kingdom, Verdi composed his original *Aida* in 1871, a story of love amid slavery that was borrowed by Sir Elton John (b. 1947; *Billy Elliot the Musical, The Lion King*) and Sir Tim Rice (b. 1944; *Joseph and the Amazing Technicolor Dreamcoat, Jesus Christ Superstar*) for their 1998 musical of the same name (see *Elton John and Tim Rice's Aida: Live Footage). Puccini's 1896 *La Bohème*, based on a collection of vignettes about young Bohemians living in Paris's Latin Quarter in the 1840s, was a major influence on Jonathan Larson's (1960–1996) famous *Rent* (1996), which opened on *La Bohème's* 100th anniversary (see *RENT 1996 Tony Awards).

Of course, the 14 popular comic operas, or operettas, of British librettist William Gilbert (1836–1911) and composer Arthur Sullivan (1842–1900), were created in the late 1800s and are still performed today, largely unchanged. Have a listen to perhaps their most famous song from their most famous opera, the patter song "I Am the Very Model of a Modern Major General," from the 1879 *The Pirates of Penzance*, as sung by John Reed (1916–2010) for the D'Oyly Carte Opera Company in their 1968 album with the New Symphony Orchestra of London, at *Gilbert and Sullivan I Am the Very Model of a Modern Major General. For more great fun, watch seventies rock icon, multi-instrumentalist, and record producer Todd Rundgren (b. 1948), with New York string quartet Ethel (formed 1998), (mostly) nail "Lord Chancellor's Nightmare Song," another patter tongue-twister, from 1882's *Iolanthe*, at *Todd Rundgren with Ethel.

During the approximately 100 years between the early 1800s and early 1900s, primarily in the United States but also in Europe and England, many of these older forms of entertainment evolved into

English comedian, composer, singer and actor George Grossmith (1847–1912), dressed up as the original Lord Chancellor in Gilbert and Sullivan's 1882 light opera *Iolanthe*, in the outfit he wore to sing "Lord Chancellor's Midnight Song."

what became a variety of new and unique popular traditions. They include many performing frameworks and styles, some of which were clearly similar to each other and some quite distinct. Known as aggregates, or hybrids of styles, they often included combinations of separate single acts such as dance, music, song, theatre, comedy and juggling, and they helped create the milieu within which the true musical developed.

True precursors to the musical as we know it today, many of the innovations they initiated can be identified in the contemporary musicals of our time *if* we know what to look for. They include at least twenty forms of entertainment, or venues where the entertainment was showcased, with performances ranging from mainstream dramatic theatre to the revues that became a 20th century phenomenon.

Mainstream Dramatic Theatre evolved in spite of the fact that colonial travel in the 1600s and 1700s was confined to horseback and boat (it took two days for Benjamin Franklin to go by sea between Philadelphia and Boston). Individual performers such as jugglers and magicians and clowns and sword dancers and tight-rope walkers and other novelty acts took their shows on the road: true peripatetic forms of entertainment. In spite of theatrical events being banned in Massachusetts, Pennsylvania, and then in all stateside theatres by the First Continental Congress of 1774, by the mid–1700s, touring productions of Shakespeare, with imported British actors, had become popular in the United States. Of course, when things are banned, as always throughout history, what happens? They find a way. (Prohibition, beginning in 1919 and continuing until 1933 in the United States, is a perfect case in point.)

Indigenous short comedies and farces soon traveled the land via floating theatres (later called Showboats), especially on the Erie Canal (completed in 1825), and then on the Ohio and Mississippi Rivers, too. Incorporated into the middle of virtually any form of play and, eventually, operas and operettas, audiences saw variety acts that included singing, dancing, juggling, satire, and pantomime. These short entertainments were called *entr'actes*, a French phrase meaning "between acts," and is a term we still use today if something occurs at that time. One can spot *entr'actes* without the entertainments in the middle of long films such as *West Side Story* (1961) and *The Sound of Music* (1965).

Pantomimes deserve special mention. Derived from the commedia dell'arte tradition of conventional comedy in Renaissance Italy and including characters such as the Harlequin and Pulcinella (precursor to the clowns of today), the theatrical productions known as Pantomime—or, in Britain, simply Panto—presented a fairy-tale or nursery-rhyme subject that was enlivened by comedy, music and ballet. Do not confuse the more popular and ubiquitous concept of pantomime (which goes back at least as far as ancient Greece and Rome, in the plays of Aeschylus and masked dancers of Italy) with the particular way in which we use this term here. The theatrical Pantomime performances that are precursors of today's musicals hail from as far back as the 16th century, entertainments that built toward climactic, magical transformation effects that transported realistic dramas into a fantasy land.

Classic Pantomime transformations are everywhere apparent in traditional children's stories such as *Aladdin, Cinderella, Jack and the Beanstalk, Puss in Boots, Snow White, Peter Pan, Sleeping Beauty*, and other Mother Goose tales that have no clear origins. These stories have been presented on French, British and American stages for centuries. British Pantos are still popular today and include songs, dance, buffoonery, and satire in equal measure. Scenic and mechanical stage effects are used to cause the stage to magically transform into incredible visuals. Today, gauzes, quick changes, drum revolves, lasers, computerized effects, the Christmas tree growing in *The Nutcracker*, rock operas by the Who and all the Cirque de Soleil (formed 1984) shows have their roots in traditional Pantomime theatre. Lighting designers owe a debt of gratitude to this long tradition of magic onstage.

In one late 17th-century production, stage soldiers grouped together to form the figure of a huge elephant with shields—a predecessor to many of choreographer Busby Berkeley's (1895–1976) stage and screen effects from the early 1930s. In Charles Dickens's (1812–1870) *A Christmas Carol* (1843), we see Pantomime-type transformations in the form of the Ghosts of Christmas past, present, and future, as well as Scrooge's spiritual transformation from a miser to a philanthropist.

An example from the comedian-singer-actor Eddie Cantor film (né Edward Israel Itzkowitz; 1892–1964) *The Kid from Spain* (1932) shows just such a Pantomime-like transformation effect twice—first, with the offensive blackfaces painted on top of the girls' heads, and second, a "jigsaw puzzle" effect with the girls carrying placards to simulate a giant bull's head, at *Eddie Cantor What a Perfect Combination. The number, "What a Perfect Combination," was written by the composer-lyricist team of Harry Ruby (1895–1974) and Bert Kalmar (1994–1947) and choreographed by Busby Berkeley.

Likewise, in *Billy Elliot the Musical* (2008), the "Angry Dance" has a Pantomime-like transformation straight out of the Berkeley tradition at *Billy Elliot 2009 Tony Awards Angry Dance. Toy soldiers coming to life and ordinary people and objects turning into strange creatures are all easily recognizable today in shows such as the traditional *Nutcracker* (1892) and *Babes in Toyland* (1903 Broadway; 1934 film).

Lyman Frank Baum (1856–1919) published the first of over a dozen Oz novels on his 44th birthday, May 15, 1900, and called it *The Wonderful Wizard of Oz*. After he died, his successors kept the series going with another 30-plus books. Intended as a Pantomime for young and old, it was the biggest hit of the 1903 season, touring on the road for six years. In a way, it was America's first real fairy tale; it was made into two silent films in 1910 and 1925, the classic Hollywood production (1939), and the all-black *The Wiz* (1975) on Broadway and in Hollywood (1978). Early footage from just seven years after the show appeared on Broadway can be seen at *Wizard of Oz 1910 and twenty-two years later in 1925 at *Wizard of Oz 1925. Both give us a good idea of what the stage productions might have looked like, although as always, the film medium can do things that can't be done on stage (and vice versa). Of course, the Broadway show *Wicked* (2003) is yet another one of the latest versions of Pantomime at its finest (and an Oz backstory, to boot).

The ultimate example of Pantomime transformation, of course, comes from that very favorite American fairy tale, 1939's Hollywood version of *The Wizard of Oz*, particularly Dorothy's entrance into the Land of Oz at *Judy

A 1910 still from the first of a seemingly endless number of film adaptations based on L. Frank Baum's original 1900 novel *The Wonderful Wizard of Oz*. Two unknown actors as Kansas farm animals frame actors Robert Z. Leonard (1889–1968) as the Scarecrow (possibly) and Bebe Daniels (1901–1971) as Dorothy (possibly).

Garland the Cyclone Scene. Note how the movie exploited recent improvements in color by starting the film in black and white (actually, a sepia tone mimicking black and white) and then stunning its audience when Judy (née Frances Ethel Gumm; 1922–1969) as Dorothy opens the front door—an incredible example of cinematic Pantomime. (Also watch Miss Gulch turn into the Wicked Witch of the West on the back screen as seen through Dorothy's bedroom window.)

The Minstrel Show, beginning in the 1830s and persisting far too long into the 20th century, was another important example of aggregate 19th-century entertainment traditions, a collection of comic and musical elements dating back to at least the Middle Ages and Renaissance in Europe, when it was simply called minstrelsy. Multi-talented singers, storytellers, and performers traveled the countryside working for food and lodging. By the early 19th century, the separate acts had become organized very loosely around a fixed format, consisting of three main sections.

In Act One, a group of performers in blackface seated in a semi-circle were dominated by a central emcee, known as The Interlocutor, who traded jokes and gags with two disruptive end men, Tambo (on tambourine) and Bones (on sticks). The group presented a program of song, dance and comedy tied to a heavily mythicized vision of the antebellum (pre–Civil War) South. Examples of several of their typical jokes follow, many of which were precursors to the Vaudeville and Burlesque puns that were to come in the following century:

> Why is a man that's got gout like a window? Because he's full of *panes.*
> Why is a dog like a tree? 'Cause it *barks.*

> INTERLOCUTOR: I saw you walking with a young lady yesterday.
> END-MAN: Yes, she's related to the Burst family. Do you know John Burst?
> INTERLOCUTOR: Very well indeed.
> END-MAN: He's got three children.
> INTERLOCUTOR: What are their names?
> END-MAN: Alice May Burst, James Wood Burst, and Henry Will Burst. [*Laughs.*]
> INTERLOCUTOR: They must be full of hot air and gas.

> END-MAN: What business are you in? I saw you with a lot of old tin cans going into a grocery store.
> INTERLOCUTOR: I'm in the canning business, canning pears, peaches, and tomatoes.
> END-MAN: Is that so? I'm in the wholesale dry goods business. So you're in the canning business, are you? What do you do with such a whole lot of pears and peaches?
> INTERLOCUTOR: Well, we eat what we *can,* and what we can't eat, we *can.*
> END-MAN: Eat what you can, and what you can't eat, you can! Just like my business.
> INTERLOCUTOR: How?
> END-MAN: We *sell* an order when we can *sell* it, and when we can't *sell* it, why, we *can-cel* it. Eat what you can and what you can't eat, you can! You're a can can kind of chump, you are.

In addition to the pun-filled, terrible-by-today's-standards jokes, Minstrel audiences came to hear songs. Minstrelsy contributed the most popular songs of the period, the best of which have survived today to become some of the most beloved "folk" songs in the American repertory. One such song was composed by Dan Emmett (1815–1904) around 1846 called "Blue-Tail Fly" (or "Jimmy Crack Corn"). As with most Minstrel songs, the composer structured lyrics and melody to end in a lively refrain, contrasting markedly with the opening section. American radio and television singer Burl Ives (1909–1995) introduced many of these folksy Minstrel songs to children of the 1950s and 1960s, including me, whose parents sang them day in and day out when we were growing up. Have a listen to that very song at *Blue Tail Fly (Jimmy Crack Corn), Live 1964.

> When I was young I used to wait
> At master's side and hand his plate
> And pass the bottle when he got dry
> And brush away the blue-tail fly.
> Jimmy crack corn and I don't care,
> Jimmy crack corn and I don't care,
> Jimmy crack corn and I don't care,
> Ol' master's gone a-way.

"Polly Wolly Doodle" (1840s), another favorite from that era (sometimes also credited to Dan Emmett), was performed by the Depression-era child actress Shirley Temple (1928–2014) in the feature film *The Littlest Rebel* (1935), at *Shirley Temple Polly Wolly Doodle, with famed tap dancer-actor Bill "Bojangles" Robinson (1878–1949) accompanying her on banjo.

> Oh, I went down south
> For to see my Sal
> Sing Polly wolly doodle all the day
> My Sal, she am
> A spunky gal
> Sing Polly wolly doodle all the day.
> Fare thee well
> Fare thee well
> Fare thee well my fairy fay
> For I'm off to Lou'siana
> For to see my Suzy-anna
> Sing Polly wolly doodle all the day.

"Old Dan Tucker" (1830) and "Dixie" (1859) were also written by Emmett, the latter, interestingly, becoming both a beloved *and* hated hymn of the Civil War, its sentimentality overcoming politics. A smash hit in New York when it came out, new lyrics were added and the song was subsequently adopted as the Confederate battle anthem!

> I wish I was in de land o' cotton
> Old time dar am not forgotten
> Look away! Look away! Look away! Dixie Land.
> In Dixie Land whar I was born in
> Early on one frosty mornin'
> Look away! Look away! Look away! Dixie Land

Stephen Foster (1826–1864) lived, worked and died in the North, especially around Pittsburgh, and he was determined to become the best "Ethiopian" writer of songs, composing over 200 of them that included major 19th-century hits such as "Oh! Susanna" (1848), "Camptown Races" (1850), "Old Folks at Home (Swanee River)" (1851), and "My Old Kentucky Home" (1953). In blackface, Al Jolson sings "Camptown Races"—and six African

Americans in blackface tap dance to it—in the 1939 biopic of Stephen Foster, *Swanee River*, at *Camptown Races Al Jolson.

Many of these songs have been adapted and performed since the 19th century up through today. During the "$99,000 Answer" television episode (January 28, 1956) of *The Honeymooners*, starring Jackie Gleason (né John Herbert Gleason; 1916–1987) and Art Carney (né Arthur William Matthew Carney; 1918–2003), their alter-egos Ralph Kramden and Ed Norton hysterically deal with a piano version of "Old Folks at Home" at *The Honeymooners Swanee River. American songwriter James Taylor (b. 1948), on his 1971 premiere album *Sweet Baby James*, sings a lovely acoustic version of "Oh Susanna" at *Oh Susanna James Taylor. And the Louisville, Kentucky, a cappella group Linkin' Bridge (formed 2016) update "Old Kentucky Home" into rich 2017 harmonies at *My Old Kentucky Home Linkin' Bridge.

James Bland (1854–1911), one of the most celebrated of all Minstrel Show songwriters with over 600 songs, came up with two big hits: "Carry Me Back to Old Virginny" (1868) and "Oh, Dem Golden Slippers" (1879), the latter of which is danced to and sung in the 1951 film *Golden Girl* at *Mitzi Gaynor Golden Girl Golden Slippers.

These songs depended on a lot of repetition that provided little expressive depth or theatrical function. Nevertheless, their sound remains catchy, and they are the precursors of popular tunes we are more familiar with in the musicals of the 20th and 21st centuries.

Act Two, the middle section of the Minstrel Show, was called the Olio (or Fantasia). It was a series of specialty variety acts that included songs, dances, comedy numbers, jugglers, and other short pieces and is reminiscent of the entr'acte discussed earlier. An example of a typical Olio act appears in the 1934 film *Kid Millions*, starring Eddie Cantor, a song-and-dance man who exploited his huge eyes and exaggerated expressions for comedic effect. The song that the scene revolves around is "Mandy," at *Kid Millions Mandy, an Irving Berlin (né Israel Baline; 1888–1989) tune written for the *Ziegfeld Follies of 1919*, one of the most popular of all the revues that the great impresario Florenz Ziegfeld (1867–1932) produced on Broadway. The song also stars a young Ethel Merman (née Ethel Zimmermann; 1908–1984) who, protesting the use of blackface, only tans her face up, while Cantor goes full black. Look, too, for some typically fabulous tap dancing by the young Nicholas Brothers, Harold (1921–2000) and Fayard (1914–2006).

The Afterpiece, a one-act skit, was the third section, and usually involved a type of parody or burlesque of a previous act, a recent social or political event, or an important personality. A shortened theatrical version of Harriet Beecher Stowe's (1811–1896) novel *Uncle Tom's Cabin* (1852) became a frequent Afterpiece. (See the Tom Show below.)

In summary, the Minstrel Show was a conglomerate of diverse yet self-contained units strung together by a sketchy format with no narrative cohesive force. Most excerpts of Minstrel Shows that appear in early film musicals usually include the first bantering section with the Interlocutor and Tambo and Bones or the occasional blackface song-and-dance number. These can be seen in many of the early Eddie Cantor films he made for Samuel Goldwyn's United Artists series from 1930 to 1936, and Al Jolson's films at Warner Brothers, beginning with the first part-talky *The Jazz Singer* (1927). Cantor and Jolson, brought up as Vaudevillians in the early days of Broadway, frequently found unlikely ways to get themselves made up in blackface at least once per film. (As did Bing Crosby, even into the 1940s.) Seen today, these sequences are uncomfortable to view at best, in spite of their relative public acceptance among both whites and blacks at the time.

Because African Americans were mostly excluded from public performances in the 1800s, even blacks had to put on blackface, particularly after Emancipation in 1865, an even more insulting practice than whites in blackface. The ostensible reason was that this was show biz, and since African Americans were not permitted to perform as blacks in the predominantly white entertainment industry, they had to "black up" to become acceptable characters. Prejudices such as these persisted at least through the 1950s, not only in night clubs but throughout society, and even until Martin Luther King's Civil Rights Act of 1965, and beyond.

Even the great Fred Astaire, in his homage to black tap dancer extraordinaire Bill "Bojangles" Robinson, dressed up in blackface during his "Bojangles of Harlem" number from the 1936 film *Swing Time*, at *Bojangles of Harlem Astaire. But this was one of the few (if not only) times that a white performer actually honored a real man with his performance rather than via a racist and insulting stereotype.

Although it continued into the early parts of the 20th century, by the 1870s, after the Civil War, Minstrelsy had lost its creative energy. The Act Two variety acts segment, the Olio or Fantasia, eventually grew into Vaudeville, whereas Act One specialty acts led to the Revue format; Act Three burlesque parodies led to Burlesque.

The Tom Show, in its heyday in the latter part of the 19th century, involved touring companies that presented a condensed dramatic version of the popular Harriet Beecher Stowe novel *Uncle Tom's Cabin* (1852), as well as including variety acts such as song, dance and juggling. A unique version, "The Small House of Uncle Thomas," was created for the Rodgers and Hammerstein 1951 Broadway show *The King and I* as a narrative ballet by Jerome Robbins (1918–1998). It transferred wholly intact to the 1956 film of the same name but is unavailable on YouTube because of copyright restrictions. You may need to purchase or rent the film to access the ballet, in the chapter of the same name.

How and why might such a famous show incorporate Stowe's story? The 1951 Broadway show *The King and I* was based on a 1946 film called *Anna and the King of Siam*, itself based on the 1944 Margaret Langdon (1903–1993) book of the same name. That book grew out of an 1862 story, "The English Governess at the Siamese Court," and other stories written by a woman named Anna Leonowens (1831–1915). Who was Anna Leonowens? She was the real governess of the actual King Mongkut of Thailand (known in the West as Siam, until 1949), about whom the more familiar *King and I* story revolves. Anna Leonowens questioned the king's use of slaves during her time in Siam, and a story about the quest for freedom from slavery fit perfectly into the musical.

Medicine Shows, prevalent from the middle to the end of the 19th century, were touring, small-scale variety act productions that performed out in the hinterlands, especially during the westward expansion. As early as the 14th century, traveling medicine shows sold bogus curatives. In the United States, Medicine Shows involved glib pitchmen (quacks) who sold rattlesnake oil, a variety of tonics, salves, and so-called miracle elixirs, but the shows themselves also offered comedy, music, juggling, and other entertainments. One of the most famous was the Kickapoo Indian Medicine Company (originating out of Connecticut, of all places) that sold a product called Sagwa that was supposed to be a blood, liver and kidney renovator. On a personal note, during the summer of 1974 I toured upstate New York county fairs as a singer and puppeteer for Dr. Edison's Traveling Medicine Show, a bogus (but extremely enjoyable) gig where we sold Dr. Edison's Electric Elixir, guaranteed to cure everything from warts to hemophilia. It was simple tap water that we sold in small jars for a buck a bottle.

One of many examples from Broadway that are familiar is the flim-flam peddler Ali Hakim from *Oklahoma!* (1943 Broadway, 1955 film) and, of course, actor Frank Morgan's (1890–1949) character Professor Marvel in the beloved 1939 film *The Wizard of Oz* ("acclaimed by the crowned heads of Europe … let him read your past, present and future in his crystal … also juggling and sleight of hand … balloon exhibitionist"), before he turned into the smoke-and-mirrors Wizard himself.

Certainly, we continue to see all kinds of similar advertising to this day, especially on late-night TV and spoofed in *Saturday Night Live* skits, shilling so-called curative products. Who can forget Canadian comedian Dan Aykroyd's (b. 1952) classic 1972 "Bat-o-Matic" routine at *Dan Aykroyd Bat-o-Matic? In fact, the bogus medicine shows of the 1800s contributed to the American government responding in 1906 with the Pure Food and Drug Act, followed 22 years later by the Food, Drug and Cosmetics Act of 1938, to help get a handle on the authenticity and quality of drugs and other tonics.

P. T. Barnum's "Museums" and Circuses. Phineas Taylor Barnum (1810–1891) was the original super-size-me showman. From 1841–1868, Barnum ran what he called the Dime Museum in New York City (although he charged a quarter), where he piled as much diversity as possible under one roof (so much so that it contributed to two burn-to-the-ground fires). Rather than trying to figure out what his customers wanted, Barnum operated on the principle of overwhelming them by including everything under the sun: a natural history museum, scientific displays, a theatre showing continuous performances of singers, acrobats, animal acts, popular plays, melodramas, educated dogs, performing fleas, jugglers, ventriloquists, gypsies, albinos, fat people, giants, dwarves, rope-dancers, pantomime, instrumental music, dancers, dioramas, panoramas, models, mechanical inventions, and you name it. Barnum's goal was to overwhelm customers with a superabundance of stimulants, so people were compelled to return with their friends to try to see the rest of it.

With the completion of the transcontinental railroad in 1869, Barnum decided to take the museum to the audience rather having the audience come to the museum. Beginning in 1871 until his death 20 years later, Barnum developed the traveling circus concept along with other leading showmen, such as James Anthony Bailey (1847–1906), with whom he would eventually partner in 1881. Their work together evolved into what became the world-famous Ringling Brothers and Barnum & Bailey Circus (1919–2017), in which hundreds of performers paraded around in one, two, and eventually three rings, saturating audiences with their spectacle. Today's immensely popular Cirque de Soleil shows, begun in 1984 and touring all over the world, are most definitely carrying on Barnum's tradition.

Barnum was the first real impresario America had, and he did everything in a huge way—big, bigger, biggest—an attitude still prevalent. Overwhelming spectacle was his credo, and he set the stage for similar approaches on Broadway, film, and throughout our entire culture. As of 2018, there have been two musicals on the great impresario: 1980's *Barnum*, on Broadway, and 2017's *The Greatest Showman*, in film. (See below in respective years for more details on each.)

Wild West Shows, primarily a late 19th-century phenomenon, involved combinations of elements from circuses and variety acts. The most famous one was called Buffalo Bill Cody's (1846–1917) Wild West Show, beginning in 1883 and touring for thirty years, until 1913. These traveling productions offered up romanticized images of a disappearing frontier and involved such acts as trick riding, music, drama, cowboys and Indians in mock battles, buffaloes, horses, sharpshooters, and Melodramas (see below). One of the best examples we have of the Wild West Show is from the 1950 Technicolor extravaganza *Annie Get Your Gun* film, based on Irving Berlin's 1946 Broadway

GREAT TRAVELING WORLD'S FAIR FOR THE CAMPAIGN OF 1873.

After his two American museums burned to the ground, and the transcontinental railroad was completed in 1869, Phineas Taylor (P. T.) Barnum (1810–1891) took his surfeit of sights "on the road," eventually merging into Ringling Brothers and Barnum & Bailey circus.

show and itself loosely based on the real-life story of one of the greatest sharpshooters the Wild West ever knew, Annie Oakley (1860–1926), from Ohio. Look for the "Dazzling Display" chapter from the 1950 film with Betty Hutton (née Elizabeth June Thornburg; 1921–2007) as Annie (unavailable on YouTube).

Melodrama, the most popular theatrical form of the 19th century, depended heavily on stage effects that involved the use of wings, traps, bridges, cuts and lighting to produce the illusion of three-dimensional depth, called, ironically, "naturalism," on stage spaces that were, at the time, quite limited in size. However, during the latter part of the 19th century, producer-directors such as David Belasco (1853–1931), who named a theatre after himself in 1910, on 44th Street, adapted his stage for large-scale battle scenes, floods, fires, storms, huge ballets, and even chariot races with real horses. Shows such as *The Black Crook* (1866), *The White Fawn* (1867), *Humpty Dumpty* (1868), and *The Twelve Temptations* (1869) were created for their spectacle possibilities (shades of Barnum again), with hundreds of plays written solely as vehicles for magic, special effects, and elaborate trap doors. Today, our *Cats, Miss Saigon, Les Misérables, Phantom of the Opera*, and *Lion King* have brought back similar huge set elements to the stage with real helicopters, giant chandeliers, and stupendous animal puppets. These Melodrama productions were quite unlike today's use of the term, in which the story, according to the dictionary, is "marked by exaggerated emotions, stereotypical characters, and interpersonal conflicts." Today's Soap Operas may be called contemporary melodramas, but the 19th-century version, still used, were about creating and presenting spectacular "naturalism" onstage.

Burlesque, from the 1840s through the 1940s, was an aggregate of music, dance, comedy, and parody that also included the display of the female body. Not just the strip show that we think of today, Burlesque was an art form (if still primarily prurient) that included spoofs on the current topics of the day. Burlesque is a direct descendant of the commedia dell'arte, where principal characters would carry a *burle*—a stick with a padded end—with which they would slap the other players for comic effect (the origin of slapstick comedy).

According to the *American Heritage Dictionary* the verb *burlesque* means to imitate, satirize or parody. Involving pastiche and great wit, the genre traditionally included comic sketches often lampooning the social attitudes of the upper classes, but alternated with dance routines by scantily clad women. By the 1880s, the genre had created some rules for itself: minimal costuming, often focusing on the female form; sexually suggestive dialogue, dance, plotlines and staging; quick-witted humor lacking complexity; and short routines or sketches with minimal plot cohesion.

Famous Burlesque performers from the 20th century include the comedians Bud Abbott (1895–1974) and Lou Costello (1906–1959). In their classic "Who's on First?" number, seen it its entirety from their 1945 film *The Naughty Nineties* at *Who's on First Naughty Nineties, the skit epitomizes Burlesque's use of quick wit and puns (very bad ones) to great effect. I dare you to not laugh.

Mae West (1893–1980) literally embodied the Burlesque elements of sexual teasing and innuendo with subtle face and body gestures that melted grown men in their tracks. Even though she was already over 40 years old, the nine films she made for Paramount Pictures beginning in 1932 (*Night after Night*, her premier) through 1940 (the classic *My Little Chickadee*, with co-star W. C. Fields) showcase her talents at their height. However, she was still acting the part at the age of 85 in 1978 in the hard-to-watch *Sextette*. See

Miss West work her magic during a side show fairground act at *Tira the Incomparable Sister Honky Tonk, from the film *I'm No Angel* (1933).

The more prurient Burlesque strip tease (down to underclothes) is accurately rendered in composer Jule Styne (né Julius Kerwin Stein; 1905–1994) and lyricist Stephen Sondheim's tune "Let Me Entertain You," from the Broadway show *Gypsy* (1959), re-created for the film three years later, at *Let Me Entertain You Gypsy.

Opera and Operetta, while not precisely in the musical theatre canon, have some similarities to the form. From its birth in the 1800s, the musical has certainly spoofed as well as appropriated elements of opera. Comic operas like John Gay's *The Beggar's Opera* (1728), already discussed, remain popular today, as well as the fourteen William S. Gilbert (1836–1911) and Arthur Sullivan (1842–1900) light operas such as *H.M.S. Pinafore* (1878), *The Pirates of Penzance* (1879), and *The Mikado* (1885). And, as noted earlier, dramatic opera composers such as Wagner, Bizet, Berlioz, Puccini, and Verdi had some of their work updated, particularly Puccini's *La Bohème* and Verdi's *Aida* by Jonathan Larson and Elton John, respectively.

It should be remembered that notions of unity and narrative consistency did not matter much then, because of the aggregate nature of many of these entertainments. Operettas such as the 1888 Broadway revival of *Prince Methusalem*, by Johann Strauss (1825–1899), added totally incongruous songs, dances or poems into the shows; in this case, the Ernest Thayer (1863–1940) baseball poem "Casey at the Bat," written the same year, was recited in the middle of act 2.

Even though there were earlier musical-rich formats such as Minstrelsy and Medicine Shows, 1866's part opera–part ballet *The Black Crook* is generally acknowledged as the first true musical, and rightly deserves credit for bringing dance, music and theatre together into one unit. Ironically, it was a stroke of pure luck—the accidental burning down of the Academy of Music in New York City—that caused a visiting French ballet company full of 70 scandalously clad ballerinas (for that time, anyway; they were only in tights) to be hastily incorporated into sections of the long-winded (five and a half hours), generally dull drama. Nevertheless, *The Black Crook* went on for many profitable revivals over the next 25 years. True, its plot, music, dance, spectacle, and display of female anatomy had been derived from long established stage traditions, but in this one show, the beginnings of what we know today as a musical were clearly evident.

In season 5, episode 1, of his *Omnibus* (1952–1961) television series, classical and Broadway composer Leonard Bernstein (1918–1990) shares a bit of background on *The Black Crook* and includes a watered-down excerpt of "You Naughty, Naughty Men"—with music by George Bickwell and lyrics by Theodore Kennick—a rather apologetic account of men's manly wiles perpetrated on women, at *Omnibus Bernstein Discusses The Black Crook. A steamier version of the song can be heard at *You Naughty, Naughty Men from The Black Crook, re-created on piano by the music director of the New York Public Library Adam Roberts and sung by the Austin, Texas, singer Libby Dees.

Hippodramas involved circus-like equestrian maneuvers incorporated into flimsily plotted staged dramas and spectacles. Originally an ancient Greek (and Roman) horse or chariot race, this colorful entertainment as a musical precursor came into being in the first half of the 19th century and continued until 1939. Spectacular plays were presented in which animals, especially horses, were given definite parts, sometimes leading actions, and sometimes getting better reviews than their human counterparts! Often, these shows were presented in the New York Hippodrome, a huge theatre on Sixth Avenue between 43rd and 44th Streets. Built in 1905, it was equipped with state-of-the-art technology and could seat 6000 people. Thinly plotted productions featured circus animals, auto races, staged battles, patriotic spectacles, Martians in Wars of the Worlds, and nautical extravaganzas with bevies of beautiful swimmers. Its last gasp came in 1935 with *Jumbo* (1962 film, the last by Busby Berkeley), produced by impresario Billy Rose (1899–1966) and with a musical score and lyrics by Richard Rodgers (1902–1979) and Lorenz Hart (1895–1943). Rehearsals for opening night of the original 1935 *Jumbo*, starring Jimmy Durante underneath a reclining elephant, can be seen at *Rehearsal Footage of Jumbo 1935.

Aquadramas were created to re-enact sea battles on stage, and often were performed at the Hippodrome, too.

Dioramas were created for audiences to watch a revolving or moving platform or set that gradually disclosed large-scale scenic paintings enhanced with lighting effects. Barnum used them as early as the 1850s, and they show up in Broadway productions from time to time. There is an early example of a painted moving set Diorama in the 1948 MGM film *Easter Parade*, a story based on a couple of Vaudevillian performers played by Fred Astaire and Judy Garland. Their Diorama-inflected song-and-dance number is set to an old-fashioned tongue-in-cheek tune, "A Couple of Swells," by Irving Berlin, at *A Couple of Swells Fred Astaire and Judy Garland.

Les Misérables (1987) employs a large revolving turntable that rotates during the show to reveal various sets (see *Behind the Scenes at Les Misérables). So, too, does the 2017 revival by the National Theatre of London of Stephen Sondheim's 1971 *Follies*, which can be glimpsed in action at *National Theatre Live Follies Trailer. In an even more innovative vein, the artists of Broadway's *The Lion King* (1997) transformed the idea of revolving into platforms of carved wooden wildebeests that "stampede" toward Simba and the audience via a *horizontally-rotating drum*, which can be seen at *The Lion King from Cub to King.

Panoramas involve stationary platforms where audiences sit or stand and turn themselves around to see a 360-degree painting. The museum underneath the St. Louis Gateway Arch (opened 1965) is one such example, where the museumgoer slowly walks down a spiraling ramp as more and more images reveal themselves with each new curve. All planetariums are Panoramas, requiring participants to turn not only their heads but bodies around in order to see all the projected skies on the ceiling. The CinemaScope and VistaVision type wide-screen film formats, developed in 1953 and 1954, respectively, remain to this day—along with the huge IMAX screens (debuted in Toronto in 1971; 89' by 66')—versions of Panorama, asking viewers to move their eyes if not their entire heads to catch all the action. And, of course, most iPhones have a Panorama feature on their cameras.

Amusement Parks were an important venue for entertainment that could be considered a precursor to today's musicals, with Coney Island's Steeplechase Park in Brooklyn, New York, opening in 1897 (home of the first hot dog), a prime example (see *Coney Island Park). An Amusement Park is a collection of rides and other attractions assembled for the purpose of entertaining a fairly large group of people; they're also called Theme Parks.

An Amusement Park is more elaborate than a simple city park or playground, as it is meant to cater to adults, teenagers, and small children. It may be permanent or temporary and is usually periodic, taking place over a few days or weeks per year. The temporary (often annual) Amusement Park with mobile rides and so on is often called a Fair or Carnival. The oldest Amusement Park in the world was opened in 1583 in Bakken, Denmark, and the oldest that still exists is in the Tivoli Gardens in Copenhagen, dating from 1843. Take a three-minute tour at *Tour of Tivoli Gardens.

Theme Parks are a more narrowly defined category of an Amusement Park, and are permanent facilities that use architecture, signage, and landscaping to help convey the feeling that people are in a different place or time. Often, a Theme Park will have various "lands," or sections of the park, devoted to telling a particular story. Alternatively, an Amusement Park often has rides with little in terms of theming or additional design elements. For the most part, Theme Parks are the highest quality forms of Amusement Parks. The name of the Six Flags Entertainment Corporation, founded in 1961 in Texas, evokes the six nations that ruled Texas over the years: Spain, France, Mexico, Republic of Texas, Confederate States of America, and the United States of America. Take your own animated rides on a few 2018 Six Flag state parks at *New for Six Flags Theme Parks.

Fairgrounds travel all over the country and are sometimes referred to as simply a fair, county or state. They are small to medium-sized traveling fairs primarily composed of amusement rides. Barnum started his career in

Fairgrounds, and Mae West, as noted earlier, performs in one at the beginning of *I'm No Angel* (1933).

Extravaganzas, begun in the 1700s, were used as afterpieces in Minstrel Shows, entr'actes, or full-length performances of their own. They downplayed plots almost to the point of total exclusion, while scenic effects similar to those found in Melodramas or Pantomimes became the most important elements. Imagine taking just the scenic effects from shows and creating entire productions based on spectacle alone—that would be an Extravaganza. Our use of the term today still implies as much: "an elaborate spectacle or display." Scenery was so elaborate that the actors sometimes found themselves crowded out completely from the stage, the manager relying solely on the magic of paint and canvas to pack the house.

The Black Crook, with its full ballet company onstage, incorporated Extravaganza at that point. Cirque du Soleil stories are often overwhelmed by the enormity and superabundance of the Extravaganza production elements and special effects. Have a look at an excerpt from the Cirque show *Love* (2006) at *Cirque du Soleil Lucy in the Sky with Diamonds, or the water show during *O*, in permanent residence since 1998 at the Bellagio in Las Vegas, Nevada, at *The Water Stage O Cirque du Soleil. Extravaganza rules.

Two

Late 19th and Early 20th Centuries

To carry on with our discussion of the forms and venues of entertainment that can be seen as precursors to the contemporary musical, this chapter will cover Vaudeville, The Music Hall and Revues.

Vaudeville, beginning around the 1880s and continuing into the 1930s, was originally an extension of the Minstrel Show's middle section, the Olio, a series of separate acts in music, comedy, and novelties. American Vaudeville differed from its French and British equivalents, called Music Halls, in which the latter were less diversified than their American counterparts and tailored for specific social classes. Directed more towards establishing a sense of intimacy and rapport with the audience, Music Halls still exist in England today, and I remember going to one a few years ago—the audience and emcee were boisterously responsive to each other at times, and it was great fun, even though I didn't understand half of the topical and local references. (Of course, they speak British English in England, not American English.)

American Vaudevillian acts were more varied, pitched towards a heterogeneous mass audience, and succeeded each other with little or no introduction or bridging element. Usually consisting of between seven and nine acts, there were, however, loose principles of logic, design, pacing, and orchestration, and an awareness geared towards audience response that created an overall impression of diversity and abundance similar in tone to Barnum's excesses. The kinds of acts were as varied as there were performers: magic, dance, song (popular, opera, classical), comedy, knife throwers, jugglers, (relatively) trained animals, flea circuses, you name it. To see some early silent films showing a guy wrestling a mule, a monkey playing violin, a slapstick fight between two men with bags of flour and soot, a woman dancing with a chair in her mouth, and many other sights we don't often see today, take a look at *Before There Was Television: Vaudeville, Early American Entertainment.

Urban America in the late 19th and early 20th centuries was a true melting pot of immigrants from all over the world, including Western European nations, the British Isles, Asia, India, China, Japan, Russia, and Africa. The seven years of Ireland's Great Famine (1845–1852) "was a period of mass starvation, disease and emigration.... By 1850 the Irish made up a quarter of the population in Boston, New York City, Philadelphia, and Baltimore" ("Great Famine (Ireland)"; https://en.wikipedia.org/wiki/Great_Famine_(Ireland)#Emigration; retrieved August 9, 2015). In order to connect to broader groups of people, entertainments in the States then, and to a large degree today, required more variety than their British or French counterparts.

Not surprisingly, people in the two major religious groups in America, the Jews and Catholics, populated Vaudeville extensively. Al Jolson (né Asa Yoelson, 1886–1950), a Jew born in Lithuania, and Eddie Cantor (né Israel Itzkowitz, 1892–1964), the son of Russian Jewish immigrants and born in New York City, are two of the most famous examples. See Cantor sing one of his Vaudeville hits, "Makin' Whoopee" (1928), complete with his signature eye rolls, in the early 1930 two-tone color film *Whoopee!* at *Eddie Cantor— Makin Whoopee.

Catholics with Irish ancestry such as George M. Cohan (1878–1942), born in Providence, Rhode Island, and Jimmy Cagney (1899–1986), born in New York City, were also well represented among these early performers. Likewise, many of the composers who eventually created music in Broadway and Hollywood were themselves first- or second-generation immigrants, too (except for Cole Porter, a local boy from Peru, Indiana), and they include Irving Berlin (born Israel Baline in Tyumen, Russia) and George Gershwin (born Jacob Gershovitz in Brooklyn, a son of Russian immigrants).

> Between 1880 and 1919, 5.5 million immigrants from Europe made their home in New York. More than 1.2 million newcomers arrived in 1907 alone—a million of them Jews.... Soon Irishmen, Jews, Germans, and Italians all learned that show business let them leap the hurdles placed before them in the New World; "Where else," Minnie Marx, the mother of the Marx Brothers, reasoned sensibly, "can people who don't know anything make money?" ... The ethnic numbers always went over particularly well. No one took offense because to be singled out as a Jew or an Italian or an Irishman in a comedy song was not to be excluded, but to be *included* [Kantor and Maslon, 2010, pp. 4–7; italics added]

This politically-incorrect-for-our-century attitude is what allowed the Jewish Al Jolson to be accepted as a black man in blackface singing about going home to the Swanee River in Florida and Georgia (the real river is called the Suwannee), set to the tune "Swanee" (1919) composed by fellow second-generation Russian George Gershwin. The same attitude allowed second-generation Irishman George M. Cohan to claim all of America for himself through such patriotic songs as "Yankee Doodle Boy" (1903), written by Cohan himself. (There are no videos of him singing the song but Jimmy Cagney does a first-rate job with it while playing Cohan in 1942's film *Yankee Doodle Dandy*, at *Yankee Doodle Dandy.) The attitude also permitted Israel "Izzy" Baline to write an Italian dialect song, "Marie from Sunny Italy," in 1907, the first of over 1200 songs written over his long 101 years on this planet. (The printer of the song's sheet music misspelled Baline's name as "I. Berlin," and Izzy thought it sounded good and kept it.)

It was also typical of Berlin, and many other early 20th-century composers in Tin Pan Alley, to write black-dialect "coon songs" and a variety of Yiddish songs. For a true sense of that kind of acceptance in the early 20th century, take a look at Al Jolson in blackface singing "My Mammy" (1921), with music by Walter Donaldson (1893–1947) and lyrics by Joe Young (1889–1939) and Sam M. Lewis (1885–1959), from the first part-talkie film *The Jazz Singer* (1927), at *Mammy—Al Jolson. Again, while the song may be pleasant, it's difficult to watch with our 21st-century eyes.

Another important point about traditional theatre beginning in the late 19th century: While Medicine and Minstrel and Wild West shows were traditionally held outdoors, in open spaces or under tents, the apron stage (or, in the case of movies, the rectangular screen) literally placed a frame around the performers, putting the action within a more self-contained and enclosed setting. With this creation, a more fully controlled environment existed, allowing more elaborately composed experiences to be on display.

Aside from the development of arc lamps in the 1880s and the building of dozens of theatres before and during the turn of the 20th century, another important event that happened was a commitment on the part of New York City to build a series of underground railways—a subway system—that would traverse the entire island of Manhattan and allow people to travel quickly anywhere. The New York City Transit subway system opened in early November 1904 and was centered at the crossroads of the theatre district at Times Square—the corner of 44th Street and Broadway—just before George M. Cohan's biggest hit opened, *Little Johnny Jones*, at the Liberty Theatre. His song "Give My Regards to Broadway," at *Give My Regards to Broadway James Cagney, couldn't have been written at a more propitious time. (It is ironic to note, however, that only a fraction of all of Broadway's theatres are actually on Broadway.)

Interestingly, the most important part of the early 20th-century Broadway milieu wasn't actually on Broadway but began 14 blocks south of 42nd Street on a short strip of West 28th Street between Broadway and Sixth Avenue. This little street was called Tin Pan Alley and was where most of the song publishing businesses rented offices and storefronts. A cacophony of pianos could be heard all day and all night. Why was it called Tin Pan Alley? Because after the Civil War, American homes had become the center of family entertainment, and every middle-class and lower-middle-class family with aspirations to middle-class life had to have a piano in the parlor. (In fact, all of my grandparents, who were born near the beginning of the 20th century, and my father and mother, born in 1930 and 1933, respectively, inherited that very American of habits, and I was forced to take piano lessons at the tender age of ten in 1963 in my home on Long Island, in New York, hating every minute of it. Of course, today I thank them profusely, because it instilled a love of music in me that owes its existence to that tradition.)

Tin Pan Alley shops sold sheet music to thousands of piano-owning homeowners. There was a Song Plugger, who played songs anywhere—offices, bars, theatre lobbies, backstage, and the backs of trucks, a Stooge singing the song back to the performer to prove how catchy it was, and house arrangers, musically gifted piano players who would embellish the original song in some innovative way. See part 1 of the 1929 film *Glorifying the American Girl*, at *Glorifying the American Girl 1929 Part I, beginning at the five-minute mark, for a realistic example of song plugging in a department store at that time.

Vaudeville stars became voracious consumers of these songs, taking them across the country while the publishers tripped all over themselves to get their songs placed with them, and vice versa. (Noted above, Al Jolson's 1919 appropriation of the early George Gershwin classic "Swanee," and Eddie Cantor's rendition of "Makin' Whoopee," are two such examples.) Each song had its own story, its own conceit or cliché, and few of them were written for specific stage productions (Kantor and Maslon, 2010). Remember that this was a time before the ubiquity of records and radio and even sound movies, all things we take for granted today, for the cylinder phonograph had only recently been invented by Thomas Alva Edison (1847–1931) in 1877 and the gramophone record in 1888; the radio console was developed in the early 1920s and the talking picture in 1927.

Some of the big hits of the time were catchy, easy-to-sing-along-to melodies still heard today—sentimental ballads, novelty numbers, ethnic songs, romanticized songs of innovative technology (such as a bicycle), and nostalgia tunes:

- "Daisy (A Bicycle Built for Two)" (1892), written by British-born Harry Dacre (1857–1922), is given a peppy Nat King Cole (1919–1965) treatment on his 1963 version at *Nat King Cole Bicycle Built for Two. It was also poignantly sung by the HAL computer, of all things, in Stanley Kubrick's (1928–1999) science fiction epic film *2001: A Space Odyssey* (1968) at *HAL 9000 sings Daisy;
- "The Sidewalks of New York" (1894), written by Irish-born Vaudevillian Charles B. Lawlor (1852–1925), as sung by *House* television series alumni (2004–2012) Robert Sean Leonard (b. 1969) at *The Sidewalks of New York;

- "The Band Played On" (1895), with music by Charles B. Ward (1865–1917) and lyrics by John F. Palmer (b. 1870), can be heard as performed by the Guy Lombardo (1902–1977) Trio, with Kenny Gardner (1913–2002) on vocals, on their 1941 version at *The Band Played On Guy Lombardo Trio;
- "Bill Bailey, Won't You Please Come Home?" (1902), written by Hughie Cannon (1877–1912), became a number one hit in a 1902 recording sung and played by Arthur Collins (1864–1933) at *Bill Bailey Won't You Please Come Home;
- "In the Good Old Summertime" (1902), with music by Welsh-born immigrant George Evans (1870–1915) and lyrics by Ren Shields (1868–1913), was also the title of a Van Johnson (né Charles Van Dell Johnson; 1916–2008) and Judy Garland 1949 film that not surprisingly takes place at the turn of the 20th century. As sung in 2010 by Athens-born Julien Neel (b. 1979), via his one-man Barbershop Quartet Trudbol, his four-part harmonies ring like a bell at *Trudbol a Cappella In the Good Old Summertime;
- "Take Me Out to the Ballgame" (1908), with music by Albert Von Tilzer (né Albert Gumm; 1878–1956) and lyrics by Jack Norworth (1879–1959), can be heard the very year it was written as sung by Edward Meeker (1874–1937) at *Take Me Out to the Ballgame 1908. Gene Kelly (1912–1996) and Frank Sinatra (1915–1998) do an energetic song-and-dance to the tune in their second of three films together, the 1949 movie of the same name at *Frank Sinatra Gene Kelly Take Me Out to the Ballgame.

The Music Hall, as noted above, remains the British equivalent of Vaudeville. Beginning around 1830 and continuing to today, variety acts were the rage: contortionists, dwarf equestrians, singers, comics, and character acts all performed in front of a very rowdy and responsive homogeneous crowd. Some sense of its history can be seen in part 1 of 6, "The Story of the Music Hall," at *Musical Contexts the Story of the Music Hall.

Today's stand-up comedy hails from that time, and many habits such as heckling, finishing on a song, and familiar, repeatable comedy numbers date back to the Music Hall. Radio programs such as the British *Goon Show* (1951–1960) made extensive use of the tradition and were important influences on surreal troupes such as Monty Python's Flying Circus (formed 1969) and the Firesign Theatre (1966–2012) from the United States. A radio episode of the *Goon Show* from October 25, 1955, starring goon stalwarts Peter Sellers (1925–1980), Spike Milligan (1918–2002), and Harry Secombe (1921–2001), is at *The Goon Show Rommel's Treasure. The classic "Dead Parrot Sketch," from Monty Python's first season, episode 8, first aired on December 7, 1969, can be seen at *The Parrot Sketch. *Don't Crush That Dwarf, Hand Me the Pliers*, the Firesign Theatre's third album (1970), captures their lunacy logic in total at *Don't Crush that Dwarf Firesign Theatre.

Revues. Some of the shows already discussed continued on into the early 1900s, and Vaudeville into the early 1930s—with circuses, Amusement Parks, and fairs continuing to this day—but Revues are truly an early 20th-century phenomenon, as they lasted a mere 30 years or so, until the beginning of sound pictures.

Highly flexible and amorphous, the Revue, spelled thus and not r-e-v-i-e-w, owes its existence to Vaudeville, Music Halls, Burlesque, and the Olio section of the Minstrel Show. It was a mixture of self-contained acts with a general emphasis on music and comedy. However, unlike Vaudeville, the Revue's format was more solid and anchored and its acts linked by a tenuous plot, a general theme, a musical score, the décor, or a producer's unique idea for that production. The same performers would often appear several times during a Revue, with a strong star or host figure somewhat dominating the proceedings. Comedian W. C. Fields (né William Claude Dukenfield; 1880–1946), entertainer and French Resistance agent Josephine Baker (née Freda Josephine McDonald; 1906–1975), and cabaret crooner Maurice Chevalier (1888–1972) all played this kind of role in early Revues. Unlike Vaudeville, the material was usually unique and written specifically for that one production.

Fields was both consummate juggler and comedian, and two such numbers from the Revue format can be seen in his 1934 full-length film *The Old-Fashioned Way*, at *The Old-Fashioned Way Fields Juggling, and in the 1933 comedy short *The Pharmacist*, at *The Pharmacist WC Fields. To get a sense of the eroticism on display at the time, Baker's topless dancing at the Parisian Folies Bergères can be seen from a 1927 excerpt of her "Banana Dance," wearing some coverings, at *Josephine Baker's Banana Dance. And Chevalier's uniquely ingratiating style in "I'm an Apache," from the early Rodgers and Hart 1932 musical *Love Me Tonight*, can be seen at *Maurice Chevalier I'm an Apache.

Rather than the Vaudeville's regional and even national touring circuit, the Revue stayed put in one theatre space. In this way, the producer could utilize all the resources in that one theatre rather than relying on portable props that needed to be carried from house to house. The most popular Revues of the 20th century were the Ziegfeld Follies, housed at the New Amsterdam Theatre on Broadway (the theatre is still there, even though the Follies are not). We are today familiar with the term "follies," as in the *Folies Bergères* (1869–1920s) in Paris, which combined a contemporary, much more risqué version of Burlesque within a Revue-type format. The *Folies Bergères* are paid homage in both Moulin Rouge movies—the primary theatre, founded in 1889 and still going strong, where the cancan dance originated—*Moulin Rouge* (1952), starring José Ferrer (1912–1992) and helmed by famed noir director John Huston (1906–1987), and *Moulin Rouge!* (2001), starring Scot Ewan McGregor (b. 1971) and Australian Nicole Kidman (b. 1967) and directed by fellow Aussie Baz Luhrmann (né Mark Anthony Luhrmann; b. 1962).

Still, even if there were a loose theme or musical idea weaving the acts together, a Revue was not bound by the constraints of a narrative, and the most elaborate production could still be fully indulged with minimal regard for integration, plot sequence, or simple logic. Like Vaudeville or the Olio, a Revue could include a comedy piece followed by a song, a dance, or a novelty act, and that was fine. Again, watch either film mentioned above for 20 minutes or more and you'll see this kind of variety in action.

The original Revues, as the French spelling indicates, began in the Paris of the 1840s or so. Their earliest phases were based on topical humor and included a series of satirical sketches and songs aimed at current events, which if you'll recall, was also an important hallmark of Burlesque. Frequently, Revues would make fun of the previous theatre season through the use of lampoons or even straight excerpts told in exaggerated fashion. Hence, the English version of the word, "review," like the French form, denotes an actual *review* of the past season.

For example, an early British Revue from 1863 was called *The Sensations of the Past Season, with a Shameful Revelation of Lady Somebody's Secret.* Yearly versions became popular, particularly in the United States, such as the *Ziegfeld Follies of 1907, 1908*, and so on, and this practice of yearly dating, if not actually following the Revue format, was carried over into early film musicals such as those at Warner Brothers, which used titles such as *Gold Diggers of 1933*, *Gold Diggers of 1935*, and *Gold Diggers of 1937*. MGM Studios had their own *The Broadway Melody* (from 1929), *Broadway Melody of 1936*, *Broadway Melody of 1938*, and *Broadway Melody of 1940*. Unfortunately, only the titles of these films reminded people of the Revue format, for the films themselves did, in fact, have plots (albeit slight ones).

The first American Revue is generally acknowledged to be *The Passing Show* in 1894, performed at New York's Casino Theatre, but Revues didn't reach the zenith of popularity until over a decade later when, in 1907, Florenz Ziegfeld began producing the first of 83 Revues until his death in 1931. These were known as the Ziegfeld Follies, and even though there were hundreds of other Follies Revues around, Ziegfeld's name became most synonymous with the format.

Impresario Florenz "Ziggy" Ziegfeld (1869–1931) was to the 20th-century Revue what P. T. Barnum was to the 19th-century circus and Extravaganza. *Ziegfeld Follies of 1907* was a typical Ziegfeld production full of comedy, satire, spectacle, pretty girls, and melodies. It included a jungle number satirizing President Teddy Roosevelt's hunting expeditions, a showgirl circling above the audience in a miniature airplane, 48 showgirls wearing battleship-model headgear, complete with twinkling lights, and a finale that involved the whole cast throwing 500 balls out onto the audience.

Unequalled in his time, Ziegfeld was the consummate showman, self-promoter, and coordinator of talent. The son of German immigrants, Ziggy became fascinated at an early age with Buffalo Bill Cody's Wild West Show, which seemed to epitomize the New World American style he was in love with. He eventually tried out a number of aggregate forms, working his way through Amusement Parks, Vaudeville, and early Revues. Ziggy had visited the *Folies Bergères* in 1905 and began his own Follies two years later, hiring women no shorter than six feet tall. The pre-eminent Vaudevillian, African American Bert Williams (1874–1922), was hired by Ziegfeld in 1910. His contract stipulated that he would not have to tour the South or be onstage with white women, leading him to declare, "I have never been able to discover that there was anything disgraceful in being a colored man, but I have often found it inconvenient," in an article he wrote, "The Comic Side of Trouble," for *The American Magazine* (1918; Vol. 85, p. 34).

Right from the start, Ziegfeld outdid every other producer in the business. His women (the Ziegfeld Girls, as he called them) wore the most elegant costumes imaginable—green and rose velvet, silks, and real sable and ermine—and some of the performers had to change gowns eight times a night, onstage, with only the chorus girls as a screen. Ziegfeld was the first producer to effectively merge the objectification of women begun in Burlesque with the loosely connected Revue format, but rather than having only an occasional woman onstage, he displayed chorus upon chorus of them for his audience.

Between 1907 and 1931, almost all of the great composers and performers who eventually made the transition to Broadway and film musicals spent at least some time with Ziegfeld's Follies: Will Rogers (1879–1935), Maurice Chevalier, Eddie Cantor, Josephine Baker, Al Jolson, Billie Burke (1884–1970; Ziegfeld's second wife, who played Glinda the Good Witch of the North in 1939's *The Wizard of Oz*), Irving Berlin, W. C. Fields, George and Ira Gershwin (1896–1983), Fred Astaire, Fannie Brice (1891–1951), Ed Wynn (1886–1966), Jimmy Durante (1893–1980), and a host of other great talent.

In 1946, Fred Astaire introduced the Ziegfeld style in glorifying his girls in the third of three films on the man and his shows, *Ziegfeld Follies*, with a bevy of beauties cavorting atop live horses as they rode on a rotating carousel (straight out of Diorama) to the tune of "Here's to the Girls," composed by Roger Edens (1905–1970) and lyrics by Arthur Freed (1894–1973). Complete with a young Lucille Ball (1911–1989) and even younger Cyd Charisse (née

Tula Ellice Finklea; 1922–2008), the number can be experienced at *Here's to the Girls—Ziegfeld Follies. From the early sound picture *Glorifying the American Girl* (1929), the only full-length film produced by Ziegfeld himself and showcasing his actual performers, you can watch an authentic version of his Revue format in action, albeit in poorly recorded action, at *Ziegfeld Style Finale (1929).

Jerome Kern (1885–1945), a native New Yorker (though his father was a Jewish German immigrant), worked during the early years of the 1900s in London with Music Halls and Revues and in Operettas and Revues in the States, writing over 700 songs in a career that included scores for 39 Broadway musicals. Countering the waltz rhythms of the European influence in city shows, his songs often used four beats to the bar and fit better with the burgeoning fox-trot dances here at home. He also incorporated American ragtime and other syncopations into his tunes, helping the indigenous art form to grow.

In the 1905 American version of the British Revue *The Earl and the Girl*, Kern wrote "How'd You Like to Spoon with Me," with lyrics by Edward Laska (1894–1959). Re-created for the loose biopic of Kern's life in the 1946 *Till the Clouds Roll By*, it was performed by 20-year-old Angela Lansbury (b. 1925) in the typically breezy Revue-style manner, seen at *How'd You Like to Spoon with Me Till the Clouds Roll By Angela Lansbury. With *The Girl from Utah*, from 1914, Kern had his first big hit, the tender and exquisite "They Didn't Believe Me," with lyrics by Herbert Reynolds (né Michael Elder Rourke; 1867–1933), which helped "revolutionize the style of American show songs, replacing the European operetta-inflected style with a more lyrically long-lined, ballad style" (Hemming, 1986, p. 87). Turned into a standard sung by dozens of crooners, watch Dean Martin (né Dino Paul Crocetti; 1917–1995), during one of his many television specials in the 1960s, swing it up at *Dean Martin They Didn't Believe Me.

Kern's songs were really the first in the American musical theatre world to be integrated into the plot—albeit loosely—and, in fact, helped advance it at times. (Gilbert and Sullivan's operettas were strong predecessors in this development.) After Revues such as *Very Good Eddie* (1915), *Oh, Boy!* (1917), and *Oh, Lady! Lady!!* (1918), Kern's star continued to rise with the smash hit *Sally* (1920). The classic song from that show, "Look for the Silver Lining" (lyrics by B. G. "Buddy" DeSylva; 1895–1950), is gorgeously rendered by Judy Garland (1922–1969) playing Marilyn Miller (1898–1936), star of *Sally*, in the same 1946 biopic mentioned above at *Look for the Silver Lining—Till the Clouds Roll By.

Of course, no one had any idea what the result would be after Kern joined with Oscar Hammerstein II (1885–1960)—he of later Rodgers and Hammerstein fame—on developing the Edna Ferber (1885–1968) novel *Show*

New York–born composer Jerome Kern (1885–1945) hit the big time with the 1920 musical *Sally*, starring Marilyn Miller (1898–1936) in the title role, and his paean to optimism in "Look for the Silver Lining" (lyrics by B. G. DeSylva).

Boat, a story about racism, alcoholism, and misogyny. Produced by none other than Florenz Ziegfeld, primarily known for glorifying the American girl via Revues, a close examination

of "Show Boat" [December 27, 1927,] reveals that it is actually quite progressive for a show that was written in 1927. The plot, involving a woman who is prohibited from performing on the show boat because she is bi-racial and is married to a white man, is compelling, as is the song "Ol' Man River," which is the complete antithesis of the more upbeat tunes popular at a time when many whites did not wish to acknowledge their injustice to African Americans. "Show Boat" was made into a film musical three times—in 1929, 1936, and 1951. In 1954 it became part of the New York City Opera's standard repertory—the first musical to be adopted by an opera company ["Broadway Stars; Jerome Kern"; http://www.pbs.org/wnet/broadway/stars/kern_j.html; retrieved January 19, 2018].

Have a look at the great baritone singer Paul Robeson (1898–1976), from the 1936 film, singing "Ol' Man River" at *Ol' Man River Paul Robeson.

Stephen Sondheim himself, who was mentored by Kern's collaborator Oscar Hammerstein II, said,

What Oscar did was to marry European operetta and American musical comedy tradition. One of the reasons *Show Boat* turned out as well as it did is that Kern knew what Oscar was trying to do, and he was just as interested in doing it—attempting to tell some kind of story about character [Kantor and Maslon, 2010, p. 114].

Prior to *Show Boat*, no musical

had ever been adapted from a serious novel, none had had to deal with a three-generation time span in the story, none had to bring a story from the past to the present, and certainly none had dealt with white characters and black characters sharing the stage as full dramatic entities [Kantor and Maslon, 2010, p. 114].

To put this in perspective, the dramatic dilemma at the core of the biggest hit musical that same year, *Good News!*, was whether the football captain could win the big game, pass his astronomy exam, and get a date with the girl.

Kern went on to compose some of his greatest songs in the 1930s and 1940s, particularly the elegiac "Smoke Gets in Your Eyes" (lyrics by Otto Harbach, 1873–1963) for the 1933 Broadway show and 1935 film *Roberta*, with Fred Astaire and Ginger Rogers. Listen to the classic 1958 Doo Wop version of the tune by the Platters at *The Platters—Smoke Gets in Your Eyes and almost any song from the 1936 film *Swing Time*, also with Astaire and Rogers, to get a sense of the wonderful tunes Kern created for those two films. His lyrical collaborator on the latter was Dorothy Fields (1905–1974), who would later write the lyrics to 1966's *Sweet Charity*, and they struck gold with every tune: "Pick Yourself Up," "The Way You Look Tonight" (Oscar winner), "A Fine Romance," "Waltz in Swing Time," and the heartbreaking "Never

Irving Berlin's (1888–1989) "A Pretty Girl Is Like a Melody" became the theme
song for the *Ziegfeld Follies of 1919*, one of over 2000 tunes the composer and
lyricist wrote for dozens of Broadway and Hollywood musicals.

Gonna Dance," performed by Fred and Ginger at *Never Gonna Dance— Swing Time.

Two other Kern highlights over the years include "The Shorty George," with lyrics by Johnny Mercer (1909–1976), from the 1942 film *You Were Never Lovelier* with Rita Hayworth (née Margarita Carmen Cansino; 1918–1987) and Fred Astaire at *Fred Astaire and Rita Hayworth—The Shorty George, and so many songs from the wonderful *Cover Girl* (1944), with lyrics by Ira Gershwin and E. Y. "Yip" Harburg (1896–1981), especially the jaunty "Make Way for Tomorrow" with Gene Kelly, Rita Hayworth, and Phil Silvers (1911– 1985) at *Make Way for Tomorrow—Gene Kelly.

Around the same time as Kern's foray onto Broadway, a young whippersnapper (by three years) made a huge splash with the 1911 tune "Alexander's Ragtime Band" (even though it was a march), shortly followed by his own Broadway debut in the Revue *Watch Your Step* (1914). The young man's name? Irving Berlin. The show exploited his innovative "double song" composition "Play a Simple Melody," which juxtaposed two melodies simultaneously. Have a listen to the pure-throated tones of pop singer Jo Stafford (1917–2008) in 1950 with the Star-lighters on backing vocals at *Jo Stafford—Play a Simple Melody. Berlin's show was full of ragtime, fox-trots, tango, polka, an opera medley, and syncopation.

Berlin had the "ability to capture and represent the human experience in a simple, direct way," said Robert Kimball (2001, p. xvi), and no less a composer than Jerome Kern, his elder, said that "Irving Berlin has no place in American music: he *is* American music." His was an art for the everyday person, and he said so himself:

> My ambition is to reach the heart of the average American, not the highbrow nor the lowbrow but that vast intermediate crew which is the real soul of the country. The highbrow is likely to be superficial, overtrained, and supersensitive. The lowbrow is warped, subnormal. My public is the real people [Berger, 1989, pp. 1, 48].

After the United States entered World War I in 1917, Berlin contributed the songs "Mandy" and "God Bless America" (which he didn't use until 20 years later, when it nearly became a second national anthem, popularized by Kate Smith, 1907–1986) to a show entitled *Yip Yip Yaphank*, shortly followed by the theme song for the *Ziegfeld Follies of 1919*, "A Pretty Girl Is Like a Melody." You can see Eddie Cantor singing the bouncy "Mandy" in his signature blackface from *Kid Millions* (1932) at *Kid Millions—Mandy, and the latter performed with Barnum-like excess at *A Pretty Girl Is Like a Melody 1936 from the 1936 film *The Great Ziegfeld*.

All told, Berlin composed over 2000 songs, many of which made it into 21 Broadway scores (5 adapted to the screen) and 11 films. As Berlin never learned to read or write music, all his songs were composed in the key of F-sharp so he could always stay on the black notes of a piano. Fond of deceptively simple tunes about the weather such as blue skies, getting caught in the rain, and the snow around Christmastime, the best of his work "is a simple, exquisitely crafted street song whose diction feels so natural that one scarcely notices the craft…. For all of their innovation, they seem to flow straight out of the rhythms and inflections of everyday speech" (Holden, 1987, p. 230).

For Berlin, the hits just kept coming:

- His 1924 ballad of longing and heartbreak "What'll I Do?" is jazzed up a bit in a bluesy version by the Nat King Cole Trio in 1947 at *What'll I Do Nat King Cole;
- "Blue Skies" (1926) made its screen debut in the part-talkie *The Jazz Singer* (1927) and was sung, pounded out (mimed) on the piano, and jazzed up by Al Jolson, mercifully without blackface, at *Blue Skies—Al Jolson;
- The 1932 "Puttin' On the Ritz" is worth seeing in at least three extraordinary circumstances from three films: *Idiot's Delight* (1939), with Clark Gable, of all people, singing and tap-dancing at *Clark Gable Putting On the Ritz; *Blue Skies* (1946), with Fred Astaire (and Bing Crosby, né Harry Lillis Crosby, Jr.; 1903–1977), at *Fred Astaire Putting On the Ritz; and *Young Frankenstein* (1974), with Gene Wilder (né Jerome Silberman; 1933–2016) and Peter Boyle (1935–2006) as Frankenstein's monster, at *Young Frankenstein—Putting On the Ritz;
- *As Thousands Cheer* (1933) was a 21-number Revue based on newspaper headlines that introduced "Easter Parade," "Heat Wave" (the weather report) and "Supper Time," the latter a song about an African American woman, played by Ethel Waters, awaiting a husband who doesn't come home due to his lynching;
- All songs from *Top Hat* (1935), arguably the greatest of the Fred and Ginger movies, including "No Strings (I'm Fancy Free)," "Isn't This a Lovely Day (To Be Caught in the Rain)," at *Isn't This a Lovely Day—Top Hat, 1935, "Top Hat, White Tie, and Tails," and "Cheek to Cheek";
- Most of the songs from *Follow the Fleet* (1936), another top notch Astaire-Rogers RKO hit: "We Saw the Sea," "Let Yourself Go," "I'd Rather Lead a Band," "I'm Putting All My Eggs in One Basket," and "Let's Face the Music and Dance," the latter at *Fred Astaire and Ginger Rogers: Let's Face the Music and Dance 1936;
- The plaintive "Change Partners," nominated for an Academy Award, from the Astaire-Rogers vehicle *Carefree* (1938) at *Change Partners—Fred Astaire;
- The classic "White Christmas," sung by Bing Crosby, in the Astaire-Crosby showcase *Holiday Inn* (1942);

- *Annie Get Your Gun* (1946/1950), including the show biz anthem "There's No Business Like Show Business," a song that took over the role from Berlin's earlier "A Pretty Girl Is Like a Melody" for *Ziegfeld Follies of 1919*, at *There's No Business Like Show Business—Annie Get your Gun 1950;
- The film *Easter Parade* (1948) with "Drum Crazy," "Steppin' Out with my Baby," and the title song, at *Judy Garland & Fred Astaire Easter Parade.

Right up until the first day of the 1920s, the nineteen teens were a pivotal time culturally and politically in the United States, as well as in the world. A law passed in 1913 represented the beginning of something in this country we now take for granted and curse at all the time. As high as 77 percent during World War I and 91 percent during World War II, a national income tax of 1 percent was levied in 1913 for the first time ever. Producers like Ziegfeld had to be even more efficient with staging costs, knowing that more and more of his money would be going to the federal government for important community benefits.

The following year saw the start of World War I, with the United States trying desperately to stay out of it. But on April 2, 1917, President Woodrow Wilson (1856–1924) announced that we must "make the world safe for democracy" in a Declaration of War delivered at a joint session of the two houses of Congress. In May of that year, another first, the Selective Service Draft Bill was initiated, and America subsequently lost over 100,000 men in aiding Western Europe in its fight with Germany. A year and a half later, in November 1918, America was hailed as the champion of world democracy, and our relative isolation from the rest of the world would never again be.

In the arts world, even though film had existed since before the 1880s, with inventors like Thomas Alva Edison (1847–1931) leading experiments, the first real movie, with a beginning, middle and ending, didn't arrive until 1903 with *The Great Train Robbery*, all twelve minutes of it (see *The Great Train Robbery 1903). It wasn't until 1919, however, that the art of movies really began coming of age. All the Broadway Revue producers started seeing their stars move west to Hollywood, in spite of the fact that the films were still all silent. Great Broadway shows would continue, but the Great White Way would never fully recover.

The contribution of major changes on the stage by film cannot be overemphasized. By the same year, labor unrest led to the development of the Actors Equity Union and its first strike. Everyone fought for improved wages except the polymath George M. Cohan (1878–1942), who believed in the school of hard knocks. Actors, musicians, stagehands, and electricians all struck, but it was over in two days, guaranteeing salaries for rehearsals, transportation home after out-of-town flops, and pay for costumes.

Prohibition, making illegal the sale, importation, and consumption of alcohol anywhere in the United States, brought in the new decade with a vengeance. On January 1, 1920, the Volstead Act was enacted. Even though optimism in the country had never been higher since we had helped win World War I, and the twenties would produce the greatest cultural renaissance our country would ever see, a reactionary counter-movement in the form of a drive towards temperance culminated in the 18th Amendment to the Constitution, and it lasted until 1933. Ironically (and not surprisingly), New York City led the nation in *not* enforcing Prohibition, for there were 3200 speakeasies alone between 42nd and 54th Streets.

Lots of changes for women occurred between 1914 and 1922. Short haircuts (bobs) and short skirts appeared as hips disappeared; backs were open and in view, while smoking and drinking further demonstrated women's newfound freedoms. Believe it or not, it took until August 18, 1920, for the 19th Amendment of the Constitution to be ratified, finally giving women the legal right to vote! People fell in love with Cinderella stories, and on Broadway, shows named after women—Irene, Sally, Rose-Marie, Nanette, Sunny, Kay, and so on—became ubiquitous. They all looked sweet but they danced hot, and none more than Marilyn Miller (1898–1936), who joined the Ziegfeld Follies in 1918 and starred in his 1920 show *Sally* (made into a film in 1929).

The twenties were a culture of optimism, a time when dreams did come true. The first year of that decade was notable for a number of Broadway shows. *The Night Boat*, with music by Jerome Kern and lyrics by Anne Caldwell (1868–1936), opened on February 2, 1920, and starred Louise Groody (1897–1961), who would become even more famous in 1925's *No, No, Nanette*.

With some songs by Richard Rodgers (1902–1979) and Lorenz Hart (1895–1943), five years before they became well-known, *Poor Little Ritz Girl* opened on July 28, 1920. Pianist and singer Larry Woodard, on KT Sullivan's 2000 album *KT Sullivan Sings the Sweetest Sounds of Richard Rodgers*, performs the rare and lovely Rodgers and Hart tune "You Can't Fool Your Dreams" from that show at *You Can't Fool Your Dreams/Out of My Dreams/I Have Dreamed.

Good Times—not to be confused with another musical of the same name seven years later—opened on August 8, 1920, at the cavernous Hippodrome. It boasted songs by Raymond Hubbell (1879–1954) and included not only diving girls but elephants and trick horses prancing about, typical of Hippodrama spectacle.

Sally (December 21, 1920), with music by Jerome Kern and lyrics by a variety of writers, made Marilyn Miller a star at the age of 22 for producer Florenz Ziegfeld. Miller herself, with co-star Alexander Gray (1891–1976), sings the big hit "Look for the Silver Lining," from the 1929 film version of the show, at *Look for the Silver Lining.

Lyricist Noble Sissle (1889–1975) and composer Eubie Blake's (1887–1983) big hit "I'm Just Wild about Harry," highlighting the first major all-black show, *Shuffle Along* (1921), introduced jazz to Broadway.

On May 3, 1921, *Two Little Girls in Blue*, about poor sisters who could only afford one ticket to India, with music by Vincent Youmans (1898–1946), was lyricist Ira Gershwin's (1896–1983) first hit (under the pseudonym Arthur Francis), a show three years before he made it big with his brother, George (*Lady, Be Good!*). The title song, at *Two Little Girls in Blue, has a beguiling poignancy rare for so early in the history of musicals.

Shuffle Along opened on May 23, 1921, with music by Eubie Blake (né James Hubert Blake; 1887–1983) and lyrics by Noble Sissle (1889–1975). "I'm Just Wild about Harry" and "Love Will Find a Way" were its two big hits, and in addition to introducing jazz to Broadway, it was the first time blacks could watch from the audience (at least in one section of the theatre). Have a listen to Eubie Blake himself syncopating his way through the first song, as recorded on a 1916 Player Piano Stroud Pianola, at *I'm Just Wild About Harry—Composed and Played by Eubie Blake. In April 2016, librettist George C. Wolfe (b. 1954) and choreographer Savion Glover (b. 1973) re-created *and* reconceived the show for 21st-century Broadway. Starring Audra McDonald (b. 1970), Brian Stokes Mitchell (b. 1957) and Billy Porter (b. 1969), an excerpt can be seen at *Show Clips Shuffle Along.

On August 9, 1921, the satirical musical *Tangerine*, about three men jailed for not paying alimony, opened with music by a variety of composers. "Sweet Lady," composed by Frank Crumit (1889–1943) and performed by Paul Whiteman and His Orchestra later that same year, captures some of the show's effervescence at *Paul Whiteman Sweet Lady 1921. Check out the women's outfits from the time, flashing by on video!

On September 22, 1921, Irving Berlin opened his first (of four) *Music Box Revue* in the Music Box Theatre, a building designed and built by Berlin and producer Sam H. Harris (1872–1941) for the express purpose of showcasing Berlin's songs. The 1923 edition, for example, demonstrated the songwriter's skill in the burgeoning jazz age with "Pack Up Your Sins and Go to the Devil," performed by the Columbians Dance Orchestra that same year at *Pack Up Your Sins and Go to the Devil the Columbians 1923. The droll double-talk speech of comedian Robert Benchley's (1889–1945) "Treasurer's Report," a typical Revue number from the same show, can be seen in a 1928 film at *The Treasurer's Report.

With songs by Hungarian-born operetta writer Sigmund Romberg (1887–1951), the Al Jolson vehicle *Bombo* (October 6, 1921) kept adding tunes from so many other composers that there were more songs than Romberg's! Out of nearly thirty, Jolson blasted out "California, Here I Come," written by Buddy DeSylva (né George Gard DeSylva; 1895–1950) and Joseph Meyer (1894–1987), at *California Here I Come Al Jolson. Likewise, the charming "April Showers," also by DeSylva and Louis Silvers (1889–1954), can be seen as performed in 1949 Chicago by Jolson at *Al Jolson April Showers.

On April 13, 1922, the musical Revue *Make It Snappy*, starring Eddie Cantor, introduced two hit songs, "Yes! We Have No Bananas," written by Frank Silver (né Frank Silverstadt; 1892 or 1896–1960) and Irving Cohn (1898–1961), and "The Sheik of Araby," with music by Ted Snyder (1881–1965) and lyrics by the now forgotten writer Harry B. Smith (1860–1936)—apparently the most prolific of all lyricists, having penned over 300 librettos and 6000 lyrics—and Francis Wheeler. The latter tune was brilliantly danced to by famed tappers the Nicholas Brothers—Harold (1921–2000) and Fayard (1914–2006)—nearly naked, and then sung by Betty Grable (1916–1973) and Alice Faye (1915–1998), both wearing perhaps just a bit more than the brothers, in the 1940 film *Tin Pan Alley* at *The Sheik of Araby from the Tin Pan Alley.

That same year saw the 4th of 16 *George White's Scandals*, a Follies-like Revue series whose popularity was eclipsed only by Ziegfeld's own Follies. As with Ziggy's shows, many entertainers became famous through their association with the *Scandals*, including comedian/juggler/actor/writer W. C. Fields (1880–1946) and Paul Whiteman and His Orchestra, in the 1922 edition; the torch singer Helen Morgan (1900–1941), in 1925; eccentric dancer Ray Bolger (1904–1987), singer/actor/bandleader Rudy Vallee (1901–1986), belter Ethel Merman, and actress/singer Alice Faye, in 1931; and exuberant tap dancer Eleanor Powell, in the 1935 film version. George Gershwin's first big hit, "I'll Build a Stairway to Paradise," with lyrics by Buddy DeSylva and Ira Gershwin, appeared in the 1922 *Scandals* (August 28, 1922), played for all its worth at *Paul Whiteman and His Orchestra I'll Build a Stairway to Paradise in a recording later that same year.

On November 13, 1922, the sentimental *Little Nellie Kelly* opened on Broadway (see also the 1940 film of the same name, starring Judy Garland) with songs and direction by George M. Cohan. "Nellie Kelly, I Love You," a bouncy and charming fast waltz, can be heard performed by the prolific Billy Murray (1877–1954) and the American Quartet at *Billy Murray and the American Quartet Nellie Kelly, I Love You.

Adele Astaire (1896–1981) and her brother Fred starred as the romantic, eventually married couple in *The Bunch and Judy* (November 28, 1922), a slight story of a wayward Broadway starlet. With lyrics by Anne Caldwell and Guy Bolton and music by Jerome Kern, "Hot Dog!" interpolated from the 1915 *Very Good Eddie*, brings pizzazz to an upbeat two-step at *Hot Dog Very Good Eddie (sung by the Company, from the 1975 revival).

Throughout the twenties, public and critical tastes were becoming more sophisticated and turned towards brasher, snappier, and more streamlined musicals onstage. And even though segregation still existed, a true renaissance began for African Americans in uptown New York's Harlem District, generally acknowledged as between 120th and 135th Streets on the west side. Re-discovering, re-creating, and reveling in their own African cultural heritage, blacks led the way in America in ragtime (1910s), jazz (1920s and 1930s), and big band music (1930s and 1940s) with performers such as the trumpeter-singer Louis Armstrong (1901–1971), pianist-composer Duke Ellington (né Edward Kennedy Ellington; 1899–1974), pianist-conductor Count Basie (né William James Basie; 1904–1984) and composer-conductor Cab Calloway (né Cabell Calloway III; 1907–1994), among a host of other top entertainers, writers, and artists. While many performers still had to sneak through the kitchen doors to get to the stage, white intellectuals were drawn to the artistry displayed and hustled their way uptown to mix chops with the performers.

Back downtown, Tin Pan Alley—28th Street, between 5th Avenue and Broadway—was home to many of the immigrant Jew and Catholic music makers. The Gershwins, Irving Berlin, and a host of other composers developed their talents there. Both places, Harlem and Tin Pan Alley, became the two most prolific areas of music and culture the world may ever know. Many of the greatest Broadway shows and tunes were written in the twenties, and many eventually were transferred, in truncated form, to the screen.

Oscar Hammerstein's lyrics and Vincent Youmans's music, among others, headlined Broadway's *Wildflower* (February 7, 1923), which was produced by Oscar's uncle, Arthur. The plot challenged Nina to keep her temper under control for six months; despite the provocations of cousin Bianca, she smiled, inherited a fortune, and married beau Guido. The title song and "Bambalina" were the two big hits of the show, and both can be heard on a contemporary recording at *Wildflower/Bambalina.

It wasn't until *The Jazz Singer* in late 1927 that sound on film became popular. But on April 15, 1923, American inventor Lee de Forest (1873–1961) filmed a number of his patented Phonofilms with Eddie Cantor, Noble Sissle, Eubie Blake, jazz bands, and many other acts in featured performances. These short sound films demonstrate just how well synchronization could work, excerpts of which can be seen at *First Sound of Movies Promo.

On August 15, 1923, the musical farce *Little Jessie James*, set in an apartment overlooking Central Park in Manhattan, opened with book and lyrics by theatre director, screenwriter, lyricist, film director, and producer Harlan Thompson (1890–1966) and music by composer and orchestra leader Harry Archer (1888–1960). The catchy ballad "I Love You" is gorgeously sung by an anonymous fellow (who is also on all the instruments and vocals!) at *I Love You Harlan Thompson (on the YouTube page of "diezungen").

September 3, 1923, saw W. C. Fields as circus barker and con man Professor Eustace McGargle attempt to promote his foster daughter Poppy as a long-lost heiress in *Poppy*. She turns out to actually be an heiress, but on the way, tunes such as "What Do You Do on Sunday, Mary?" at *American Quartet What Do You Do on Sunday, Mary, with music by Stephen O. Jones and lyrics by Irving Caesar (1895–1996), kept the story light and breezy. Fields also starred in the 1936 film version of the show, humorous excerpts of which can be seen at *Poppy 1936 Part I. One of his classic lines can be heard in the movie: "And if we should ever separate, my little plum, I want to give you just one bit of fatherly advice: 'Never give a sucker an even break.'"

On October 29, 1923, producer George White presented "America's Greatest Colored Comedians"—Miller and Lyle (Flournoy Miller

Taken circa 1906, this is a photo of the sister-and-brother act Adele (1896–1981) and Fred (1899–1987) Astaire, who started in Vaudeville shortly after they left Omaha, Nebraska, in the 1900s.

[1885–1971] and Aubrey Lyle [1884–1932])—in *Runnin' Wild*, an all-black Revue with music by James Johnson (1894–1955) and lyrics by Cecil Mack (né Richard Cecil McPherson; 1873–1944). There was one particular number, staged by choreographer Lyda Webb, that featured the all-new Charleston dance (although various historians and performers claim it had been around since before the turn of the century), set to the song of the same name. Played on a piano roll in classic Harlem stride piano style by none other than the composer himself, it can be heard at *James P Johnson the Charleston 1925, while examples of the dance can be seen at *The Charleston Dance (1923–1928). The song and dance soon swept the nation and planet, and represented the Roaring Twenties spirit like no other tune.

November 6, 1923, saw *Stepping Stones*, with Jerome Kern music and Anne Caldwell lyrics, a story of sweet little Roughette Hood in battle with hungry villain Otto DeWolfe. Along with the addition of circus, Minstrel Show, and Vaudevillian acrobat Fred Stone (1873–1950) and his actor/singer/dancer daughter, Dorothy (1905–1974)—the "stepping stones," get it?—the show boasted the plaintive "Once in a Blue Moon," which can be heard on contemporary soprano Rebecca Luker's (b. 1961) 2013 album *I Got Love—Songs of Jerome Kern* at *Rebecca Luker Once in a Blue Moon.

Starring Eddie Cantor as caddie master, bootlegger, and all-around busy-body, *Kid Boots* (December 23, 1923; silent film in 1926) presented songs by a variety of composers. Just as it opened, the hit "Dinah," with music by Harry Akst (1894–1963) and words by Sam M. Lewis (1885–1959) and Joe Young (1889–1939), was woven into the show. Trumpeter-singer Louis Armstrong (1901–1971) blasts, scats and swings his ensemble through the tune in a 1933 tour of Copenhagen at *Louis Armstrong Dinah 1933.

Lollipop (January 21, 1924), a musical comedy with music by Vincent Youmans and lyricist Zelda Sears (1873–1935), was about an adopted orphan named Lollipop who falls in love with an attractive plumber. Hijinks ensue. Its one big hit, "Take a Little One-Step," became even more popular the next year when it was interpolated into Youmans's *No, No, Nanette*. Hear it sung by 62-year-old, 1930s film tapper and singer Ruby Keeler (née Ethel Ruby Keeler; 1909–1993)—who had retired from show business in 1941!—in that show's 1971 revival at *No, No, Nanette Original Broadway Cast.

Between May 1924 and September 1927, Polish American brothers Max Fleischer (1883–1972) and Dave Fleischer (1894–1979) created the first syn-chronized animated films by pioneering follow-the-bouncing-ball sing-alongs for audiences. They brought characters such as Koko the Clown and Betty Boop to the screen in a series of 19 films, excerpts of which can be seen at *Ko-Ko Song Car-Tunes Promo. This series led to the June 1926 seven-minute film *My Old Kentucky Home* (based on the 1852 Stephen Foster tune of the same name) at *My Old Kentucky Home First Officially-Produced Sound Animation. All these films were clear precursors to the animated films of Disney to come, starting with Mickey Mouse's debut in 1928, *Steamboat Willie*, at *Walt Disney Animation Studios Steamboat Willie.

Groucho, Chico, Harpo, and Zeppo—stage names of the Marx Brothers, whose real names were Julius Henry (1890–1977), Leonard (1887–1961), Adolph Arthur (1888–1964), and Herbert Manfred (1901–1979) respectively—finally made it out of Vaudeville and onto Broadway on May 19, 1924, with the opening of the Revue *I'll Say She Is*. Never made into a film, an excerpt from the show demonstrates their typically surreal zaniness at *Marx Brothers Theatrical Agency Scene, part of a 1931 promotional film for their own upcoming *Monkey Business* movie that same year.

The Revue (with an ever-so-slight story) *Lady, Be Good!* opened on December 1, 1924, with music and lyrics by George (1898–1937) and Ira Gersh-win (1896–1983), respectively. It was the first of 14 Broadway musicals written by the brother team, and with this show, the Gershwins fully established themselves as the strongest proponents of the jazzy, pulsating sound of the twenties. About a broke brother-and-sister team, with each sibling willing to sacrifice for the other, it also was the first starring vehicle for brother Fred (1899–1987) and sister Adele (1896–1981) Astaire. Listen to Ella Fitzgerald

(1917–1996) turn the title song into a heartbreaking paean to love on her 1950 *Ella Sings Gershwin* album at *Oh, Lady Be Good Ella Fitzgerald. Then watch film star Eleanor Powell (1912–1982) tap up a storm and pirouette like crazy to a boogie-woogie version of "Fascinatin' Rhythm," the big hit from the show, in the 1941 film *Lady Be Good* at *Fascinatin' Rhythm—Eleanor Powell from Lady Be Good.

The original version of the title song was performed on stage by Cliff "Ukulele Ike" Edwards (1895–1971), recorded later the same year singing and playing his uke at *Cliff Edwards—Fascinating Rhythm. (Edwards was most famous for giving voice to Jiminy Cricket in the 1940 animated film *Pinocchio*.) Finally, "The Half of It, Dearie Blues" can be heard on a rare 1926 recording of Astaire singing and tapping, with Gershwin himself on the piano, at *The Half of It, Dearie Blues—Fred Astaire.

While *Lady, Be Good!* helped move jazz and, with Astaire, dance into the spotlight (George had composed the extraordinarily well-received jazz-inflected classical work "Rhapsody in Blue" back in February of the same year), the show remained a lightweight production typical of the decade's Revue formats, its story mercilessly silly like the soon-to-be-discussed *Good News* (1927), *Funny Face* (1927), and *Whoopee* (1928).

The songwriting team of composer Richard Rodgers (1904–1979) and lyricist Lorenz Hart (1895–1943) made it big with a pun-filled song that became their first hit, "Manhattan," in the May 17, 1925, parody Revue *The Garrick Gaieties*. Dozens upon dozens of vocalists and instrumentalists have made "Manhattan" their own in the nearly 100 years since the song was first written. Ruth Tesler and Allan Gould's straight-faced take, in the 1929 short film *Makers of Melody*, captures its mood perfectly at *I'll Take Manhattan 1929. And with the Ruby Braff–George Barnes Quartet (formed 1972) backing him on cornet, bass, and two guitars, Tony Bennett (né Anthony Dominick Benedetto; b. 1926) swings nice and easy through a jazz version of the number on his 1973 album *Tony Bennett Sings 10 Rodgers & Hart Songs* at *Tony Bennett Manhattan.

Yes, this Richard Rodgers with Lorenz Hart is *that* Richard Rodgers, the one more commonly associated with Oscar Hammerstein II for the 17 years between 1943 and 1960, the year of the latter's death. But Rodgers had actually worked with Hart seven years longer than with Hammerstein—24—from 1919 until Hart's death in 1943. The first duo became true bi-coastal songwriters, creating tunes for Broadway shows from 1925 to 1931, Hollywood from 1932 to 1935, and then back on Broadway until 1943.

No, No, Nanette (September 16, 1925), with music by Vincent Youmans and lyrics by Irving Caesar, was a farce involving several fun-loving couples at a seaside resort in Atlantic City. Two hit songs came out of the complications: "Tea for Two" and "I Want to Be Happy." The first can be heard sung by Doris Day (née Doris Mary Ann Kappelhoff; 1922–2019) in the 1950 film of the same name, at *Doris Day Tea for Two, and the second by a barely 20-year-old Ella Fitzgerald (1917–1996), in a 1937 recording with drummer Chick Webb (né William Henry Webb; 1905–1939) and His Orchestra, her first ensemble group, at *I Want to Be Happy Ella Fitzgerald.

Based on an actual Revolutionary War (1775–1783) event, in which Mary Lindlay Murray (1726–1782) delayed British General William Howe (1729–1814) long enough, by feeding him cake and wine, for George Washington (1732–1799) to regroup his forces, *Dearest Enemy* (September 18, 1925) was Rodgers and Hart's first of over two dozen musicals filled with only their songs. Before the fully integrated musicals of Rodgers and Hammerstein (beginning with 1943's *Oklahoma!*), *Dearest Enemy* did in fact make an honest effort to wed plot with time period, as represented by "War Is War," "Where the Hudson River Flows," and "Here in My Arms" at *Dearest Enemy War Is War, *Dearest Enemy Where the Hudson Flows, and *Dearest Enemy Here in My Arms, respectively.

The operetta *The Vagabond King* (September 21, 1925; filmed in 1930 and 1956) had music by Czech-born composer and pianist Rudolf Friml (1879–1972) and words by lyricist-poet Brian Hooker (1880–1946) and playwright William H. Post (1867–1930). The story revolves around a fictionalized day-in-the-life of poet and ne'er-do-well François Villon (b. 1431, disappeared 1463). From his posthumously released 1961 album *The Vagabond King*, tenor Mario Lanza (né Alfredo Arnold Cocozza; 1921–1959) belts out "Love Me Tonight," one of the many yearning Friml ballads from the show, at *The Vagabond King Love Me Tonight Mario Lanza (not to be confused with Rodgers and Hart's own later tune "Love Me Tonight," from the 1932 film of the same name).

Multi-talented Marilyn Miller (née Mary Ellen Reynolds; 1898–1936) starred in composer Jerome Kern and lyricist-librettist Oscar Hammerstein's first collaboration, *Sunny* (September 22, 1925), a story of a circus performer who falls in love with a rich fellow from a snooty family. There have been better dancers and singers and actors in the history of musicals, but during the twenties, none put the three together with quite as much endearing charm as Miller. The big song hits of the show were the title tune and "Who?" but have a look at *Marilyn Miller Tap Dance from the 1930 film version to catch a glimpse of the exuberance that must have been so infectious for audiences of her time.

The Marx Brothers' second of three Broadway shows, *The Cocoanuts* opened on December 8, 1925, and is set

> against the backdrop of the 1920s Florida Land Boom, which was followed by the inevitable bust. Groucho is a hotel proprietor, land impresario, and con man, assisted and hampered by two inept grifters, Chico and Harpo, and the ultra-rational hotel

assistant, Zeppo. Groucho pursues a wealthy dowager ripe for a swindle, played by the dignified Margaret Dumont [1882–1965; "The Cocoanuts"; https://en.wikipedia. org/wiki/The_Cocoanuts_(musical); retrieved January 22, 2018].

With over a dozen songs written by Irving Berlin, the film version (May 3, 1929), their first of 13—5 with the original four Marx Brothers—included a number of tunes that overlapped between show and film and can be heard on a 1926 recording at *Gems from Cocoanuts Irving Berlin Songs. But people came to Marx Brothers movies for the comedy, excerpts of which can be seen at *Why a Duck, *Cocoanuts Auction Scene, and *Cocoanuts Bum, respectively.

Tip-Toes, a farce involving amnesia and marital infidelity, opened on December 28, 1925, and starred the same four artists as the previous year's *Lady, Be Good!*: composer George Gershwin, lyricist Ira Gershwin, and sibling dancer-singers Adele and Fred Astaire. The composer himself can be heard playing the ragtime-esque "That Certain Feeling" on a 1926 player piano recording at *That Certain Feeling George Gershwin, while guitarist Howard Alden's (b. 1958) version of "Sweet and Lowdown" from the show, performed in the 1999 Woody Allen film version of the same name (mimed by actor Sean Penn), is charmingly rendered at *Sweet and Lowdown Playing Guitar.

Among composer Richard Rodgers and lyricist Lorenz Hart's melodious tunes—in a show about an amateur cyclist falling in love with a professional peddler's daughter—"The Blue Room," from *The Girl Friend* (March 17, 1926), stands out. It is sweetly performed by the Revelers, a 1920s and 1930s popular ensemble of four harmonists and a pianist, at *1926 Revelers The Blue Room. Also listen to Mel Tormé's (1925–1999) loving, velvety rendition of the song from a 1950 television show at *Mel Tormé Blue Room.

The musical Revue *Americana* (July 26, 1926) featured a variety of songwriters and performances, including Ira Gershwin's lyrics set to a composer other than his brother George; in the case of the cheery tune "Sunny Disposish," that writer was Philip Charig (1902–1960). Frances Williams (née Frances Jellinek; 1901–1959) does a middling-fast jazzy version of the song at *Frances Williams Sunny Disposish, while the four-part-harmony ensemble Manhattan Transfer, on their first album *Jukin'* (1971), speeds things up to Roaring Twenties zestiness at *Manhattan Transfer Sunny Disposish. *Americana* was revived in 1928 and again in 1932 (see below) with new composers and performers.

The musical comedy *Castles in the Air*, a story about two men who mistake an exclusive resort for an inn and then pretend they're nobility, opened on September 6, 1926, and featured songs by Missouri-born ragtime composer Percy Wenrich (1887–1952). One of his biggest hits was the 1912 charmer "Moonlight Bay" (not in the show, however), sung by famed turn-of-the-century quartet singers the American Quartet (1899–1925) at *Moonlight Bay 1912. In 2010, Greek musician Julien Neel (b. 1979) re-tracked his voice four times for his "group" Trudbol One Man Barbershop Quartet in a lovely a cappella version of the same song at *On Moonlight Bay a Cappella Barbershop Quartet.

October 12, 1926, saw the opening of composer Jerome Kern's *Criss Cross*, a story about an aviator who helps a colleague protect a younger woman from a devious schemer. With lyrics by Otto Harbach and Anne Caldwell and starring father-and-daughter team Fred and Dorothy Stone again (see 1923's *Stepping Stones* above), few (if any) of the songs shone more than Fred Stone's antics, so the reviews state, except for, perhaps, the bouncy "You Will, Won't You?," heard on player piano at *Weber Duo-Art You Will Won't You.

George and Ira Gershwin's songs for the Revue *Oh, Kay!* (November 8, 1926), starring Gertrude Lawrence (1898–1952) as Kay, were highlighted by a little number called "Someone to Watch over Me." Recorded the year after the show, Lawrence's tremulous version can be heard at *Gertrude Lawrence Someone to Watch over Me. Of the dozens, even hundreds, of versions of this classic over the years, listen to soprano Lea Salonga (née Maria Lea Carmen Imutan Salonga; b. 1971), of *Miss Saigon* (1989 London), *Aladdin* (1992) and *Mulan* (1998) fame, inhabit both lyrics and melody in concert at *Lea Salonga Someone to Watch over Me.

Peggy-Ann (December 26, 1926), Richard Rodgers and Lorenz Hart's second musical comedy on Broadway in 1926, was

> considered daring for its time: there was no opening chorus and no songs for the first 15 minutes. The plot, told in one long dream, focuses on Peggy-Ann's dream fantasies. She is the niece of the owner of a boarding house in New York and the fiancée of a local boy. She escapes from a hum-drum life through dreams of herself as a wealthy adventuress, with a yacht and a husband ["Peggy-Ann"; https://en.wikipedia. org/wiki/Peggy-Ann; retrieved January 26, 2018].

When the songs do come, the big hit, a typical twenties jazz band number, "Where's That Rainbow?" can be heard performed by the then-popular Frank Black (1894–1968) Orchestra at *Frank Black Orchestra Where's That Rainbow. But two other songs evoke a quieter, less-spoken tenor of the times: the New York City love letter "A Little Tree in the Park" is given a tender rendering by Celia Berk at *Celia Berk A Tree in the Park, from her 2016 album, *Manhattan Serenade*; and jazz singer Lee Wiley (1908–1975), with a voice reminiscent of Billie Holiday (née Eleanora Fagan; 1915–1959), sweetly but seriously warns the ladies about men in "A Little Birdie Told Me So," at *A Little Birdie Told Me So Lee Wiley, from her 1954 album *Lee Wiley Sings Rodgers and Hart*.

THREE

1927 through the 1930s

Rio Rita (February 2, 1927), a Ziegfeld-produced show about the relationship troubles of an Irish-American-Mexican singer, brought the comedy team of Wheeler and Woolsey together—Bert Wheeler (né Albert Jerome Wheeler; 1895–1968) and Robert Woolsey (1888–1938)—and had songs by composer Harry Tierney (1890–1965) and lyrics by Joseph McCarthy (1885–1943; not to be confused with the Cold War politician). The yearning "Sweetheart, We Need Each Other," from the 1929 part-Technicolor film version of the show, at *Sweetheart We Need Each Other Rio Rita Technicolor, remains a static if plaintive song for a full four minutes of screen time, until performers Bebe Daniels (née Phyllis Virginia Daniels; 1901–1971) and John Boles (1895–1969) break into a funny little tap dance near the end. The show was made into an Abbott and Costello film of the same name, without any of the songwriters' tunes, in 1942.

Based on the 1922 light comedy play about Navy buddies on leave and a diner owner named Looloo, *Shore Leave*, by Hubert Osborne (1881–1958), was made into the Broadway musical *Hit the Deck!* (April 25, 1927), itself adapted into three separate films over the years—in 1930 (this one is now lost), 1936, and 1955. The middle one was the wonderful 1936 *Follow the Fleet*, with songs by Irving Berlin and starring Fred Astaire and Ginger Rogers. But the original show, with music by Vincent Youmans and lyrics by Clifford Grey and Leo Robin, had several good hits itself, including "What's a Kiss Among Friends?" re-envisioned into a sexy little song and dance for Debbie Reynolds (1932–2016) and four sailors (including acrobat Russ Tamblyn) in the 1955 film version at *Hit the Deck A Kiss or Two Debbie Reynolds (with choreography by Hermes Pan). Elsewhere, "Sometimes I'm Happy" burst forth, and if you haven't seen any of the Dean Martin (1917–1995) and Jerry Lewis (né Joseph Levitch, 1926–2017) movies or television specials from the 1950s, here's your chance as they "accompany" the Norman Luboff (1917–1987) Choir on the song during one of their 1955 shows, at *Dean Martin & Jerry Lewis—Sometimes I'm Happy (1955).

The typically innocuous 1920s musical *Good News* opened on September 6, 1927, and was followed by two popular film adaptations, in 1930 and 1947. With hits by composer Ray Henderson (né Raymond Brost; 1896–1970) and lyrics by Buddy DeSylva and Lew Brown (1893–1958), the burning issue in the narrative was "whether football hero Tom Marlowe would be allowed to lead the team despite his failing grade in astronomy" (Green and Ginell 2014, p. 56). The furious energy of "The Varsity Drag," with some borrowed elements of the Charleston dance craze, can be seen in the 1930 film version of the show at *Varsity Drag—1930 Film.

Exactly one month later, on October 6, 1927, the part-talking-and-singing film *The Jazz Singer* opened at the Warner Theatre in New York City, and movies would never be the same. Ten weeks later, on December 27, 1927, *Show Boat* opened at the Ziegfeld Theatre, and *Broadway* would never be the same.

The Jazz Singer (October 6, 1927) starred Al Jolson in easily his most famous role, cantor's son Jakie Rabinowitz turned jazz singer Jack Robin. Though the narrative

> was undiluted *schmaltz* from start to finish, director Alan Crosland, by taking his cameras on location into the predominantly Jewish areas of New York's lower East Side, managed to convey an accurate picture of ghetto life and, ethnically, offered a fascinating glimpse of a community of aliens desperately trying to assimilate themselves into a new society while, at the same time, clinging fervently to the Middle-European traditions [Hirschhorn, 1981, p. 20].

The movie grossed $3.5 million, an unheard of amount for its time (although Jolson's follow-up the next year, *The Singing Fool*, netted more than $4 million), and included the hits "Toot, Toot, Tootsie!," "Blue Skies," and "My Mammy." The first tune, composed by Ted Fiorito (1900–1971) and Robert King, with lyrics by Gus Kahn (1886–1941), at *Toot, Toot, Tootsie Al Jolson, gives contemporary 21st-century audiences a perfect introduction to the extraordinary charisma Jolson held on stage. Ad-libbing the lead-in, he blasts through the tune while dancing and whistling up a storm as his own accompaniment.

The song "Blue Skies" had been written in 1926 by Irving Berlin as a

> last-minute addition to the Rodgers and Hart musical *Betsy*. Although the show ran for 39 performances only, "Blue Skies" was an instant success, with audiences on opening night demanding 24 encores of the piece from star Belle Baker. During the final repetition, Ms. Baker forgot her lyrics, prompting Berlin to sing them from his seat in the front row ["Blue Skies (Irving Berlin Song)"; https://en.wikipedia.org/wiki/Blue_Skies; retrieved August 23, 2015].

Jolson is never more endearing than when he sings the jazzy "Blue Skies" in his living room while (fake) playing piano and charming his mother at

*Blue Skies Al Jolson. Conversely, it's hard to stomach watching "My Mammy"—music by Walter Donaldson and lyrics by Sam Lewis and Joe Young—at *Mammy Al Jolson (Jazz Singer Performance) with the singer in blackface; I recommend starting the song and then closing your eyes. It's a wonderful tune, as heartfelt and catchy as the words that catch in the performer's throat, who warbles yet another tune to his dear old mom, this time in the crowd.

By the end of the twenties, film audiences could not get enough of the singing and talking pictures, and so the silents screamed their way silently into oblivion. (Only Charlie Chaplin hung tough, and successfully, with his next two pictures, both largely silent—the transcendent *City Lights*, in 1931, and the classic *Modern Times*, in 1936.)

The rate at which East Coast Broadway stars headed to Hollywood was as breakneck as Keystone Kop chases (1912–1917). By 1927, Broadway boasted 250 shows that opened in over 80 theatres—including eight new buildings that had been built to open that year alone—serving more than 20 million theatregoers. By 2015, there were less than half that number of theatres (approximately 40) and ticket holders.

Broadway's *The Five O'Clock Girl*, a story about a playboy and a poor shop girl who get to know each other through a number of late afternoon phone conversations, opened on October 10, 1927, with music and lyrics by Harry Ruby (1895–1974) and Bert Kalmar (1884–1947), respectively. In their 1950 biopic *Three Little Words*, starring Red Skelton (né Richard Skelton; 1913–1997), Fred Astaire, and Vera-Ellen (née Vera-Ellen Westmeier Rohe; 1921–1981), the plaintive "Thinking of You" from the earlier show becomes a graceful song and dance with multiple understated turns, rare-for-Astaire lifts, and even balletic *chaînées*, at *Three Little Words Thinking of You.

With music by Richard Rodgers and lyrics by Lorenz Hart, the 1889 Mark Twain (né Samuel Langhorne Clemens; 1835–1910) novel *A Connecticut Yankee in King Arthur's Court* was adapted into the musical *A Connecticut Yankee* (November 3, 1927). Conked on the head with a champagne bottle, Martin dreams he's been transported back to Camelot, where he is asked to bring them up-to-date with telephones and other handy devices. Several hit songs emerged from the show, including the bouncy two-step "Thou Swell," heard in a contemporaneous 1928 recording with tenor vocalist Franklyn Baur (1903–1950) at *1928 Hits Archive Franklyn Baur Thou Swell; and a murderous list song to rival any of Cole Porter's, "To Keep My Love Alive" is done justice—boy, is it!—by Elaine Stritch (1925–2014) in one of her many one-woman shows (2006) at *To Keep My Love Alive Elaine Stritch. A full-length version of the song, with even more clever double-entendre lines, was written for Vivienne Segal (1897–1992) in the 1943 revival, which can be heard at *To Keep My Love Alive by Vivienne Segal.

Funny Face (November 22, 1927), starring Adele Astaire and her younger brother, some guy named Fred, was a madcap story of stolen pearls and hijinks at Atlantic City. With music and lyrics by George and Ira Gershwin, respectively, the show was made into an excellent and totally different February 1957 film to showcase 27-year-old Audrey Hepburn (née Audrey Kathleen Ruston; 1929–1993) and a much older (57) Fred Astaire. It carried a handful of tunes from the original such as the wonderful "'S Wonderful" and the love-filled "He Loves and She Loves," two highlights. Listen to João Gilberto (né João Gilberto Prado Pereira de Oliviera; b. 1931) turn the first into a cool bossa nova tune on his *Amoroso* (1976) album at *S'Wonderful—Joao Gilberto, then watch Astaire croon the second to Hepburn in the film as they dance together outdoors and even glide on a small lake float among swans at *Fred Astaire—He Loves and She Loves Funny Face.

A "Babbitt" is a self-satisfied, smug, yet conventional person, while a "bromide" is a boring dullard full of platitudes. "The Babbitt and the Bromide," also from the original *Funny Face* show, was a featured dance number for Fred and Adele back in 1927, but by the time the 1946 film *Ziegfeld Follies* arrived, Gene Kelly (1912–1996) had appeared onscreen and Astaire could not resist turning the ditty into their only major duet on film, at *Fred Astaire and Gene Kelly—The Babbitt and the Bromide. Try to guess which dancer choreographed which part of this corny, typical Revue number from the twenties. (Hint: Astaire preferred turning to the right, while Kelly was the lefty.)

Based on the 1926 novel by Edna Ferber (1885–1968), *Show Boat* (December 27, 1927) showed Broadway that a new Great White Way was on the way, although it took another 16 years before one of the collaborators of that 1927 show saw that evolution come close(r) to fruition. Produced by none other than Florenz Ziegfeld, of glorifying-the-American-girl Follies fame, *Show Boat* was the brainchild of composer Jerome Kern and lyricist/librettist Oscar Hammerstein II (with some lyrics by P. G. Wodehouse). It stunned the opening night crowd … into silence.

Theatre historian Stanley Green (1923–1990) said that

> the characters were more three-dimensional [than any other show of the time], the music was more skillfully integrated into the libretto, and the plot dared to deal with such unaccustomed subjects as unhappy marriages, miscegenation, [alcoholism,] and the hard life of black stevedores [over a 50-year period; 2011, p. 60].

One need listen to no other tune but that extraordinary paean to the Mississippi River itself at *Ol' Man River Show Boat 1936 Paul Robeson, to realize how important the show and songs were to the development of musicals. Bass-baritone singer and human rights activist Paul Robeson (1898–1976), whose father at the age of 15 escaped slavery from North Carolina and eventually became a minister in Princeton, New Jersey, couldn't perform in the original owing to previous commitments, but he joined the revival as Joe in 1932 and fully inhabits the rich character of the song in the 1936 film.

> From the show's opening number "Cotton Blossom," the notes in the phrase "Cotton Blossom, Cotton Blossom" are the same notes as those in the phrase "Ol' Man River, dat Ol' Man River," but inverted. However, "Cotton Blossom" was written first, and "Ol' Man River" was written only after Kern and Hammerstein realized they needed a song to end the first scene in the show. Hammerstein decided to use the idea of the Mississippi River as a basis for the song, and told Kern to use the melody that the stevedores sang in "Cotton Blossom" but invert some of it, and slow down the tempo. This inversion gave "Ol' Man River" a tragic quality ["Ol' Man River"; https://en.wikipedia.org/wiki/Ol%27_Man_River; retrieved August 24, 2015].

African American jazz performer and civil rights activist Lena Horne (1917–2010) had petitioned MGM for the role of Julie LaVerne in their 1951 film version of the show, but she had to settle for imbuing the classic "Can't Help Lovin' Dat Man" with her trademark sultry heartbreak in the 1946 Jerome Kern biopic *Till the Clouds Roll By*, at *Can't Help Lovin' Dat Man Lena Horne. As of 2015, there had been five Broadway revivals and three films (1929, 1936, and 1951) of the show.

Part operetta and part musical comedy, *Rosalie* (January 10, 1928), about a princess from a fictional country called Romanza who visits West Point, featured songs by George and Ira Gershwin, most notably the bluesy "How Long Has This Been Going On?" (not to be confused with the 1974 Ace hit "How Long," at *Ace How Long). Pop artist Boz Scaggs (né William Royce Scaggs; b. 1944) surprises with a classy and jazzy version of the tune from his 2003 album *But Beautiful: Standards, Volume 1*, at *How Long Has This Been Going On Boz Scaggs. The show was made into a 1937 film of the same name, but dropped the Gershwin tunes for new ones by Cole Porter.

If you can understand the plot of the musical comedy *Present Arms*, the Rodgers and Hart show that opened on April 26, 1928, you're a better person than me:

> A man from Brooklyn is serving as a buck private in Pearl Harbor. He flirts with an English Peer's daughter; however, she is being pursued by a German, who raises pineapples in Hawaii. The Brooklynite pretends to be a Captain in order to make an impression, but he is found out, booted out, and loses out on the girl, until he proves himself in a shipwreck ["Present Arms"; https://en.wikipedia.org/wiki/Present_Arms; retrieved January 29, 2018].

Rodgers himself conducts the orchestra *and* plays piano on the big hit from the show, sung by Deane Janis, "You Took Advantage of Me," at *Richard Rodgers Conducts You Took Advantage of Me, recorded on the 1949 album *Rodgers–Hart Musical Comedy Hits*. In listening to the words—Rodgers himself called the tune "sassy and unregretful," and it was apparently the Prince of Wales' (future Edward VIII) favorite songs—one realizes that it could be sung by either a woman or a man.

With music by Jimmy McHugh (1894–1969) and lyrics by lyricist Dorothy Fields (1905–1974), *Blackbirds of 1928* (May 9, 1928), the longest running all-black Revue on Broadway, starred the pioneering tap dancer Bill "Bojangles" Robinson (1878–1949). The show boasted the songwriters' first hit, "I Can't Give You Anything but Love." Tony Bennett (né Anthony Dominick Benedetto; b. 1926) and Lady Gaga (née Stefani Joanne Angelina Germanotta; b. 1986) teamed up for a snappy and swinging version of the song on their 2014 album *Cheek to Cheek* at *Tony Bennett, Lady Gaga—I Can't Give You Anything but Love. The high-energy fox-trot "Diga Diga Doo" knocked the socks off the audience, performed by Goody and his Good Timers at *Digga Digga Do Goody.

Based on Brit John Gay's ballad opera *The Beggar's Opera* (1728), from exactly 200 years earlier, the German *Threepenny Opera* (August 31, 1928; 1931 film) was a groundbreaking play adapted into a socialist critique of capitalism by playwright Bertolt Brecht (1898–1956) and music by Kurt Weill (1900–1950). The big hit was "Die Moritat von Mackie Masser," better known as "Mack the Knife," and popularized by Bobby Darin (1936–1973) in 1958 at *Mack the Knife Bobby Darin. Have a listen to Brecht himself, in the original German, in a rare 1929 recording at *Mack the Knife (original).

Al Jolson's follow-up film to his uber-hit *The Jazz Singer* was *The Singing Fool* (September 29, 1928), a soaper about the rise and fall and rise and fall of a singer. Hits by Jolson *not* performed in blackface included "Sitting on Top of the World" and "There's a Rainbow 'Round My Shoulder," and in blackface, the first million-seller tune from a film, "Sonny Boy." But the one song deleted because of a lawsuit by its writer, English Music Hall performer and composer Billy Merson (1879–1947), was the comic "The Spaniard That Blighted My Life," sung as a playful duet by Jolson and Bing Crosby in 1947 at *Al Jolson and Bing Crosby The Spaniard That Blighted My Life.

A cross between a Revue and a musical with a flimsy plot about love between "proper" Massachusetts folk and Parisian actresses, *Paris* (October 8, 1928) introduced the world to Cole Porter (1891–1964) with his hit "Let's Do It (Let's Fall in Love)," the parenthetical part of the song's title forced on him by the censors. Porter waged (and often won) double-entendre battles with them his entire life. Period singer Irving Kaufman (né Isidore Kaufman; 1890–1976) captures the bubbly tenor of the original when he warbles the tune the same year it came out at *Sam Lanin Plays Cole Porter Let's Do It. Typical of Porter's list songs, "Let's Do It" has verse after verse after verse that endlessly play on the three words in the title. Porter's own early recording on vocal and piano can be heard at *Let's Do It Cole Porter. With a similar entreaty, "Let's Misbehave," originally intended for *Paris* but dropped in favor of "Let's Do It," was nevertheless recorded that year by the star of the show, Corsican American Irene Bordoni (1885–1953), at *Irene Bordoni Sings Cole Porter Let's Misbehave. The song finally made it into the show's 1962 revival.

With songs by Brown, DeSylva and Henderson, *Hold Everything!* (October 10, 1928) gave Cowardly Lion Bert Lahr (1895–1967) the vehicle for his first starring role. Like *Good News* the previous year, the show was sports-themed, but this time a boxer gets in trouble with his girlfriend because he won't fight for a charity. Bandleader Ben Selvin's (1898–1980) ensemble, the Broadway Nitelites, recorded the hit from the show, "You're the Cream in My Coffee," at *You're the Cream in My Coffee Hold Everything.

Animal Crackers (October 23, 1928), the second of three Broadway hits for all four Marx Brothers, had an anarchic book by George S. Kaufman (1889–1961) and Morrie Ryskind (1895–1985), and zany music and lyrics by Harry Ruby and Bert Kalmar, respectively. As recorded for the 1930 film version of the show, complete with Groucho's goofy dance to "Hooray for Captain Spaulding" and its inimitable double-talk, the brothers' lunacy takes off at *Hooray for Captain Spaulding.

This Year of Grace (November 7, 1928) came to Broadway from London with book, lyrics, and music by Noël Coward (1899–1973); it also starred Noël Coward. Among some 20-odd hummable tunes in the show, "A Room with a View" stands out for its lively lyric and bouncy melody, sung by the songwriter himself at *Noel Coward A Room with a View. "World Weary," another hit, was also sung by the star (with pianist Carroll Gibbons; 1903–1954) at *Noel Coward World Weary.

Treasure Girl (November 8, 1928), a forgettable Revue about a spoiled young woman (played by Gertrude Lawrence) involved in a treasure hunt, benefited from a host of lovely George and Ira Gershwin tunes, especially its hit, "(I've Got a) Crush on You," gorgeously rendered by pop superstar Linda Ronstadt (b. 1946) on her 1983 album *What's New*, at *Linda Ronstadt—I've Got a Crush on You. "I Don't Think I'll Fall in Love Today," an unheralded and deeply poignant tune, can be heard by the singing duo of actress-film director Nancy Walker (1922–1992) and David Craig on the 1952 album *Lyrics by Ira Gershwin* at *I Don't Think I'll Fall in Love Today Nancy Walker. "What Causes That?" is done up cheerily, even mock-hopelessly, by Michael Feinstein (b. 1956) on vocal and piano from his 1987 album *Pure Gershwin* at *Michael Feinstein What Causes That. "What Are We Here For?," another obscure and this time charming query tune, is updated to 2017 by Celia Berk and Karen Akers (b. 1945) at *Karen Akers/Celia Berk Gershwin Duet. And a real treat, yet another "unknown" *Treasure Girl* song, "Where's the Boy? (Here's the Girl!)," is lovingly rendered by the Gershwin brothers' younger sister Frances (1906–1999) on her 1973 album *Frances Gershwin: For George and Ira, with Love*, at *Where's the Boy? Here's the Girl! *Treasure Girl* turned out to be a real treasure.

The Ziegfeld-produced *Whoopee* (December 4, 1928), with music and lyrics by Walter Donaldson (1893–1947) and Gus Kahn (1886–1941) respectively, had two big hits with "Makin' Whoopee," sung by Eddie Cantor, and "Love Me or Leave Me," one of twenties-heartthrob Ruth Etting's (1897–1978) signature tunes. The 1930 film version of the same name, in two-tone color and with an "!" added to the end of the title, showcased Cantor's Vaudevillian style in his rendition of the first tune at *Eddie Cantor Makin' Whoopee. The film included two more winners, "My Baby Just Cares for Me" and the 1925 hit ditty "Yes Sir, That's My Baby." The pianist-singer Nina Simone (1933–2003), accompanying herself on piano and belting it out in her characteristic contralto, transforms the first song into an infectious, stride-like strut on her 1958 debut album *Little Girl Blue* at *Nina Simone My Baby Just Cares for Me. It's more than instructive (and more than a little mind-blowing) to watch Simone's evolution with this particular song, culminating in her live performance at the 1976 Montreux Jazz Festival (formed 1967) in Montreux, Switzerland, at *Nina Simone My Baby Just Cares for Me (Live at Montreux). One can clearly hear the classical music training running through the musician's fingers.

The part-talkie Warner Brothers film *My Man* (December 15, 1928) featured Fanny Brice (née Fania Borach; 1891–1951) singing her two signature tunes, "My Man," with music by Maurice Yvain (1891–1965) and lyrics by Channing Pollock (1880–1946), and "Second-Hand Rose," with music by James F. Hanley (1892–1942) and lyrics by Grant Clarke (1891–1931). Both were originally performed by Brice in the *Ziegfeld Follies of 1921*, and a 1921 recording of Brice singing the second tune at *Fanny Brice Second-Hand Rose gives us a sense of her projection skills for Ziegfeld at the time. The radio show *Good News* showcased Brice's heartbreaking version of the first tune—her biggest hit in stark, potent contrast to her comedienne persona—on their October 3, 1938, episode at *Fanny Brice My Man 1938. Another, perhaps more powerful heart tugger by Brice can be seen and heard in the 1930 film *Be Yourself* with the tune "When a Woman Loves a Man," with music by Ralph Rainger (1901–1942) and lyrics by Billy Rose, at *Fanny Brice When a Woman Loves a Man. Brice appeared in just five films, so there aren't many opportunities to experience her multiple talents.

The year 1929 started out just the same as 1928 ended—high times all around. *Follow Thru*, a Broadway show about a country club golf match, opened on January 9, 1929. Full of "contagious high spirits" (Green and Ginell 2014, p. 67), with songs penned by Brown, DeSylva and Henderson, the hit "Button Up Your Overcoat" was a typically breezy number by the trio. The tune is rendered in signature coquettish, boop-boop-a-doop style by Helen Kane (née Helen Clare Schroeder, 1904–1966), the inspiration for the caricature cartoon Betty Boop herself (formed 1930), at *Helen Kane—Button Up Your Overcoat 1929.

Broadway's *The Little Show* (April 30, 1929) was just that, a small, witty and sardonic Revue not reliant on the extravagance of a Ziegfeld to put over its intimate charm. Composer Arthur Schwartz (1900–1984) and lyricist Howard Dietz's (1896–1983) 1st of 11 Broadway musicals, it also boasted their first hit, "I Guess I'll Have to Change My Plan." The tune is lovingly reprised as a soft-shoe tap duet in the 1953 film *The Band Wagon* (1931 Broadway) by Fred Astaire and debonair, Scottish-born film and stage performer, producer and director Jack Buchanan (1891–1957), at *I Guess I'll Have to Change My Plan from The Band Wagon 1953.

Hollywood's first all-talking musical, MGM's *The Broadway Melody*, opened on June 12, 1929. A story about the relationship shenanigans between Eddie, Queenie, Hank and a certain producer Francis Zanfield (get it?), the film earned the first-ever Academy Award for Best Picture. In spite of its obviously static camera work, with music by Nacio Herb Brown and lyrics by Arthur Freed, the title tune was sung and danced (and tapped to in pointe shoes, too!) at *The Broadway Melody 1929.

The Hollywood Revue of 1929 (June 20, 1929) introduced the tune "Singin' in the Rain" to the public via ukulele player and singer Cliff Edwards (1895–1971), the Brox Sisters (1910s—1939), and a chorus of dancers staged by Sammy Lee (1890–1968) at *Ukulele Ike Singing in the Rain. With music by Nacio Herb Brown (1896–1964) and lyrics by Arthur Freed (1894–1973), the film reprised the song in two-tone Technicolor at *Singin' in the Rain Hollywood Revue of 1929.

George and Ira Gershwin wrote most of the songs (with some lyrics by Gus Kahn), singer-tapper Ruby Keeler (née Ethel Ruby Keeler; 1909–1993) and comedian-singer Jimmy Durante (1893–1980) starred, and Duke Ellington (né Edward Kennedy Ellington; 1899–1974) conducted the orchestra for Broadway's *Show Girl* (July 2, 1929), the story of a Broadway showgirl pursued by not one, not two, not three, but four suitors. The quirky "I Must Be Home by Twelve O'Clock" is winningly put over on both piano and vocals by cabaret performer Bobby Short (1924–2005) on his 1973 album *Bobby Short Is K-RA-ZY for Gershwin* at *Bobby Short I Must Be Home, while the upbeat "Harlem Serenade" can be heard on piano and vocals by historian and performer Peter Mintun (b. 1950) at *Peter Mintun Harlem Serenade.

Famed interpreter, anthropologist, and archivist of the American Songbook, pianist-singer Michael Feinstein (b. 1956) inhabits *Show Girl's* yearning-for-home blues ballad, "Home Blues," whose lyrics start with the line "An American in Paris" on the 2003 *Essential George Gershwin* album, at *Michael Feinstein Home Blues. And even though Ruby Keeler introduced the song in the show, her then-husband Al Jolson, sitting in the audience, jumped up and sang "Liza (All the Clouds'll Roll Away)" to her and then, in typical restrained fashion (not!), stole the song for his own act and reprised it from his seat on subsequent visits. He can be heard wailing the tune at *Al Jolson Liza. Even Jimmy Durante got into the songwriting act, penning four of the show's numbers, including "Can Broadway Do without Me?" Giving us a sense of his Vaudevillian performing chops, have a listen to Durante sing the tune at *Jimmy Durante Can Broadway Do Without Me.

On with the Show! (July 13, 1929) was a Warner Brothers part-backstage musical, part-comedy, and part-mystery film with two numbers written and staged specifically for blues and jazz singer Ethel Waters (1896–1977). One of them became a signature tune, composer Harry Akst (1894–1963) and lyricist Grant Clarke's (1891–1931) paean to the blues, "Am I Blue?," which can be heard at *Am I Blue Ethel Waters. It became a standard for many performers over the years, including Hoagy Carmichael (né Hoagland Howard Carmichael; 1899–1981) and Lauren Bacall's (née Betty Joan Perske; 1924–2014) potent low-key duet of the song in the 1944 film *To Have and Have Not*—with a bemused Humphrey Bogart (1899–1957) looking on—at *Am I Blue Hoagy Carmichael.

Broadway's *Sweet Adeline* opened on September 3, 1929, a show set in the Gay Nineties about a girl from Hoboken who is unlucky in love but becomes a Broadway star. The title of the show should not be confused with the 1903 Barbershop Quartet tune of the same name, which can be heard at *Friends of Yesterday Sweet Adeline by the Friends of Yesterday in a 1984 recording, a mid-20th-century harmony group. The song has music by Harry Armstrong (1879–1951) and lyrics by Richard H. Gerard (1876–1948) and can also be heard in a 1939 recording by the Mills Brothers (1928–1982) at *Sweet Adeline Mills Brothers. *Sweet Adeline* the musical had music by Jerome Kern and lyrics by Oscar Hammerstein. Boasting over 20 tunes, it included the lovely "Here Am I," which can be heard as an instrumental duo by pianist Victor Arden (né Lewis John Fuiks; 1893–1963) and composer, pianist and conductor Adam Carroll (1898–1974) at *Ampico Here Am I.

The quintessential torch singer Helen Morgan (1900–1941) introduced a hit song about loneliness, "Why Was I Born?," in *Sweet Adeline* and can be heard singing it at *Helen Morgan Why Was I Born. On his 2017 triple album *Triplicate*, a 75-year-old Bob Dylan, of all people, also sings the song—in heartbreaking fashion—at *Bob Dylan Why Was I Born. Another melancholy ballad from the show, "Don't Ever Leave Me," is crooned by film and stage actress, singer, television host and writer Polly Bergen (née Nellie Paulina Burgin; 1930–2014), who played Helen Morgan in the 1957 teleplay *The Helen Morgan Story*, at *Don't Ever Leave Me Polly Bergen.

The film musical *Gold Diggers of 1929* opened on October 5, 1929. It featured jazz guitarist-singer Nick Lucas (né Dominic Nicholas Anthony Lucanese; 1897–1982) performing his signature tune, "Tip-Toe through the Tulips," with music by Joe Burke (1884–1950) and lyrics by Al Dubin (1891–1945), in a two-tone color scene complete with goofily-dancing quintet and huge tulips opening up to reveal more singers. Accompanying himself on ukulele, eccentric musician and singer Tiny Tim (né Herbert Buckingham Khaury; 1932–1996) re-popularized the song in 1968, seen at *Tiny Tim Tip-Toe thru the Tulips.

The Cole Porter musical *Fifty Million Frenchmen* opened on November 27, 1929, and it was the second of 23 Broadway shows for which he penned both music and lyrics. The show was about an American millionaire who bets friends he can do without money for a month in Paris *and* get engaged to the girl he loves. Porter's music was "noted for his throbbing, minor-key melodies and worldly, highly polished lyrics" (Green and Ginell 2014, p. 69). One of the many standouts was the breathy ballad "You Do Something to Me." Enjoy the blonde-wigged, wholly unrecognizable Irish singer/songwriter Sinéad O'Connor (b. 1966) as she croons the tune at *You Do Something to Me Sinead O'Connor, from the 1990 AIDS benefit Porter compilation album *Red Hot + Blue*. "The Tale of the Oyster," another tune from the show about the regurgitation of a particular shellfish, is sweetly rendered by pianist William Bolcom (b. 1938) and vocalist Joan Morrison on their 1988 *Night and Day: The Cole Porter Album* at *The Tale of the Oyster Bolcom and Morrison.

Three days later, on November 30, 1929, Porter's music appeared (alongside others) in *The Battle of Paris* film, the story of a singer played by Gertrude Lawrence in the city during World War I. A rare video of her singing the bouncy "They All Fall" from the film can be seen at *They All Fall Gertrude Lawrence.

A Broadway Revue called *Wake Up and Dream* (December 30, 1929), with songs by Cole Porter again, included a Gothic number to a composition by Johann Sebastian Bach (1685–1750), a ballet set to Léo Delibes's (1836–1891) *Coppélia*, 24 different sets, 500 costumes, and a huge international cast. The title tune, a love song full of paradoxical lyrics, can be heard sung by cabaret performer Mark Nadler on his 2007 album *KT Sullivan & Mark Nadler: A Swell Party RSVP Cole Porter* at *Wake Up and Dream Mark Nadler. Its hit "What Is This Thing Called Love?" was an overnight standard for dozens of performers. Have a listen to Julie London's (née Julie Peck; 1926–2000) up-tempo jazzy version, with Howard Roberts (1929–1992) on guitar, from her 1958 album *Julie Is Her Name, Volume II*, at *Julie London What Is This Thing Called Love.

Another song from the show, this time with explicit lyrics, "I'm a Gigolo" is sung and played on piano by the composer himself from an early thirties recording at *Cole Porter I'm a Gigolo. It should not be confused with the more popular "Just a Gigolo," adapted by Irving Caesar in 1929 from an Austrian tango number the previous year. That tune was made famous by Louis Prima (1910–1978) in 1959 and accurately re-created by rock band Van Halen alum David Lee Roth (b. 1954) on his 1985 solo EP album *Crazy from the Heat* at *David Lee Roth Just a Gigolo.

By the late twenties film musicals had begun usurping their Broadway counterparts. While 1927 and 1928 reaped just 1 (*The Jazz Singer*) and 2 (*The Singing Fool, My Man*) film musicals, respectively, the year 1929 boasted a full 65 and, in 1930, over 100. Their counterparts on Broadway, however, during the 75 years between 1855 and 1930, produced only eight years of 10 or more musicals: 1903, 1906, 1917, 1923, 1925, 1927, 1928 and 1930.

Broadway's *Strike Up the Band* (January 14, 1930) was originally a political satire about a war with Switzerland over cheese; it fizzled out in 1927 tryouts in Philadelphia. With songs by George and Ira Gershwin, the show had the first of several hits in "The Man I Love," inexplicably dropped for the 1930 revival, which was now about a war with Switzerland over chocolate. Etta James (née Jamesetta Hawkins; 1938–2012), singing the lost blues song on her 1994 album *Mystery Lady: The Songs of Billie Holiday*, throatily infuses it with rich emotion at *Etta James—The Man I Love. "I've Got a Crush on You," another Gershwin standard, is presented in relatively restrained fashion by Frank Sinatra in a 1947 recording at *Frank Sinatra I've Got a Crush on You. And the yearning ballad "Soon" is rendered by pop crooner Joni James (née Joan Carmella Babbo; b. 1930) on her 1964 album *Joni James Sings the Gershwins* at *Soon Joni James.

The film version of *Strike Up the Band* (September 1940), with only the title song remaining from the show—and by this time *supporting* war rather than parodying it—was more a showcase for its stars Mickey Rooney (né Joseph Yule, Jr.; 1920–2014) and Judy Garland, its director Busby Berkeley (1895–1976), and MGM's featured band at the time, Paul Whiteman (1890–1967) and His Orchestra. Have a look at the number, which is given a rousing Big Band vibe, at *Strike Up the Band Finale.

A Broadway show about a newspaper vendor living in a fairy-tale world of his own creation, where bad news is nonexistent, *Simple Simon* (February 18, 1930) featured Vaudevillian Ed Wynn (né Isaiah Edwin Leopold; 1886–1966) at his most fumbling. In stark contrast to Wynn's fantasy, "Ten Cents a Dance," a true story about so many women during the Depression as written by composer Richard Rodgers and lyricist Lorenz Hart, tugs at our hearts in originator Ruth Etting's presentation at *Ten Cents a Dance Ruth Etting. Tina Turner's (née Anna Mae Bullock; b. 1939) bluesy "Private Dancer," from her 1984 album of the same name at *Tina Turner Private Dancer, recalls the emotions of "Ten Cents" as Turner's character sadly reminisces about her life renting time in a ballroom.

Showcasing the self-proclaimed King of Jazz, Paul Whiteman and His Orchestra (a presumptuous misnomer, although he helped popularize the form), the Revue *King of Jazz* (April 19, 1930) was Universal Pictures' two-tone Technicolor entry into the all-color, early sound film medium. Featuring huge, mobile sets and typical variety numbers such as comedy, songs, dancing and operetta, it included an entire performance of George Gershwin's 1924 "Rhapsody in Blue" at *King of Jazz Restored Technicolor Sequence, several versions of composer Milton Ager (1893–1979) and lyricist Jack Yellen's (1892–1991) springy "Happy Feet," with (among others) dancer Al "Rubber Legs" Norman (1906–1999) wildly gyrating everything from the waist down, at *Happy Feet Footage King of Jazz, and the three Rhythm Boys (1925–1931)—Bing Crosby (né Harry Lillis Crosby, Jr.; 1903–1977), Al Rinker (1907–1982), and Harry Barris (1905–1962)—nicely harmonizing on Barris's own composition "So the Bluebirds and Blackbirds Got Together," at *Bing Sings So the Bluebirds and the Blackbirds Got Together.

Hollywood's *Dixiana* (August 1, 1930), about circus performers in the antebellum south, was tap dance pioneer Bill "Bojangles" Robinson's (1878–1949) screen debut, a specialty tap number that clearly challenged the camera operator to follow his upright, high-on-the-balls-of-his-feet style at *Bill Robinson Dixiana 1930.

Girl Crazy (October 14, 1930), a Broadway show about an easterner sent to Arizona to forget about drinking and women (spoiler alert: it doesn't work), added to the Gershwin brothers' burgeoning catalogue of successes with two big hits, "Embraceable You," which made a star out of Ginger Rogers a full three years before her teaming with Fred Astaire (although Fred was called in to help some with the dancing), and "I Got Rhythm," which made a star out of Ethel Merman, who held the middle C of the song for a full 16 bars (almost ten seconds).

Twenty-six years after the show opened, Merman blasts out that first hit on a 1956 TV special at *Ethel Merman Sings I Got Rhythm. At the opening of the Manhattan Theatre back in August 1931, George Gershwin himself played the tune on the piano, recorded on film at *Gershwin Plays I Got Rhythm New York 1931. And the four-part harmony group the Happenings (1961–1970) got a 1966 pop hit out of the song at *The Happenings I Got Rhythm. The world had to wait until 1978 before a recording of Ginger Rogers singing "Embraceable You" was available, on the album *Miss Ginger Rogers*. Have a listen to Ginger (at age 66) doing a lovely job with the song at *Ginger Rogers Embraceable You. Jo Stafford (1917–2008) doesn't hurt the glorious song one bit, either, on her 1953 album *Broadway's Best* at *Jo Stafford Embraceable You.

The show's hits just kept coming. Judy Garland embraces "But Not for Me" in the 1943 *Girl Crazy* film version of the show at *Judy Garland But Not for Me, while Ella Fitzgerald purrs the heart-tugger on her 1959 album *Ella Fitzgerald Sings the George and Ira Gershwin Songbook* at *Ella Fitzgerald But Not for Me. (Two other films were made of the show, in 1932 and 1965, the former also called *Girl Crazy* and the latter, starring Herman's Hermits, Sam the Sham and the Pharaohs, Louis Armstrong, and Liberace, called *When the Boys Meet the Girls*.) I have a soft spot in my heart for the humorous, easy-going ditty "Bidin' My Time," recorded by the original onstage quartet the Foursome (1926–1941) later that year at *1930 Version Foursome Bidin' My Time, as well as Judy Garland's own low-key take in the 1943 film at *Bidin' My Time Judy Garland.

Sweet and Low, a musical Revue full of sketches and songs by a variety of performers and composers, opened on Broadway on November 17, 1930, with famed Ziegfeld performer Fanny Brice (née Fania Borach; 1891–1951) in the cast. With words by Ira Gershwin and impresario-lyricist Billy Rose (1899–1966) and music by Harry Warren, the cheerful little "Cheerful Little Earful" zips along in a hot recording of Fred Rich (1898–1956) and his New York Syncopators at *Cheerful Little Earful Frank Rich. "You Sweet So and So," with music by Phil Charig and Joseph Meyer and lyrics again by Gershwin, is endearingly put over in a contemporary recording by Jack Buchanan (né Walter John Buchanan; 1891–1957) and the Debroy Somers (né William Henry Somers; 1890–1952) Band at *You Sweet So and So Jack Buchanan.

A satire of New Yorkers such as high-society types, bootleggers, prostitutes, and con men, written by famed *New Yorker* magazine cartoonist Peter Arno (1904–1968), Broadway's *The New Yorkers* (December 8, 1930), a show with lots of Cole Porter tunes, was "something of a forerunner of *Pal Joey* [December 1940] in its amoral characters, cynical outlook, and flashy night-club atmosphere" (Green and Ginell 2014, p. 74). The faux-diet primer "I'm Getting Myself Ready for You" bounces along nicely on piano and vocals with jazz musician Peter Mintun at *Peter Mintun I'm Getting Myself Ready for You. Accompanied on piano by fellow Belgian Dirk Baert, bass-baritone Wilfried Van dan Brande, a lifelong Porter lover and interpreter, booms out the anti-outdoors ode "The Great Indoors" at *The Great Indoors Van dan Brande.

The big hit of *The New Yorkers*, "Love for Sale," another of the composer's tunes treated at the time as scandalous and in bad taste, was a straightforward account of a prostitute's life. The pop/jazz vocalists the Manhattan Transfer (formed 1969) interestingly start the song off on their 1978 album *Pastiche* with a country western, giddy-up type instrumental (courtesy of harmonica player Charlie McCoy; b. 1941, accompanying some twangy guitar) before seguing into their signature four-part harmony at *Manhattan Transfer—Love for Sale. I like to think Porter would have enjoyed this take.

Ironically, by the end of 1930, the public had tired of the rush to make film musicals—the years 1931 and 1932 reaped just 24 and 10 movie musicals, respectively. Hollywood even began cutting song-and-dance numbers out of many films completely. For example, consider what happened to the 1929

Broadway show *Fifty Million Frenchmen*, which boasted 18 Cole Porter songs; in its 1931 film adaptation, not one remained.

A satire about a girl who makes it big in silent pictures but, by the time of the talkies, the tables are reversed in her boyfriend's favor (they make up at the end, of course), Broadway's *America's Sweetheart* (February 10, 1931) had music by Richard Rodgers and lyrics by Lorenz Hart. Oh, the sweet and simple, naïve days of lyrics! Accompanied by her fifties Big Band sound, Ella Fitzgerald sings all of the bartering words of "I've Got Five Dollars" on her 1956 album *Ella Fitzgerald Sings the Rodgers and Hart Songbook* at *I've Got Five Dollars Ella Fitzgerald. In direct contrast, Hart's racy lyrics for "A Lady Must Live," while they wouldn't make 21st-century audiences blush, cut to the quick of a liberated woman's lifestyle (of the time) as sung by Great Songbook interpreter Karen Oberlin at *A Lady Must Live Karen Oberlin.

The Band Wagon (June 3, 1931), composer Arthur Schwartz (1900–1984) and lyricist Howard Dietz's (1896–1983) second big Revue (full of show number parodies), was the last time Fred Astaire and his sister Adele performed together on Broadway. Fred and ballerina actress Cyd Charisse (née Tula Ellice Finklea, 1922–2008) exquisitely embody the songwriters' elegiac "Dancing in the Dark" number from the show in the 1953 film version of *The Band Wagon* at *Fred Astaire and Cyd Charisse Dancing in the Dark. There are lyrics to the song, too. With Canadian jazz composer and pianist Oscar Peterson (1925–2007), along with five other musicians, Astaire himself gently croons the tune on his 1952 album *The Astaire Story* at *Fred Astaire Dancing in the Dark 1952. And the medium-speed fox-trot "New Sun in the Sky" number, also sung by Astaire and recorded in 1931 with violinist and bandleader Leo Reisman (1897–1961) and His Orchestra, can be heard at *New Sun in the Sky Leo Reisman.

Eddie Cantor's second of five movie musicals in the early thirties for Polish American film producer Samuel Goldwyn (né Szmuel Gelbfisz; 1879–1974) was *Palmy Days* (October 3, 1931), a story about love hijinks at a bakery factory. Busby Berkeley's camera skills continued to grow with his work at Goldwyn Studios, as demonstrated in "Yes, Yes! (My Baby Said Yes)," written by the songwriting team of Con Conrad (né Conrad K. Dobar; 1891–1938) and Cliff Friend (1893–1974), at *Eddie Cantor Yes Yes.

Composer Jerome Kern and lyricist Otto Harbach's Broadway show *The Cat and the Fiddle* (October 15, 1931) was a slight story about a composer and an opera singer. "She Didn't Say Yes," a gentle, jazzy hit full of wordplay, was sung by American singer Elisabeth Welch (1904–2003), whose career spanned seven decades, in the 1986 Revue *Jerome Kern Goes to Hollywood* at *She Didn't Say Yes Elisabeth Welch.

Everybody's Welcome (October 31, 1931), a Broadway musical about an advertising man who changes careers to become a novelist, was filled with songs primarily created by composer Sammy Fain (1902–1989) and lyricist Irving Kahal (1903–1942). But the tune most remembered in the show was written by Herman Hupfeld (1894–1951), a little number that became an overnight hit 11 years later in the 1942 film *Casablanca*. As sung and played by Dooley Wilson (né Arthur Wilson; 1886–1953) in the movie, "As Time Goes By" can be seen and heard (Dooley's piano playing is dubbed, but that's his voice) at *Play It, Sam As Time Goes By.

Flying High (November 14, 1931), a story about the hijinks surrounding the invention of an "aerocopter," was an MGM film musical produced by famed *George White's Scandals* producer George White (1891–1968) and featured songs by composer Jimmy McHugh and lyricist Dorothy Fields. An early film showcasing Busby Berkeley's (1895–1976) kaleidoscopic camera technique, "I'll Make a Happy Landing" puts his high-overhead crane shot designs on full display at *Busby Berkeley 1931 Flying High.

Of Thee I Sing (December 26, 1931), a follow-up political parody to *Strike Up the Band*, was the first of seven (and counting) Broadway musicals to win the Pulitzer Prize for literature. It ran the longest of all Gershwin shows before *Porgy and Bess* (1935), although, because of its more fully integrated score, it produced fewer stand-alone hit songs.

> In his *New York Times* review of the 2006 concert revival, Charles Isherwood called *Of Thee I Sing* "a trenchant little musical satire.… [T]he laughter that greets the show today is tinged with surprise at how eerily some of its jokes seem to take precise aim, from decades back, at current affairs. A chorus of reporters sings to the new president of the '17 vacations you have had since you've been here.' A politician dismisses Abraham Lincoln's pronouncement about not being able to fool all of the people all the time by remarking: 'It's different nowadays. People are bigger suckers.' … [I]t serves as a sigh-inducing argument for the enduring follies of American politics" ["Of Thee I Sing"; https://en.wikipedia.org/wiki/Of_Thee_I_Sing; retrieved August 17, 2015].

A story about President Wintergreen and Vice President Throttlebottom, who had run and won on a "love" ticket, *Of Thee I Sing* spoofed Congress, the presidency, and the democratic process in equal measure. What a naïve concept, to imagine that "love is sweeping the country," in a song with the same title. Ella Fitzgerald embodies its idealism on her 1959 album *Ella Fitzgerald Sings the George and Ira Gershwin Song Book* at *Ella Fitzgerald Love Is Sweeping the Country.

A 1932 version of the title song is jazzed up, baby, by Frank Luther with the Victor Arden–Phil Ohman Orchestra at *1932 Arden & Ohman Of Thee I Sing. "Here's a Kiss for Cinderella," a farewell to fooling around, is cheerily bounced about by Bobby Short on piano and vocal from his 1970 album *Nobody Else but Me* at *Bobby Short Here's a Kiss for Cinderella. And on her 1995 album *This Is Anita O'Day*, Anita O'Day (née Anita Bell Colton; 1919–

2006) brings her inimitable rhythm and dynamics to the big hit "Who Cares?" at *Anita O'Day Who Cares. In the neoclassical George Balanchine (1904–1983) ballet *Who Cares?*, from 1970, Balanchine's homage to the Gershwins is a pas de deux by Melinda Roy and Ronald Perry set to the tune "Who Cares?" It appears at the 14-minute mark of a 1993 New York City Ballet version at *George Gershwin Balanchine Who Cares.

Uncanny precursor to the 2001 hit *The Producers*, the Broadway show *Face the Music* (February 17, 1932) was a satirical story about a presumed flop that becomes an unlikely hit. Among the high-spirited songs by Irving Berlin were two winners, "Let's Have Another Cup of Coffee" and "Soft Lights and Sweet Music," but who could have guessed that the songwriter who gave us weather reports like "Heat Wave," "Blue Skies" and "White Christmas" could write such a funny and biting chunk of irony like "Torch Song," simultaneously spoofing Porter's recent "Love for Sale" ditty *and* torch song singer Helen Morgan? Have a listen to Adèle Anderson's (b. 1952) tongue-in-cheek rendition of the tune from her 2008 album *Everything Happens to Me* at *Torch Song Adele Anderson.

Horse Feathers (August 10, 1932), the four Marx Brothers' fourth of five films at Paramount Pictures, was ostensibly a story about college football and a rival game between two fictional schools, but the narrative was just a loose skeleton for the boys to perpetrate their miraculous pre–Censorship Code mayhem upon all the participants. Equally talented at music as well as comedy, the brothers invariably found time in their films to straightforwardly perform on their respective instruments: Harpo on the harp (although you can see him playing clarinet in *The Cocoanuts* and piano in a couple of their films, too), Chico on piano, Groucho on guitar, and Zeppo on vocals. Composer Harry Ruby and lyricist Bert Kalmar's hit song for the film, "Everyone Says I Love You," is sweetly rendered by each brother at *Marx Brothers Everyone Says I Love You, with Harpo even whistling it at one point. To see him perform the song on his preferred harp, look at *Harpo Marx in Horse Feathers. Woody Allen made a film with the same title as the song in 1996, and it was full of classic tunes, including that one, sung mostly by the actors themselves (see below).

As with Berlin before them, composer Richard Rodgers and lyricist Lorenz Hart headed out to the West Coast in the early thirties to try their hand at films. Starting with *Love Me Tonight* (August 18, 1932), it starred French actor, singer, and cabaret performer Maurice Chevalier (1888–1972), playing a tailor who poses as a nobleman, and opera soprano Jeanette MacDonald (1903–1965), the princess he falls in love with. The song "Isn't It Romantic?" at *Isn't It Romantic, was innovatively integrated into the film's story, via cuts and segues, by Armenian American director Rouben Mamoulian (1897–1987). Beginning with Chevalier singing it in his tailor shop, the song is then taken up by a patron moving out into the street, passed off to a taxi driver and his client (who happens to be a songwriter), who is soon further composing and singing the song while sitting in a train surrounded by soldiers, who join in as a chorus, followed by them marching over a hill and then along some country roads still in full voice. A violinist who had joined the group breaks away to run across a field to meet his gypsy friends around a fire, whereupon he plays the tune and they join in humming and then singing the words. The camera pans right across another field to the princess's castle, where soprano Jeanette MacDonald goes out onto her balcony to hear it and somehow, miraculously, knows all the words and belts it out as a solo that connects the lovers from the start to the finish of the six-minute song. Two other hits became standards—"Mimi" and "Lover"—but "The Son of a Gun Is Nothing but a Tailor," at *The Son of a Gun Is Nothing but a Tailor, is also given the fully integrated treatment, sung by not only co-stars Charles Butterworth (1896–1946) and C. Aubrey Smith (1863–1948) but by what looks like the castle's entire household, made up of dozens of minor actors called on to (happily) perform.

Flying Colors (September 15, 1932), with music by Arthur Schwartz and lyrics by Howard Dietz, was a Broadway Revue full of sketches and tunes that included a projected film behind the dance number "Louisiana Hayride" at the end of act 1. Originally an upbeat fox-trot, "A Shine on Your Shoes" was one of the show's hits. Mel Tormé gives it the Big Band treatment on his 2001 album *Mel Tormé's Finest Hour* at *A Shine on Your Shoes Mel Tormé, while Fred Astaire and real-life shoe shiner Leroy Daniels (1928–1993) dance up a storm to it in the 1953 *Band Wagon* film at *Shine on Your Shoes Astaire.

The song "Brother, Can You Spare a Dime?" from *Americana* (October 5, 1932), a musical Revue with music by Jay Gorney (né Abraham Jacob Gornetzsky; 1894–1990) and lyrics by Edgar Yipsel (E. Y.) "Yip" Harburg (né Isidore Hochberg; 1896–1981), turned out very quickly to become the anthem of the Great Depression. Gorney, born in Bialystok, Russia, based the tune on a lullaby he had heard as a child. Most famous for his lyrics on *The Wizard of Oz* (1939) and *Finian's Rainbow* (1947), the song was also Harburg's first big hit. Bing Crosby recorded the tune the same year the show came out, at *Bing Crosby Brother Can You Spare a Dime, and it's easy to see that the times were beginning to bring some reality to musicals.

The Big Broadcast (October 14, 1932), the first of four Big Broadcast films at Paramount Pictures, was a story revolving around casual radio singer Bing Crosby (in his first full-length film role) with co-stars George Burns (né Nathan Birnbaum; 1896–1996) and Gracie Allen (1895–1964) contributing the comedy. With music by Harry Woods (1896–1970) and lyrics by Howard Johnson (1887–1941), the First Lady of Radio, contralto Kate Smith (née Kathryn Elizabeth Smith; 1907–1986), sang a calm and soothing version of one of its tunes as her theme show song, "When the Moon Comes over the

Mountain." It can be heard at *The Kate Smith Hour When the Moon Comes over the Mountain in a swinging, upbeat version, complete with a fun trio of candy-stripe-jacketed, dancing male harmonizers bouncing around behind her, from her fifties television show.

Cab Calloway (1907–1994) and His Orchestra were also on hand in the film to sing, dance and scat about smoking opium on "Kicking the Gong Around," with music by Harold Arlen (né Chaim Arluck; 1905–1986) and lyrics by Ted Koehler (1894–1973), at *Cab Calloway Kicking the Gong Around. The Mills Brothers (1928–1982) also appeared, singing speedo four-part harmony (and an even faster-than-Calloway scat at one point) on "Tiger Rag," a tune copyrighted in 1917 (with a truly labyrinthine history) by the Original Dixieland Jass Band (formed 1916), at *Mills Brothers Tiger Rag.

Broadway's *Music in the Air* (November 8, 1932), with music by Jerome Kern and lyrics by Oscar Hammerstein, compared the charms of rural simplicity with the challenges of urban sophistication. "The Song Is You" quickly became a classic, as song stylist Nancy Wilson (b. 1937) demonstrates on her 1963 album *Yesterday's Love Songs/Today's Blues* at *Nancy Wilson The Song Is You. Pop singer Keely Smith (née Dorothy Jacqueline Keely; 1928–2017) does equally fine justice to the tune on her 1958 album *Politely!* at *The Song Is You Keely Smith.

Cole Porter's songs spruced up *Gay Divorce* (November 21, 1932), a Broadway show about an American writer in love with a woman who mistakes him for the husband of her best friend. "Why Marry Them?" makes a pretty good argument for keeping men around awhile until you get tired of them. It is properly rendered by Wilfried Van den Brande and Dirk Baert on vocals and piano, respectively, at *Why Marry Them Gay Divorce. The same duo presents a precursor to Burton Lane (1912–1997) and E. Y. Harburg's 1947 "When the Idle Poor Become the Idle Rich" (from *Finian's Rainbow*) in the song "Mr. and Mrs. Fitch," also from the show, at *Mr. and Mrs. Fitch Van den Brande.

The only song to make the jump to the October 1934 film version, renamed *The Gay Divorcee*—gay divorces couldn't pass muster with the censors, but a divorcée could still have fun—was the incomparable "Night and Day," here sung by Fred Astaire and then danced by him and his new screen partner, a woman who had already achieved some fame already in 20 films—Ginger Rogers—at *The Gay Divorcee 1934 Night and Day. Astaire can also be heard on a contemporary recording from the time singing the typically clever Porter lyrics of "I've Got You on My Mind" from the show at *Gay Divorce I've Got You on My Mind.

The Broadway musical *Take a Chance* (November 26, 1932), with music by Nacio Herb Brown (1896–1964) and Richard A. Whiting (1891–1938) and lyrics by Buddy DeSylva, was a story about two small-time gamblers who would prefer to work in legitimate theatre. "Eadie Was a Lady," a song about a dead prostitute sung in the show by Ethel Merman in her best Mae West impression, became a 1932 hit for Cab Calloway at *Eadie Was a Lady Cab Calloway. And Lillian Roth (née Lillian Rutstein; 1910–1980) belts it out (with all of its racy lyrics on display this time) in the 1933 pre-Code film version of the show at *Lillian Roth Eadie Was a Lady.

The film was also notable for introducing composer Harold Arlen and lyricists E. Y. Harburg and Billy Rose's fabulous fantasy hit "It's Only a Paper Moon" to the wider public, as performed by Cliff "Ukulele Ike" Edwards in a 1932 recording at *It's Only a Paper Moon Cliff Edwards. The Beatles' singer-songwriter Paul McCartney (b. 1942) does a nifty little job on the tune on his 2012 album *Kisses on the Bottom* at *It's Only a Paper Moon Paul McCartney.

Walk a Little Faster (December 7, 1932), with music by Belarus-born Vernon Duke (né Vladimir Aleksandrovich Dukelsky; 1903–1969) and lyrics by E. Y. "Yip" Harburg, was a Broadway Revue with varied songs and sketches that included innovative curtain designs by set designer Boris Aronson (1898–1980). The lovely "A Penny for Your Thoughts" is graciously, even gently, sung by British-born Sandra King (née Sandra Fairbrass; b. 1950), with Pat Smythe (1923–1983) accompanying on piano, on her live 1983 album *A Concert of Vernon Duke Songs* at *A Penny for Your Thoughts Sandra King. "April in Paris," the major hit of the show and a standard of the American Songbook, became a powerhouse trio for Mel Tormé, Judy Garland and the Count Basie (né William James Basie; 1904–1984) Orchestra, with Basie at piano on Judy's second television special from July 7, 1963, at *Judy Garland, Mel Tormé The Judy Garland Show.

Al Jolson starred in the Hollywood film *Hallelujah, I'm a Bum* (February 3, 1933), a simultaneously romanticized and satiric look at the hobo lifestyle so many people were forced to experience during the Depression. Filled with composer Richard Rodgers and lyricist Lorenz Hart tunes and performed in an interestingly rhythmic, sing-song style throughout, "You Are Too Beautiful" was the one real love ballad, rendered in heartfelt fashion by Jolson at *Al Jolson You Are Too Beautiful.

If the glut of film musicals due to the advent of sound pictures had peaked by 1930—remember, 1929 and 1930 boasted over 50 and 60 Hollywood musicals, respectively—and their rejection because of oversaturation led to their dearth (and near death) in 1931 and 1932—respectively 24 and 11—the years 1933 and 1934 surprised everyone with their *resurgence*. Why? Two names in particular answer that question: Busby Berkeley (né Berkeley William Enos; 1895–1976) and Fred Astaire (né Frederick Austerlitz; 1899–1987), both of whom wedded their talents to the burgeoning improvements in film technology as more and more Broadway artists (singers, songwriters, designers, etc.) added to the westward expansion.

The backstage Hollywood musical *42nd Street* (March 9, 1933) was the first film for Canadian-born dancer/singer Ruby Keeler (née Ethel Ruby Keeler; 1909–1993) and the first time that choreographer Busby Berkeley, composer Harry Warren, and lyricist Al Dubin worked together with director Lloyd Bacon (1889–1955) at Warner Brothers studios. The title number, at *Come Meet Those Dancing Feet 1933, is first powerfully tapped to by Keeler (in her hard-soled shoes, a distinct change from the light touch of the high-up-on-the-toes taps of Bill Robinson) and then expanded into a mini-musical about the denizens of the street, complete with an attempted rape and a successful murder! Berkeley would soon innovate his stage-bound dance scenes beyond even the largest of studio spaces into pure fantasy numbers possible only on film.

"Young and Healthy" gives us a sense of that evolving direction, at *42nd Street Young and Healthy. It starts on a proscenium stage sung solo by thirties-heartthrob Dick Powell (1904–1963), then builds to include more and more men and women dancing on a revolving platform (shades of Diorama) as the camera continues to pull back to the kaleidoscopic high-overhead crane shot that was fast becoming a signature film technique of Berkeley's. The climax finds the camera dollying between the spread legs of dozens of bare-legged chorine girls to finish in a close-up of Powell and Toby Wing (née Martha Virginia Wing; 1915–2001) lying on the platform grinning at us. This finale is re-created and updated during the "Gutterballs" musical number, starring actor Jeff Bridges (b. 1949) and Julianne Moore (b. 1960) and set to the Mickey Newbury–penned (né Milton Sims Newbury, Jr.; 1940–2002) 1968 hit for Kenny Rogers (b. 1938) and the First Edition (1967–1977), "Just Dropped In (To See What Condition My Condition Was In)," at *Gutterballs, from the 1998 crime comedy film *The Big Lebowski*.

Silent film comedians Stan Laurel (1890–1965) and Oliver Hardy (1892–1957) easily adapted their gentle Music Hall humor to sound movies in the 1930s, starring in MGM's film operetta *Fra Diavolo (The Devil's Brother)* (May 5, 1933), which was based on French composer Daniel Auber's (1782–1871) 1830 opera of the same name. Full of Auber's music as instrumentals and vocals, the film also gave Stan a chance to show off his physical dexterity, and Ollie's signature "slow burn" towards the camera, in two scenes: "Kneesy, Earsy, Nosey" and "Finger Wiggle," at *Laurel & Hardy Kneesy Earsy Nosey and *Laurel & Hardy Finger Wiggle, respectively.

Based on the James Avery Hopwood 1919 play *The Gold Diggers*, the Hollywood musical *Gold Diggers of 1933* (May 27, 1933) was one of the few Depression-era films that actually addressed the decade's troubles in a semi-realistic way. Starring the same crew that were involved in the earlier 1933 film *42nd Street*—Keeler, Powell, Warren, Dubin, and Berkeley—all four of the extravagant song-and-dance numbers highlighted the talented artists at their best: "We're in the Money," at *We're in the Money Gold Diggers of 1933, opens with a pre-Astaire Ginger Rogers singing Pig Latin and dancing with her female colleagues dressed up in huge coins; the risqué, pre–Censorship Code naked silhouettes in the "Pettin' in the Park" number are severely truncated by the YouTube censors (buy or rent the Warner Brothers film) at *Pettin in the Park Gold Diggers; the electrically lit violins of "The Shadow Waltz," at *Gold Diggers of 1933 The Shadow Waltz, among other cinematic effects, make for a startling black-and-white Extravaganza vision; and in "Remember My Forgotten Man," Berkeley poignantly, even heartbreakingly, reprises Gorney and Harburg's "Brother, Can You Spare a Dime?" message from the previous year's *Americana* by putting out-of-work World War I veterans front and center through Warren and Dubin's powerful seven-minute, mini-musical paean. (Look for the brief use of a rolling Diorama treadmill as the "fresh" bodies speed off stage right to replace the slow-moving injured stage left.)

Broadway's *As Thousands Cheer* (September 30, 1933)—not to be confused with the September 1943 Hollywood musical, *Thousands Cheer*, with a wonderful duet dance between Gene Kelly and a mop—was another Irving Berlin (1888–1989) songfest Revue directed by Berlin's frequent early collaborator and librettist, Moss Hart (1904–1961). This Revue was uniquely structured in the form of a newspaper with each sketch's song and dance based on an actual headline. It was a typical Berlin production, short and sharp, but more politically aware than anything he had done before or since. Yes, *that* Irving Berlin, he of the patriotic and simple love songs. Aside from the provocative "Supper Time," about an African American wife (sung by Ethel Waters) waiting for a husband who will never come home because he has just been lynched—at *Ethel Waters Supper Time—other hits included "Easter Parade" and "Heat Wave," the pun-filled, Porter-like latter tune sung by Waters again, recorded the same year as the show at *Ethel Waters Heat Wave.

Berlin had seen Waters sing composer Harold Arlen and lyricist Ted Koehler's "Stormy Weather" that April in Harlem's Cotton Club; he immediately hired her. She stole the show with both tunes from popular performers Marilyn Miller, Clifton Webb (né Webb Parmelee Hollenbeck; 1889–1966), and Helen Broderick (1891–1951), and when the three of them refused to take bows with her because of her skin color, Berlin said, "Fine. There need be no curtain calls at all, then" (Webb and Smith, 2011). Shamed, they relented.

Footlight Parade (October 21, 1933) was Warner Brothers' third film of the year starring Ruby Keeler, Dick Powell, composer Harry Warren and lyricist Al Dubin's songs, and Busby Berkeley's choreography. This one also had Jimmy Cagney (1899–1986) as a pressured director of Broadway musicals,

A 1921 ad about songstress Ethel Waters (1896–1977) in the *Chicago Defender,* the nation's most widely read newspaper by African Americans at the time.

culminating in the song-and-tap duet between Cagney and Keeler, "Shanghai Lil," at *Footlight Parade Shanghai Lil. "By a Waterfall," with music by Sammy Fain and lyrics by Irving Kahal, was a ten-minute Berkeley tour de force in a huge water tank with over 100 swimmers, shot in his inimitable kaleido-scopic fashion at *Footlight Parade By a Waterfall.

A Broadway show about the denizens of a clothing store that make famous gowns, *Roberta* (November 18, 1933) was filled with the songs of com-poser Jerome Kern and lyricist Otto Harbach and included their hit "Smoke Gets in Your Eyes." Updated into a gorgeous doo-wop ballad 25 years later by the Platters (formed 1954) in 1958, watch a rare version of the tune by the group from the 12th season of the *Ed Sullivan Show* (March 1, 1959) at *The

Platters Smoke Gets in Your Eyes. Broadway's *Roberta* was made into a Hollywood musical less than two years later (February 1935) with Fred Astaire and Ginger Rogers (billed third and fourth). More compositions by Kern and Harbach were added to the film, along with lyricists Dorothy Fields, Bernard Dougall (on "I'll Be Hard to Handle") and Oscar Hammerstein II (on "I Won't Dance"). If you listen carefully to "I'll Be Hard to Handle," sung by Ginger and then seemingly spontaneously danced to by the stars at *Roberta I'll Be Hard to Handle, their laughter and taps can be heard recorded live on the freshly built wooden stage. And "I Won't Dance" is jazzily, frenetically played on piano, live again, by none other than Fred, followed by the song sung by Ginger (and Fred) and then Astaire tapping a fiery solo to the song at *Roberta I Won't Dance Fred.

Going Hollywood (December 22, 1933) was a Paramount Pictures musical about a crooner headed to Hollywood to make a movie. It starred Bing Crosby and Marion Davies (1897–1961) as the lead couple in and out of love, as well as a host of character actors coming in and out of the picture. While most songs written by composer Nacio Herb Brown and lyricist Arthur Freed were in a light, romantic vein, their brooding, minor-key "Temptation," at *Temptation Bing Crosby, was one of those rare early thirties tunes integrated into the film plot as Crosby downs tequila in a Tijuana bar while staring lustily into Davies' eyes. On the very first episode of PBS Television's *The Muppet Show* (April 25, 1977), Miss Piggy herself does a pretty good rendition, complete with backing four-part harmony dum-da-da-da-dum's, at *The Muppet Show Temptation.

In the first of three films titled *Moulin Rouge* (January 14, 1934; also 1952 and 2001), with music by Harry Warren and lyrics by Al Dubin, United Artists pulled out all the stops with "The Boulevard of Broken Dreams," an extravagant mini-musical full of partially clad women on display plus multi-talented actress Constance Bennett (1904–1965) leading the festivities at *The Boulevard of Broken Dreams. It was choreographed by Russell Markert (1899–1990), the man who had founded (and became the long-time director of) the Radio City Music Hall's Rockettes in New York City's Rockefeller Center two years earlier, in 1932.

A slight story about the goings-on in a knock-off couture shop in Paris, *Fashions of 1934* (February 14, 1934) ostensibly starred William Powell (1892–1984) and Bette Davis (née Ruth Elizabeth Davis; 1908–1989)—the latter almost unrecognizable in false eyelashes and platinum-blonde hair—but really featured Busby Berkeley's choreography for camera and his geometrically objectified women yet again. Extravagant en masse ostrich feathers plus barely covered near-nude dancers suffuse the bizarrely surreal "Spin a Little Web of Dreams," with music by Sammy Fain and lyrics by Irving Kahal, at *Fashions of 1934 Preview Clip.

Paramount Pictures' pre–Code film musical *Murder at the Vanities* (May 21, 1934) was based on the long-running Revue *Earl Carroll's Vanities*, with a murder mystery thrown in. (Known as "the Troubadour of the Nude," Earl Carroll (1893–1948) produced 11 *Vanities* shows on Broadway, replete with the most lightly clad women in town.) The song-and-dance number "Sweet Marijuana," sung by Gertrude Michael (née Lillian Gertrude Michael; 1911–1964) and with music by Arthur Johnston (1898–1954) and lyrics by Sam Coslow (1902–1982), featured giant cactus plants and topless women (with their arms crossed) strewn about; it has to be seen to be believed at *Sweet Marijuana Murder at the Vanities. Duke Ellington and His Orchestra's subversive "Ebony Rhapsody"—including dozens of African American dancers choreographed by Larry Ceballos (1887–1978) and LeRoy Prinz (1895–1983)—happily displace an all-too-serious, all-white classical music performance for the film's finale at *Duke Ellington 1934 Ebony Rhapsody.

Life Begins at 8:40 (August 27, 1934), a Broadway Revue with music by Harold Arlen and lyrics by E. Y. Harburg and Ira Gershwin, featured Bert Lahr *and* Ray Bolger five years before they appeared in *The Wizard of Oz* (also with Arlen/Harburg tunes). "Let's Take a Walk Around the Block" was filled with Harburg's (and, in this case, Gershwin's, too) typically clever word play, set to a lively Arlen composition, and heard by Ella Fitzgerald on her 1961 album *Ella Fitzgerald Sings the Harold Arlen Songbook* at *Let's Take a Walk Around the Park Ella Fitzgerald. Another punny tune, "I'm a Builder Upper," is put across bouncily with jazz trombonist and singer Pee Wee Hunt (né Walter Gerhardt Hunt; 1907–1979) on vocals, backed by Glen Gray (né Glen Gray Knoblauch; 1906–1963) and the Casa Loma Orchestra, at *1934 Glen Gray I'm a Builder Upper.

The Paramount Pictures film musical *She Loves Me Not* (August 31, 1934) was a story about a cabaret dancer who witnesses a murder and then disguises herself as a male Princeton student to hide out (sounds like a precursor to the 1959 film *Some Like It Hot* and the 1992 film *Sister Act*). Its big hit, "Love in Bloom," written by Leo Robin and Ralph Rainger, was sung by Bing Crosby and singer, actress, and spokeswoman for the arts Kitty Carlisle (née Catherine Conn; 1910–2007) at *Bing Sings Love in Bloom. But it's the jaunty and jazzy "After All, You're All I'm After," written for the film by Arthur Schwartz (music) and Edward Heyman (lyrics; 1907–1981) but not used, that is put over with the most pizzazz by Al Bowlly (1898–1941) on guitar and vocals, backed by Ray Noble (1903–1978) and his New Mayfair Dance Orchestra, at *Arthur Schwartz After All You're All I'm After.

Berkeley, Keeler, Powell, Warren, Dubin, and the rest returned to Warner Brothers for the September 1, 1934, Hollywood film *Dames*, a story about a millionaire fighting immorality deep in the heart of New York City. Among the hits was the typical Berkeley fantasy number "I Only Have Eyes for You," complete with dozens of huge Ruby Keeler face photographs and stairways reminiscent of M. C. Escher (1898–1972) surrounding a Ferris wheel full of evening-gowned dames, of course, all moving about on revolving Diorama platforms. Look fast for a film example of Pantomime transformation at *Dames I Only Have Eyes for You. An elegant, Doo-Wop version of the tune by the Flamingos (formed 1953) reached number 11 on the U.S. pop charts in 1959, heard at *Flamingos I Only Have Eyes for You.

On both coasts, 1934 was Cole Porter's year. Not only had his big Broadway hit from 1932, *Gay Divorce*, been turned into a bigger hit in Hollywood, *The Gay Divorcee*, on October 12, 1934, but the following month, on November 21, 1934, *Anything Goes* knocked it out of the park back East on Broadway.

Anything Goes boasted not one ("I Get a Kick Out of You"), not two ("All through the Night"), not three ("You're the Top"), but four ("Anything Goes") hit Porter songs and was the fourth-longest-running show in 1930s Broadway (behind *Hellzapoppin, Pins and Needles*, and *Of Thee I Sing*). With a madcap book by English humorists Pelham Grenville "P. G." Wodehouse (1881–1975) and Guy Bolton (1884–1979), American librettists Howard Lindsay (né Herman Nelke; 1889–1968) and Russel Crouse (1893–1966) added a host of clever revisions before it opened to rave reviews.

Even if you've heard both versions, it's great fun to contrast Ethel Merman's original rendition of that first snob-busting hit at *Ethel Merman I Get a Kick Out of You (1934) with Frank Sinatra's classic take on his 1954 album *Songs for Young Lovers*, at *Frank Sinatra I Get a Kick Out of You. Porter himself does pretty good justice to both the title song at *Anything Goes Performed by Cole Porter (recorded the same year as the show) and "You're the Top," recorded the following year at *You're the Top Cole Porter (1935). Yes, that's Porter's own piano playing on both renditions.

About Porter's songwriting character, theatre historian Ken Bloom and actor Frank Vlastnik, in their *Broadway Musicals: The 101 Greatest Shows of All Time*, said that his

> songs achieved a markedly higher level of sophistication than the books [for the librettos were] mainly an excuse to bridge the spaces between Cole Porter's outstanding songs. [From] the sinuous ballads … to delightful list songs full of up-to-date references, [his lyrics were loaded with] incredibly shocking double entendres that blissfully sailed over the heads of all but the most inside audience members [2008, pp. 17–18].

Film director/producer/screenwriter Michael Kantor and Tisch School of the Arts professor Laurence Maslon, in their *Broadway: The American Musical*, noted that if

> Porter had done nothing else for musical theater, he made it safe for sex—never depicted, of course, but wittily implied. His risqué material often got him in trouble with the censors and the bluenoses—the lyrics to "Love for Sale," a prostitute's torch

song, were banned from the radio for twenty-five years—but it was rarely gratuitous. Porter's view of sex is unapologetic, passionate, and healthy…. He had a gift for deeply yearning, aching ballads, often using Latin rhythms and unexpectedly long and complicated musical structures, as in "Begin the Beguine." His patter songs [such as "You're the Top" and "Anything Goes"], catalogues of metaphorical or topical ideas spun endlessly in refrain after refrain, proved him to be the wittiest lyricist since W. S. Gilbert [2004, p. 1366].

Based loosely on composer Victor Herbert's (1859–1924) music and libretto for the 1903 Broadway musical *Babes in Toyland*, the 1934 film version of the same name starred comedians Stan Laurel and Oliver Hardy (November 30, 1934). Populated with fairy-tale characters such as Mother Goose, Little Bo Peep, the Three Little Pigs, Little Jack Horner, and a monkey dressed up to look like Mickey Mouse, who had only recently (1928) been invented by the Walt Disney Company (formed 1923), all ends happily ever after when the March of the Toy Soldiers finally overcomes the Bogeymen army at the end. Have a look at the Cat and the Fiddle cheering the soldiers on at *March of the Wooden Soldiers Cat and the Fiddle.

The Broadway Revue *Thumbs Up!* (December 27, 1934) was packed with songs by nearly a dozen composers and lyricists, including James F. Hanley's (1892–1942) hit "Zing! Went the Strings of My Heart," jauntily put over by vocalist Joey Nash backed by Richard Himber (1899–1966) and his Ritz-Carlton Orchestra at *Richard Himber Zing. Apparently, "Zing!" was the song Judy Garland sang at her 1935 audition for MGM president Arthur Freed, reprised in the 1938 film *Listen, Darling* at *Judy Garland Zing. "Autumn in New York" was the other big number, a dreamy meditation on the Big Apple written by Vernon Duke. It can be heard reverently rendered on piano and vocals by Peter Mintun at *Peter Mintun Autumn in New York.

The first of nearly 20 full-length film musicals written specifically for child singer, dancer, actress, and eventual diplomat Shirley Temple (1928–2014), *Bright Eyes* (December 28, 1934), a comedy drama about an orphaned girl and the fight for custody, helped ease the Great Depression during its just-over-one-hour length. Already an "old" pro, having appeared in 12 films since 1932 when she was three years old, her six-year-old charms are on display in a colorized version of "On the Good Ship Lollipop," with music by Richard A. Whiting and lyrics by Sidney Clare (1892–1972), at *Shirley Temple On the Good Ship Lollipop.

On the same day (December 28, 1934), Eddie Cantor's fourth of five early thirties films for producer Samuel Goldwyn, *Kid Millions*, the story about a Brooklyn boy's search for his inheritance in Egypt, opened in Hollywood. In spite of the insult that Cantor's blackface alongside them must have caused, Harold (1921–2000) and Fayard Nicholas (1914–2006) tap up a storm to a tune Cantor first introduced in the *Ziegfeld Follies of 1919*, Irving Berlin's "Mandy," at *The Nicholas Brothers Mandy 1934.

In their first of four films together at Fox (and then 20th Century–Fox), Bill Robinson and Shirley Temple tap their hearts away in *The Little Colonel* (February 22, 1935), a film about family intrigues in the South just after the Civil War. Two numbers stand out: "O Susanna," Stephen Foster's 1848 antebellum tune, in a charming tap duet with Robinson and Temple "trading fours" (alternating eight-count solos) at *The Little Colonel Tap Duet, and their famous "Stair Dance" at *Shirley Temple Bill Robinson Tap on Stairs, with Robinson humming several Foster-type tunes as accompaniment.

The operetta film *Naughty Marietta* (March 8, 1935), based on the 1910 Broadway operetta of the same name, would not normally be included in this book about musicals, but the tune by Victor Herbert, "Ah, Sweet Mystery of Life," sung by soprano Jeanette MacDonald in the film at *Naughty Marietta, Ah Sweet Mystery of Life, has had legs, as they say, in popular culture since then—most notably, as sung by fellow soprano Madeline Kahn (1942–1999) to Frankenstein's monster (actor Peter Boyle; 1935–2006), in Mel Brooks's 1974 film *Young Frankenstein*, at *Elizabeth's Abduction Oh Sweet Mystery. Kahn's version of the song, just as the monster begins to make love to her onscreen, may have made Herbert roll over in his grave. Another "homage" to the song shows Edith, Gloria and Michael letting it rip in season 4, episode 5, "Archie the Gambler" (October 13, 1973), at about the two-minute mark, during the popular TV sitcom *All in the Family* (1971–1979) at *Archie the Gambler.

With 56 men dressed in black crouching underneath, rhythmically rolling them all over the place, 56 all-white grand pianos "dance" in Busby Berkeley's rendition of "The Words Are in My Heart" at *Dancing Pianos Berkeley, one of composer Harry Warren and lyricist Al Dubin's songs in *Gold Diggers of 1935* (March 16, 1935). The film was Warner Brothers' second of four unrelated musicals with the words "Gold Diggers" in the title. Perhaps the most famous of all Berkeley creations, "The Lullaby of Broadway" is filled to the brim with 126 tap dancers pounding away, an excerpt of which can be seen at *Lullaby of Broadway (buy the film to see the entire 15-minute number).

Hooray for Love (June 14, 1935) was an RKO film musical that starred Gene Raymond and Ann Sothern, but it featured the song "Living in a Great Big Way," with music by Jimmy McHugh and lyrics by Dorothy Fields. Performed by Bill "Bojangles" Robinson, Jeni LeGon (née Jennie Bell; 1916–2012), and Fats Waller at *Jeni LeGon Bill Robinson Fats Waller Living in a Great Big Way, they steal the show with a fab tap duet accompanied by Fats on the piano.

Top Hat (September 6, 1935) was arguably Fred Astaire and Ginger Rogers's most famous, and possibly best film together (out of ten). Featuring songs written by Irving Berlin (his first complete film score since the 1930 flop, *Reaching for the Moon*), all 5 songs in the film were in the top 15 of *Your Hit Parade* for the week of September 28, 1935. Have a listen and watch the dances to all 5: "No Strings (I'm Fancy Free)," at *Top Hat No Strings, a mini-musical with Fred dancing all around his hotel room declaring his love for Ginger and eventually soft-shoeing her (and himself) to sleep; "Isn't This a Lovely Day (To Be Caught in the Rain)?" at *Top Hat Isn't This a Lovely Day, reveals them both falling in love through Berlin's finest ballad (he said so himself) as Fred sings it to Ginger first and then they dance, the pace doubling and tripling; "Top Hat, White Tie and Tails," at *Top Hat White Tie and Tails, has Astaire tapping up a solo storm (with some Jimmy Cagney–recommended improvisation, who had stopped by the set) and then shooting down his cho-rus dancers, a number pilfered from a rare Astaire flop, the 1930 Broadway show *Smiles*; "Cheek to Cheek," at *Top Hat Cheek to Cheek, tests Fred's vocal range in the heavenly ballad, followed by the sublime "feather" dance, Ginger's back bends in delicious pause, pose, and repose; and finally "The Piccolino," at *Top Hat Piccolino, the grand finale via Berlin's "spoof" of Italianate tunes, a grand affair replete with dozens of dancers in numerous arrangements cul-minating in another of Astaire-Rogers's inimitable ballroom/tap duets. Throughout the film, enjoy art designer Van Nest Polglase's (1898–1968) fan-tastic (and wholly impossible) Art Deco sets, inspired by his visit to a Paris Beaux Arts exhibit earlier that decade.

Broadway Melody of 1936 (September 18, 1935), the second of four unre-lated MGM film musicals with "Broadway Melody" in the title, featured music by Nacio Herb Brown and lyrics by Arthur Freed. The film was also the first of three *Broadway Melody* pictures to star the extraordinary tap dancer (and singer) Eleanor Powell (1912–1982), who impersonates a French actress and dancer in order to impress her beau into hiring her for his new musical. The clarity of her taps are never on better display than in "You Are My Lucky Star" at *Eleanor Powell Lucky Star.

The Big Broadcast of 1936 (September 20, 1935), the second of four Para-mount Pictures film musicals with "Big Broadcast" in the title, was another Revue-type story about radio singers and their shenanigans. It featured a slew of songs by a variety of songwriters, including one with lyrics by witty poet, critic and satirist Dorothy Parker (1893–1967), of all people: "I Wished on the Moon" (music by Ralph Rainger), sung by Bing Crosby with the Dorsey Brothers' Orchestra, at *I Wished on the Moon Bing Crosby. The rarely recorded "Why Stars Come Out at Night," with words and music by English bandleader and composer Ray Noble, is intimately delivered in a mellow and heartfelt 2008 vocal by Kurt Reichenbach at *Kurt Reichenbach Sings Why Stars Come Out at Night.

The daring and racially controversial folk opera *Porgy and Bess* (October 10, 1935) featured an entire cast of classically trained African Americans. It was based on Charleston, South Carolina, author DuBose Heyward's (1885–1940) 1925 novel *Porgy*, about a disabled black street beggar who attempts to rescue Bess from her violent lover Crown and the drug dealer Sportin' Life. Even though it was a financial flop at first, overnight standards such as "Summertime," "I Got Plenty o' Nuttin,'" and "It Ain't Necessarily So" have been interpreted by literally hundreds of artists over the years. It was, sadly, George Gershwin's last Broadway score, for he died of a brain hemorrhage at the age of 38 on July 11, 1937.

Have a listen to one of many definitive versions of "Summertime" by Ella Fitzgerald and Louis Armstrong on their 1957 album *Porgy and Bess* at *Ella Fitzgerald Louis Armstrong Summertime. Baritone Norm Lewis (b. 1963) inhabits "I Got Plenty o' Nuttin'" in influential theatre and opera director Diana Paulus's (b. 1966) 2011 revision *The Gershwins' Porgy and Bess*, at *Norm Lewis Performs I Got Plenty o' Nuttin' The Rosie Show. "It Ain't Necessarily So" is performed by the man that Gershwin himself had written the part of Sportin' Life for but who didn't play it until the 1952 revival: Cab Calloway, at *It Ain't Necessarily So Cab Calloway.

Two nights later, in a story about the royal family of a fictional European country, Cole Porter's bubbly musical *Jubilee* (October 12, 1935) opened. The hits? "Just One of Those Things" was one. Rosemary Clooney's (1928–2002) bouncy jazz version of the song, on her 1982 album *Rosemary Clooney Sings the Music of Cole Porter*, can be heard at *Rosemary Clooney Just One of Those Things. Another was "Begin the Beguine," which, after a very cool female quartet, the Music Maids, harmonize on it, the number was put over no better than Eleanor Powell tapping away with Fred Astaire working hard to keep up with her in sadly their only film together, *Broadway Melody of 1940* (February 1940), at *Begin the Beguine Fred Eleanor.

Singer, songwriter, actor, musician, rodeo performer and business tycoon Gene Autry (né Orvon Grover Autry; 1907–1998), the singing cowboy and a pioneering figure in the history of country music, made 93 films (mostly B-Westerns at Republic Pictures), 91 television episodes (*The Gene Autry Show*; 1950–1956), and innumerable radio performances in his career. *The Melody Trail* (October 21, 1935), just his fifth movie, was a typical story of Autry's character falling in love with a woman and the hijinks they share before marriage. "On the Melody Trail," written by Autry's frequent sidekick Smiley Burnette (né Lester Alvin Burnett; 1911–1967), is likewise a typical (and lovely) tune crooned by Autry at *Gene Autry On the Melody Trail.

November 16, 1935, saw Rodgers and Hart's spectacular circus musical *Jumbo* open at the 5000-seat Hippodrome, re-opened for the occasion, on 43rd Street and 6th Avenue. Highlights include the big finale, "Little Girl Blue," with "The Most Beautiful Girl in the World" a close second. But have a listen to the low-key "My Romance," elegiacally put over by the incomparable Tony Bennett on his 1999 *Tony Bennett Sings the Rodgers & Hart Song-book*, at *Tony Bennett My Romance. At the end of each show, star Jimmy Durante allowed Jumbo the Elephant to "lie" on top of him, seen in rehearsal footage from the original show at the 3:53 point of the film at *Rehearsal Footage of Jumbo 1935.

The Littlest Rebel (November 22, 1935) was the second of four film musical pairings between Shirley Temple and Bill Robinson. The first took place post–Civil War but this one just as the war was starting. The duo's "Shim Sham Variation" showcases Shirley's improving tap vocabulary and syncopation skills, at *Bill Robinson Shirley Temple Shim Sham, set to a harmonica jam on the soundtrack.

The title song from RKO's film musical *I Dream Too Much* (November 27, 1935), about the relationship between an aspiring singer and struggling composer, is one of Jerome Kern's loveliest (with lyrics by Dorothy Fields), lovingly rendered by Peter Mintun on piano at *I Dream Too Much Peter Mintun.

The film musical *King of Burlesque* (January 3, 1936), a story about a former Burlesque producer who wants to go legit, won an Academy Award for choreographer Sammy Lee (1890–1968) in Best Dance Direction, a category that lasted only three years—1935, 1936, and 1937—and then was discontinued. Glimpses of his work can be seen at *Dixie Dunbar Dances Fats Waller Piano, a showcase for pixie-esque tap dancer and singer Dixie Dunbar (née Christine Elizabeth Dunbar; 1919–1991), along with dozens of her male consort tap accompanists and, especially, scat-singing Fats Waller and His Orchestra (with Fats on piano and vocals), in their high-energy performance of composer Jimmy McHugh and lyricist Ted Koehler's jazzy "I've Got My Fingers Crossed."

Much of Cole Porter's music from Broadway's *Anything Goes* (1934) was substituted in the first of two film versions (January 24, 1936) with new songs, a Hollywood practice that in this case brought mixed results rather than profits to Paramount's own publishing house. A few hits remained, fortunately, including the title song, "I Get a Kick Out of You," and "You're the Top," the latter put over with lively interplay and adapted, ever-topical lyrics (Porter's words were often updated on a yearly, even monthly, basis in order to more accurately skewer some political or social persona or event). The singers? Original Broadway star Ethel Merman and Paramount's resident star Bing Crosby, at *Ethel Merman Bing Crosby Sing You're the Top.

Based on the 1922 play *Shore Leave* by Hubert Osborne (1881–1958), surprisingly about two seamen on shore leave, *Follow the Fleet* (February 20, 1936) was Fred Astaire and Ginger Rogers's fifth of ten film musicals together. With Irving Berlin songs such as "I'm Putting All My Eggs in One Basket" and "Let's Face the Music and Dance," the film was full of several Fred and

Ginger highlights, but Ginger's only tap solo in their movies, set to an instrumental of "Let Yourself Go" at *Follow the Fleet Let Yourself Go Ginger Dances, and Fred's tap solo (with chorus) to "I'd Rather Lead a Band," with ever-increasing rhythmic complexities, have an unabashed and straightforward artistry on display. They remain my personal favorites.

A story about a lighthouse keeper and his adopted little girl, the film musical *Captain January* (April 24, 1936) was based on the 1891 children's novel by Laura E. Richards (1850–1943). "At the Codfish Ball," a perky tune full of fish puns by composer Lew Pollack (1895–1946) and lyricist Sidney Mitchell (1888–1942), becomes a traveling song and dance (in the colorized version) for Shirley Temple and Buddy Ebsen (né Christian Ludolph Ebsen, Jr.; 1908–2003) at *At the Codfish Ball Temple Ebsen. At one point they clearly perform a cute variation of Fred Astaire and Ginger Rogers's "stepping dance," on two chairs and a table, from the finale of the film musical *The Gay Divorcee* (1934), which can be seen at *Fred and Ginger Gay Divorcee Ending Montage. It was a number Fred and Claire Luce had done in the 1932 Broadway version, *Gay Divorce.*

Composer Richard Rodgers and lyricist Lorenz Hart kept the hits coming with *On Your Toes* (April 11, 1936), a star vehicle not only for eccentric dancer Ray Bolger but also recently arrived Broadway and neo-classical ballet choreographer George Balanchine (1904–1983). Originally written for Astaire but turned down out of fear his public wouldn't like him without a top hat, white tie, and tails, Bolger starred in the jazz ballet "Slaughter on Tenth Avenue" with Balanchine's then protégé (and wife) Vera Zorina (née Eva Brigitta Hartwig; 1917–2003). It was the first time ballet had been used as an integral part of a Broadway story, pre-dating Agnes De Mille's "Laurey Dream Ballet" in *Oklahoma!* by seven years. Interestingly, Astaire would shortly parody the ballet world in RKO's *Shall We Dance* (1937), in which he plays a famous ballet choreographer (which we don't believe for a second).

See a two-minute excerpt of Balanchine's "Slaughter" from the mostly lost 1939 film version of *On Your Toes* at *Vera Zorina in Slaughter on Tenth Avenue. Gene Kelly, whose initial fame was due to another Rodgers and Hart show (see *Pal Joey*, 1940), pays homage to both songwriters in his own version of "Slaughter" (with another Vera, Vera-Ellen [née Vera-Ellen Westmeier Rohe; 1921–1981]), from the December 1948 biopic on the songwriters, *Words and Music*, at *Vera & Gene in Slaughter on Tenth Avenue.

Rodgers and Hart shows were usually ridiculous stories, but their songs—articulate, thrilling, witty, personal, intimate, heart-wrenching—supplied art for a desperate population. Their work tried to get more deeply into human experience, such as in "Where or When," from [*Babes in Arms*]. Lorenz Hart, or "Larry," as he preferred to be called, was an enigmatic genius, personally tortured and professionally brilliant.... Hart's unhappiness with his looks and problems in accepting his homosexuality were not helped by Rodgers's stoicism…. The Nicholas Brothers appeared in their first book musical, *On Your Toes*, singing the Rodgers and Hart song, "All Dark People (Are Light on their Feet)." The song has inexplicably been deleted from the film version and subsequent stagings of the show [Bloom and Vlastnik, 2008, p. 27].

Other wonderful tunes from the show include "There's a Small Hotel," "It's Got to Be Love," and "Glad to Be Unhappy," the latter rich with Hart's typically lyrical contradictions about love. The tune is fully inhabited by Eydie Gormé (née Edith Garmezano; 1928–2013) on her 1967 album *Softly as I Leave You* at *Eydie Gorme Glad to Be Unhappy. And, with more zingers about the poor and rich than Harburg in his "When the Idle Poor Become the Idle Rich," from the 1947 Broadway musical *Finian's Rainbow*, Elaine Stritch and Palestine-born Ben Astar (1909–1988), in the 1954 *On Your Toes* revival, supremely skewer both classes in "Too Good for the Average Man" at *Too Good for the Average Man 1954 On Your Toes.

The Great Ziegfeld (September 4, 1936) was the first of three film musicals loosely based on impresario Florenz Ziegfeld's life. Full of Revue-type numbers such as "If You Knew Susie," "Shine On, Harvest Moon," and "Look for the Silver Lining," "A Pretty Girl Is Like a Melody" was the theme song for the producer and an Irving Berlin tune highlighted in the Broadway Revue *Ziegfeld Follies of 1919*. In the grandest of P. T. Barnum's spectacle traditions, the song highlights the film's grand finale at *MGM Musicals A Pretty Girl Is Like a Melody. It features a 100-ton, 175-step towering volute (spiral staircase), 180 performers, and 4300 yards of rayon silk curtains, and it cost $220,000, or nearly $3 million in 2017 dollars.

On the same day (September 4, 1936), Fred Astaire and Ginger Rogers's sixth of ten film musicals opened, *Swing Time*, a story about a gambler/dancer who is engaged to the wrong girl, of course. Composer Jerome Kern and lyricist Dorothy Fields never wrote better popular songs than for this film: "Pick Yourself Up," a paean to second and third and fourth tries until you get it right, is humorously sung and then brilliantly danced by Fred and Ginger at *Swing Time Pick Yourself Up; "The Way You Look Tonight," their gorgeous, Oscar-winning love ballad, is sung by Fred while sitting at a piano, a goofily shampooed Ginger behind him, at *Swing Time The Way You Look Tonight; "Waltz in Swing Time" is an instrumental that drives the duo to ecstatic circles around the fab Van Nest Polglase Art Deco ballroom, at *Swing Time Waltz in Swing Time; "A Fine Romance" is a funny ribbing they alternately make to each other in song, with Astaire doing his best Stan Laurel impersonation, at *Swing Time A Fine Romance; "Bojangles of Harlem," at *Swing Time Bojangles of Harlem, Astaire's only (partial) blackface number he duets with himself in a trick-photography scene conceived by longtime collaborator Hermes Pan, an homage less to Bill "Bojangles" Robinson and more to the hard-tapping style of his hero John W. Bubbles (né John W. Sublett; 1902–

1986), who had just played Sportin' Life in the previous year's *Porgy and Bess*; and "Never Gonna Dance," perhaps the most heart-rending and poignant of all Astaire-Rogers duets (her feet were bruised and bleeding by the end of rehearsals), at *Swing Tim Never Gonna Dance.

The story of a young 19th-century street busker separated from her pick-pocket grandfather, *Dimples* (October 16, 1936) was Shirley Temple's third of four film musicals in 1936 alone. "Hey, What Did the Blue Jay Say?" with music composed by Jimmy McHugh and lyrics by Ted Koehler, is sung and then danced by Temple to Bill Robinson–choreographed steps in his typically light, high-up-on-the-toes style at *Shirley Temple Hey, What Did the Blue Jay Say. As her syncopated rhythms and confidence became more sophisticated with each film, we can almost picture Robinson standing just off camera gazing approvingly at Shirley while she proudly dances for her mentor.

If not a hit show, Cole Porter's next Broadway musical, *Red, Hot and Blue!* (October 19, 1936), a story about a former manicurist and wealthy young widow named Nails O'Reilly Duquesne, produced three hit songs: "Ridin' High," "It's De-Lovely," and "Down in the Depths (on the Ninetieth Floor)." For the first, have a listen to Benny Goodman (1909–1986) and His Orchestra's upbeat swing recording from November 1936 at *Ridin' High Benny Goodman. The second, as staged by Nick Castle, Sr. (1910–1968), features Mitzi Gaynor (née Francesca Marlene de Czanyi von Gerber; b. 1931) and Donald O'Connor (1925–2003) interweaving wonderfully syncopated dance moves into their singing of the tune on a prop-filled cruise ship set in the 1956 *Anything Goes* film at *Mitzi Donald It's De-Lovely. The third, from the 1990 Porter compilation fundraiser for AIDS research, *Red Hot + Blue*, showcases English singer Lisa Stanfield (b. 1966) at *Lisa Stanfield Down in the Depths.

In a story about a singer wrongly imprisoned who makes a promise to a condemned jail mate, composer Arthur Johnston and Johnny Burke's hit standard, "Pennies from Heaven," from the film musical of the same name (November 25, 1936), is endearingly introduced by Bing Crosby at *Pennies from Heaven Bing Crosby. And in "Skeleton in the Closet," nary a soul is around to dance—except, perhaps, a spirit or two—as the swinging tune comes rattling out of Louis Armstrong's trumpet and voice (backed by his band, with Lionel Hampton on vibes) at *Pennies from Heaven Louis Armstrong Skeleton.

In addition to grooving on Eleanor Powell's power taps in the showcase tunes "Rap, Tap on Wood" and "Swingin' the Jinx Away," one could also enjoy Jimmy Stewart's gentle crooning, of all things, in Cole Porter's easygoing "Easy to Love" in the film musical *Born to Dance* (November 27, 1936), at *Born to Dance Easy to Love. Look for him tapping a bit, too, and not all that badly, actually (alongside real tappers Powell, Buddy Ebsen, and others), in "Hey, Babe, Hey" at *Buddy Ebsen Eleanor Powell Jimmy Stewart.

On the Avenue (February 12, 1937), a film musical with story and song by Irving Berlin, is about the putting on of a Broadway show called *On the Avenue*. With choreography by Seymour Felix (1892–1961), the Ritz Brothers (Al, Jimmy, Harry) sing and tap up a storm (while also filching some lines from Berlin's "Cheek to Cheek," in 1935's *Top Hat*) in the hyperactive "He Ain't Got Rhythm" as performed in front of a giant telescope—if you have to ask, you haven't seen it yet, but it makes no sense anyway—surrounded by dozens of chorines at *The Ritz Brothers He Ain't Got Rhythm. Great fun!

Ready, Willing and Able (March 6, 1937), a Warner Brothers film musical starring Ruby Keeler and Lee Dixon (1914–1953), about a college girl who impersonates a British star to land a Broadway role, was most notable for the song and dance "Too Marvelous for Words," with music by Richard A. Whiting and lyrics by Johnny Burke. It featured some marvelous words dug out of Webster's Dictionary, and Keeler and Dixon's fabulous tap dance on a giant typewriter, built to scale, can be viewed at *Too Marvelous for Words Ready Willing Able.

As much as 1934 Broadway was owned by Cole Porter, the same could be said for Rodgers and Hart in 1937. A story about staging a Revue and a celebration of the younger generation, *Babes in Arms* (April 14, 1937) had more hits (five) in it than even *Anything Goes* (four): "The Lady Is a Tramp," "I Wish I Were in Love Again," "Where or When," "Johnny One Note," and the incomparable "My Funny Valentine." The warm lyricism of Barbara Cook's (1927–2017) soprano rings out in her version of "Where or When," from *Barbara Cook Sings from the Heart* (1959), at *Rodgers & Hart Where or When. And which other version besides the one by the Chairman of the Board, Frank Sinatra, on his 1957 album *A Swingin' Affair*, should one listen to for "The Lady is a Tramp"—at *The Lady Is a Tramp Frank Sinatra—a song he swung to in October of that same year in the film version of *Pal Joey*? Likewise, nobody put over "I Wish I Were in Love Again" better than Mickey Rooney and Judy Garland, who starred in the 1939 *Babes in Arms* film version, performing that tune in that duo's last of ten films together, *Words and Music* (1948), a glossed over biopic on Lorenz "Larry" Hart himself. Have a look and listen to the two of them at *Judy Garland Mickey Rooney I Wish I Were in Love Again.

For a poignant change of pace, experience director Robert Altman's (1925–2006) extraordinary filming in *The Company* (2003) of Neve Campbell (b. 1973) and Domingo Rubio, the latter from the Joffrey Ballet (formed 1956), in a dance adagio choreographed by Lar Lubovitch (b. 1943), of "My Funny Valentine" at *The Company My Funny Valentine. Set to live piano and cello, the number is performed outdoors under a (staged but very effective) developing thunderstorm. Trumpeter and singer Chet Baker (1929–1988) also captures the ache in Hart's lyrics with his two-minute rendering of the song on his 1954 album *Chet Baker Sings* at *Chet Baker My Funny Valentine.

Full WORDS & MUSIC of

YOU MADE ME LOVE
YOU! I DIDN'T WANT TO DO IT.
I DIDN'T WANT TO DO IT.

SUNG BY	THE GREATEST	SUNG BY
Miss Ellaline Terriss	SONG OF THE YEAR	Miss Lillian Shelley
George P. Britt		Miss Florence Smithson
Charley Manny and Bob Roberts	THE RAGE OF THE REVUES.	Miss Maud Tiffany
The Ragtime Octette	WILL APPEAR IN	Miss Grace La Rue
		Miss Victoria Monks
Miss Fannie Brice	NEXT SUNDAY'S	Miss Ella Retford

NEWS OF THE WORLD

BEST OF ALL SUNDAY PAPERS.

☞ **SPECIAL NOTICE.** As there will be an exceptionally large demand for the "News of the World" on Sunday next, intending purchasers who are not already regular readers should order copies now to prevent disappointment.

The song that Judy Garland sang to a photo of Clark Gable in *The Broadway Melody of 1938*, "You Made Me Love You," made her a star one year before *The Wizard of Oz*. An ad for the song is seen here in the British newspaper *News of the World*. The song was written in 1913 by composer James Monaco and lyricist Joseph McCarthy.

The RKO film musical *Shall We Dance* (May 7, 1937) was chock full of the Gershwin brothers' hits: "(I've Got) Beginner's Luck," "They All Laughed," "Let's Call the Whole Thing Off," and the Academy Award nominated "They Can't Take That Away from Me." Enjoy Ginger Rogers singing "They All Laughed" first, then dancing with Astaire to the tune at *They All Laughed Shall We Dance. For more great fun, listen and watch Fred and Ginger sing the pun-filled "Let's Call the Whole Thing Off" and roller skate dance to its orchestration at *Fred and Ginger Let's Call the Whole Thing Off. Finally, Fred croons the elegiac "They Can't Take That Away from Me" to a rapt Ginger while on a mist-filled ferry at *Fred and Ginger They Can't Take That Away from Me.

The Marx Brothers' seventh film, MGM's *A Day at the Races* (June 11, 1937), featured Groucho as veterinarian Hugo Z. Hackenbush, inadvertently hired at the Standish Sanitarium (for humans). In between all the typical Marx hijinks—"Hold me closer, closer, closer!" "If I hold you any closer, I'll be in back of you"—dance ensemble Whitey's Lindy Hoppers, founded in 1935 by Herbert "Whitey" White, make their mark at *Lindy Hop A Day at the Races. Need a laugh? Have a gander at some of the boys' Vaudevillian chops at *The Marx Brothers in a Day at the Races.

RKO's film musical *New Faces of 1937* (July 2, 1937) was a story that Mel Brooks would borrow (translation: steal) thirty years later for his 1968 film *The Producers*—a crooked producer deliberately stages a lousy show that's already sold itself to investors. Ann Miller (née Johnnie Lucille Collier; 1923–2004), age 14, taps it up in her first film appearance to the title tune, written by Charles Henderson, at *Tap Dance 1937 Ann Miller.

Broadway Melody of 1938 (August 22, 1937), the third of four "Broadway Melody" pictures at MGM—at best, they were Revue-type shows with little story, but full of songs and dances—was notable for some fun tapping numbers with Eleanor Powell, George Raft, and Buddy Ebsen ("Follow in My Footsteps," "I'm Feeling Like a Million," "Your Broadway and My Broadway"), all written by composer Nacio Herb Brown and lyricist Arthur Freed. But the big hit was a song Judy Garland had sung to Clark Gable on his 36th birthday off screen, "You Made Me Love You (I Didn't Want to Do It)," with music by James V. Monaco (1885–1945) and lyrics by Joseph McCarthy (originally written in 1913), interpolated into the film at *Judy Garland Dear Mr. Gable.

Double or Nothing (September 17, 1937), a Bing Crosby film musical about a millionaire philanthropist who bets people are basically good, featured a host of tunes, specialty acts, and dances by numerous artists. Songwriters Al Siegel (1906–1966) and Sam Coslow's (1902–1982) "After You" is an action-packed scat-challenge between pianist-vocalist Frances Faye (née Frances Cohen; 1912–1991), comic actress-singer Martha Raye (1916–1994),

Bing, and faux band leader Harry Barris (1905–1962), who was one of Paul Whiteman's original Rhythm Boys alongside Crosby, at *Frances Faye Martha Raye Bing Crosby After You. You want eccentric dancing? Have a look at Ames and Arno—Elsie Ames (1902–1983), comic film partner of Buster Keaton, and Nick Arno—perform their daredevil act at *Double or Nothing Ames and Arno.

Varsity Show (October 4, 1937), another song-and-dance packed film musical from Warner Brothers, ostensibly featured ubiquitous crooner Dick Powell in several numbers but is fully worth the price of admission to see rarely recorded Vaudevillian performers Buck and Bubbles—Ford Washington Lee (1903–1955; Buck), on piano and vocals, and John W. Sublett (1902–1986; Bubbles)—on taps and vocals. Bubbles was Fred Astaire's favorite tapper, and it's clear to see why—it can be argued that his syncopations were truly the most sophisticated and easily rendered of all dancers. At *Buck and Bubbles Varsity Show, the video is a mash-up of their two spotlighted numbers, an informal piano-tap jam to "You've Got Something There," followed by their version of "On with the Dance," both written by composer Richard Whiting and lyricist Johnny Mercer.

Ali Baba Goes to Town (October 29, 1937) is an Eddie Cantor film musical in which he dreams he's entered a movie about the Arabian Nights. If you can stand to see Cantor in blackface, trying to be black, "Swing Is Here to Stay," at *Ali Baba Swing Is Here to Stay, written by Mack Gordon and Harry Revel, has a fabulous tap dance by Jeni LeGon and three-part harmonies by the Peters Sisters, an African American singing trio who can tap pretty well, too.

I'd Rather Be Right (November 2, 1937), a Depression-era satire about politics that takes place in New York City, starred George M. Cohan as Franklin Delano Roosevelt and boasted tunes by composer Richard Rodgers and lyricist Lorenz Hart. The big hit "Have You Met Miss Jones?" is put over in silky four-part harmony by the Hi-Los (formed 1953)—plus Rosemary Clooney—on the latter's 1956 musical variety television show *The Rosemary Clooney Show* at *1956 Have You Met Miss Jones Hi-Los Rosemary Clooney.

An overlooked and underappreciated film, in large part because the audience missed Fred without his seemingly ubiquitous 1930s RKO partner, Ginger, *A Damsel in Distress* (November 19, 1937) was loosely based on humorist P. G. Wodehouse's 1919 novel of the same name, a story about a bet on who Lady Alyce Marshmorton will marry. With music by composer George Gershwin and lyricist Ira Gershwin, *Damsel* was almost as bounteous with tunes as *Shall We Dance* earlier in the year, also with Gershwin songs: "Put Me to the Test" is a jaunty tap trio for Astaire, Gracie Allen and George Burns—the latter two no tap slouches themselves—at *Fred Astaire, George Burns, Gracie Allen Tap Routine; "Stiff Upper Lip," a Hermes Pan–choreographed, Academy Award–winning trip through a fun house for the trio; "Things Are Looking Up," a lovely ballad sung by Astaire and then danced by him and a 19-year-old Joan Fontaine, the latter gamely jogging with and being graciously partnered with Astaire; and "Nice Work If You Can Get It," at *Nice Work If You Can Get It A Damsel in Distress, a bouncy jazz number sung through with four-part harmonies. Check out Astaire's whirlwind tap and drum solo later in the film to the same tune, shot all in one take, at *Fred Astaire's Best Scene A Damsel in Distress. As stated, it may very well be his best scene ever. You decide!

Pins and Needles (November 27, 1937), with songs by Harold Rome (1908–1993) and directed by African American choreographer Katherine Dunham (1909–2006), was a (generally) lighthearted Revue of current events from a pro-union perspective—specifically, the then-striking International Ladies Garment Workers' Union—that was performed at the White House the next year for the Roosevelts. The show was full of accessibly melodic songs that had a bite. "Sunday in the Park," at *Sunday in the Park Jack Carroll, a paean to workers' one day off a week, is charmingly sung by Jack Carroll (né Vincenzo Riccio; 1921–2005) and ensemble on the 25th-anniversary 1962 soundtrack. From the same album, Barbra Streisand inhabits the bluesy "What Good Is Love?" at *What Good Is Love Barbra Streisand. Rome's "Doing the Reactionary," as jauntily warbled by Cab Calloway (backed by his orchestra), predates songwriter Sherman Edwards's (1919–1981) "Cool, Cool Considerate Men" (*1776*, from 1969) by 32 years in its liberal stance toward right-wingers at *Cab Calloway Doing the Reactionary.

Elsewhere, Rose-Marie (née Rose Marie Mazzetta; 1923–2017) straight-forwardly sings "Sing Me a Song with Social Significance" (hmm, what could that one be about?), also from the 25th anniversary album, at *Rose-Marie Sing Me Song Social Significance. "Four Little Angels of Peace," sweetly sung (almost as a carol, but dripping in irony) by characters standing in for Mussolini, Hitler, and the Japanese, can be heard at *Four Little Angels of Peace. And Streisand's "Not Cricket to Picket" nails the unpleasantness that complaining to one's boss can be at *Not Cricket to Picket. Inequality is always topical, I'm afraid.

Hooray for What! (December 1, 1937) was an anti-war satire with music by Harold Arlen and lyrics by E. Y. Harburg. "Down with Love" was the hit, and Barbra Streisand powers through it in a truly rousing manner on the October 3, 1963, Judy Garland Show at *Barbra Streisand Down with Love. Whew!

Walt Disney Productions' first full-length animated musical, *Snow White and the Seven Dwarfs* (December 21, 1937), re-envisioned the 1812 Brothers Grimm "Snow White" fairy tale by expanding the parts of and giving names to the seven dwarfs. (The film was such a gamble that Walt had to re-mortgage

German painter and illustrator Alexander Zick's (1845–1907) detailed artwork for the Brothers Grimm 1812 story *Snow White*, which was partial inspiration for Disney's first animated feature, *Snow White and the Seven Dwarfs* (1937).

his house to help pay for its costs.) The Academy Award–nominated score was written by composer Frank Churchill (1901–1942) and lyricist Larry Morey (1905–1971) and includes the eternal hits "Heigh-Ho," at *Heigh-Ho Snow White, "Whistle while You Work," at *Whistle While You Work Snow White, and the love ballad "Someday My Prince Will Come," sung with an operatic vibrato by Adriana Caselotti (1916–1997), at *Someday My Prince Will Come.

The next day, the moderately successful Broadway musical, *Between the Devil* (December 22, 1937), with music and lyrics by Arthur Schwartz and Howard Dietz respectively, introduced the songs "Triplets" and "By Myself," both of which appeared in the songwriters' biggest hit, the 1953 film *The Band Wagon*. In classic Vaudevillian style, the first tune is humorously put over by Fred Astaire, Nanette Fabray (née Ruby Bernadette Nanette Fabares; b. 1920), and Jack Buchanan (1891–1957), who not coincidentally starred in the show from which the song originated, at *Triplets Fred Astaire, Nanette Fabray, Jack Buchanan.

The Goldwyn Follies (February 4, 1938), about a film producer who hires an "average" person to judge his films from an everyday perspective, was the final film musical and project that composer George Gershwin and his brother Ira worked on together before George's tragic death on July 11, 1937. Their last hit, "Our Love Is Here to Stay," another standard in the Great American Songbook, swings in a slow and easy way as sung by Rosemary Clooney at a 1993 outdoor concert at the White House at *Rosemary Clooney Our Love Is Here to Stay. Pianist Bill Evans (1929–1980) jams out on the same tune with Eddie Gómez (b. 1944) on bass and Marty Morell (b. 1944) on drums on his 1969 album *You're Gonna Hear from Me* at *Bill Evans Our Love Is Here to Stay. "I Love to Rhyme," a throwaway tune in the film, is nicely resurrected by Peter Mintun on vocals and piano at *Peter Mintun I Love to Rhyme.

I Married an Angel (May 11, 1938) was a Broadway musical based on a novel of the same name by Hungarian Vaszary János (1899–1963), a story about a love-weary Budapest banker who thinks that only an angel will do. Unfortunately, until she becomes somewhat more human, she is all-too-honest and ruins his life. With music by Richard Rodgers and lyrics by Lorenz Hart, the elegiac "I'll Tell the Man in the Street" is sung with her usual impeccable flair by soprano Rebecca Luker at *Rebecca Luker Man in the Street. An effusive cabaret singer and Hart lover who died much too soon, Mary Cleere Haran (1952–2011) likewise sings a transcendent version of the tune, with longtime British composer and accompanist Richard Rodney Bennett (1936–2012) on piano, from her 1995 album *This Funny World* at *Mary Cleere Haran I'll Tell the Man in the Street.

The 20th Century–Fox film musical *Little Miss Broadway* (July 29, 1938) starred Shirley Temple as yet another orphan looking for a place to call home.

With music by Harold Spina (1906–1997), lyrics by Walter Bullock (1907–1953), and some nifty camera work by cinematographer Arthur C. Miller (1895–1970), Temple does a neat tap duet with George Murphy (1902–1992), singing and dancing all around the ground floor of a mansion to "We Should Be Together," at *Shirley Temple We Should Be Together.

Possibly inspired by the real bandleader Alexander "King" Watzke (1872–1919) of New Orleans and taking its name from the 1911 Irving Berlin hit, the film musical *Alexander's Ragtime Band* (August 5, 1938) traces an incomplete history of music from ragtime to jazz to swing, all with 26 of the popular composer's tunes as signposts—without any mention of African Americans, of course. The title tune is shown in a fictional process of creation at *Alexander's Ragtime Band.

Carefree (September 2, 1938) was Fred Astaire and Ginger Rogers's eighth of ten film musicals together. A story about mistaken identities between a psychiatrist, his friend, and his friend's fiancée, the movie was the third and final time (after 1935's *Top Hat* and 1936's *Follow the Fleet*) one of their films boasted tunes by old friend Irving Berlin. Astaire's skill at hitting golf balls is on display with an instrumental of the song "Since They Turned Loch Lomond into Swing" at *Fred Astaire Carefree Golf Dance. In order to make up for the fact that Fred rarely kissed Ginger onscreen—preferring instead to sing and dance the romance—he agreed to one long smooch at the end of a dream sequence to "I Used to Be Color Blind" at *A Romantic Dream Carefree. And "Change Partners," at *Carefree Change Partners, was the big love ballad duet of the film and the last big love duet the partnership sang and danced to at RKO.

The musical Revue *Hellzapoppin* (September 22, 1938) was packed with songs, jokes, impersonators, dancers, humorous interactions with the audience, magicians, comedians, and Whitey's Lindy Hoppers, the latter of which, after a name change to the Harlem Congeroos, followed Slim and Slam (plus band)—multi-instrumentalists Bulee Gaillard (1916–1991; Slim) and Leroy Eliot Stewart (1914–1987; Slam)—in the 1941 film version of the same name. I'm not sure there is a better recording of high-flying Lindy Hopping anywhere than at *Hellzapoppin Slim and Slam Harlem Congeroos. To get a sense of the surreal insanity that the original show undoubtedly was, have a look at the opening number of the film at *Hellzapoppin Wild Slapstick Opening Scene.

Knickerbocker Holiday (October 19, 1938), a Broadway musical with songs by composer Kurt Weill and lyrics by Maxwell Anderson, was loosely based on Washington Irving's 1809 satire *A History of New York*, but it was really a thinly veiled allegory that skewered Franklin Delano Roosevelt's New Deal of the 1930s. "September Song," the heartbreaking paean to days winding down, was originally sung in a straightforward way in the show by actor Walter Huston (1883–1950), of all people—yes, *that* Walter Huston, film director John Huston's father—at *September Song Walter Huston. In a nice touch, his granddaughter, actress Anjelica Huston (b. 1951), sang it 74 years later, at *Anjelica Huston September Song, during the 2012 "Previews" episode for the TV series *Smash*, a poignant connection between two relatives who'd missed each other by one year. Of course, as a standard, hundreds of other musicians have also taken the tune to heart. One definitive version was sung by Weill's two-time wife and longtime collaborator, Lotte Lenya (1888–1981), on her 1958 album *Lotte Lenya*, at *Lotte Lenya September Song. And if one could be blown away by one performance alone—is it possible to choose just one?—it might be Judy Garland's deeply pensive search through nature for a sign, anywhere a sign, in "It Never Was You," a hidden gem of a song from *Knickerbocker* that she sings in her last film, the 1963 *I Could Go on Singing*, alone on a stage at *Judy Garland It Never Was You.

Leave It to Me! (November 9, 1938), a Broadway musical about a late thirties American ambassador to Russia who only wants to go home to Topeka, Kansas, but inadvertently is hailed as a hero for every faux pas he perpetrates, had songs by Cole Porter and introduced Mary Martin to audiences (1913–1990)—with a young Gene Kelly in the chorus, too. "Get Out of Town," a love warning if ever there was one, is given a straightforward yet potent treatment by singer, music director, and keyboard player Clark Baxtresser (b. 1988) at *Clark Baxtresser Get Out of Town. The big hit, "My Heart Belongs to Daddy," full of Porter's typical double entendres, is gloriously put over in 1939 by Martin and Eddie Duchin (1909–1951) and His Orchestra at *My Heart Belongs to Daddy Mary Martin Eddie Duchin.

The Broadway musical *The Boys from Syracuse* (November 23, 1938), which was producer, director, and playwright George Abbott's (1887–1995) adaptation of Shakespeare's 1594 *The Comedy of Errors*, was itself an adaptation of Roman playwright Plautus's (c. 254–184 BCE) *Menaechmi, or the Twin Brothers*. A comedy about two pairs of twins who are mistaken for each other, it was full of composer Richard Rodgers and lyricist Lorenz Hart's tunes. One of the songs was "This Can't Be Love," sung and played in atypically high-speed, jazzed-up fashion by Canadian singer and pianist Diana Krall (b. 1964) on her 1993 debut album *Stepping Out* at *This Can't Be Love Diana Krall.

Set to Music (January 15, 1939), a Broadway Revue full of sketches and songs that was a revision of the 1932 *Words and Music*, was a potpourri of Noël Coward tunes, many of which were his most popular. A song about love at any age, "Mad about the Boy" is gorgeously rendered by Anita O'Day on her 1961 album *Waiter, Make Mine Blues* at *Anita O'Day Mad About the Boy. "I Went to a Marvelous Party," a breakneck recitative on party life set to piano, is sung-spoken by the composer himself on his 1957 *Noel Coward in New York* at *Noel Coward I Went to a Marvelous Party. And "The Stately Homes of England" seems to list and discuss *every* stately home in England *and* their owners and lives, sung once again by the composer at *Noel Coward Stately Homes.

Honolulu (February 3, 1939), a Hollywood musical about identical twins who switch places and realize the other's life is not quite what they expected, featured Eleanor Powell and Gracie Allen in a sweet song-and-tap duet set to the title tune, with music by Harry Warren and lyrics by Gus Kahn. Then, Eleanor grabs a jump rope and shows off her taps all over flights of stairs at *Honolulu Gracie Allen Eleanor Powell.

On August 25, 1939, the third film version of *The Wizard of Oz* opened on Hollywood and became one of the best-known movie musicals in history.

> The huge success scored by Walt Disney's *Snow White and the Seven Dwarfs* [December 1937] inevitably prompted Hollywood's leading studios to search for other children's fantasies. A logical choice was L. Frank Baum's [1856–1919] classic *The Wonderful Wizard of Oz*, written in 1900, which had been adapted as a Broadway musical in 1903 (with the title minus the word "Wonderful").… The movie made a star of 16-year-old Judy Garland, who played Dorothy, after [studio boss Louis B.] Mayer was unsuccessful in borrowing Shirley Temple from Fox [Green and Ginell 2014, p. 88].

One of the most famous scores in history was written by lyricist E. Y. Harburg and composer Harold Arlen. However, the film had a troubled shoot, including five different directors, hospitalized actors—Buddy Ebsen, who would go on to play Jed Clampett in the TV series *The Beverly Hillbillies*, was allergic to the aluminum and silver powder he wore as the Tin Man and left the production after convalescing in an iron lung; Margaret Hamilton, as the Wicked Witch of the West, caught fire in the "Help me, I'm melting scene"— and "Over the Rainbow" was almost cut because it slowed the story down. But the final product shows none of these problems, boasting timeless performances by Garland as Dorothy, Bert Lahr as the Cowardly Lion, Ray Bolger as the Scarecrow, Florenz Ziegfeld's widow Billie Burke as Glinda, the Good Witch of the North, and Frank Morgan, as the Wizard (and two other parts; see if you can spot him!).

There are literally hundreds of "Rainbow" interpretations out there, but you shouldn't even buy this book if you miss Miss Garland's original version in the film at *Somewhere over the Rainbow Wizard of Oz. As just one lovely comparison, here is James Taylor's brother, Livingston (b. 1950), with a jazzy organ version from his 1973 *Over the Rainbow* album at *Over the Rainbow Livingston Taylor. Harry Connick, Jr. (b. 1967) does a heartfelt, minor-key-tinged vocal (with piano) of "If I Only Had a Brain" on his 1987 album *20* at *If I Only Had a Brain—Harry Connick, Jr.

Too Many Girls (October 18, 1939), a Broadway musical with a story about an heiress moving between Maine and New Mexico, had songs by composer Richard Rodgers and lyrics by Lorenz Hart. (The set of the 1940 film version is where Lucille "I Love Lucy" Ball and Desi Arnaz met and fell in love.) As sung by Mary Jane Walsh at *I Like to Recognize the Tune, "I Like to Recognize the Tune" was a funny ditty listing all the composers whose melodies were being forgotten in the modern age of the late 1930s. On her 1959 album *Barbara Cook Sings from the Heart*, Cook sings yet another heartfelt Rodgers and Hart tune from the show, "I Didn't Know What Time It Was," at *Barbara Cook I Didn't Know.

Two days later, Hollywood's *At the Circus* (October 20, 1939) opened, the Marx Brothers' ninth film (and fourth without Zeppo), a story about … oh, who cares about a story in a Marx Brothers film? It takes place in and around a circus, and the brothers skewer all pretensions. Composer Harold Arlen and lyricist E. Y. Harburg's pun-filled "Lydia the Tattooed Lady" is sung and danced by Groucho in this one, at *Lydia the Tattooed Lady, not two months after Arlen and Harburg's work on *The Wizard of Oz*—not a bad year for the two of them. Harpo does a nifty jazz version of Rodgers and Hart's 1934 "Blue Moon" on the harp at *Harpo Marx Blue Moon, while Chico, on a 1929 tune by Czech composer Jaromír Vejvoda (1902–1988), plays the "Beer Barrel Polka" on the piano at *Chico Marx Beer Barrel Polka.

Directed by Vincente Minnelli (né Lester Anthony Minnelli; 1903–1986), *Very Warm for May* (November 17, 1939) was the final Broadway musical with songs by Jerome Kern and Oscar Hammerstein. The story followed a Long Island society girl hiding out from gangsters with a summer stock troupe in Connecticut. Polyglot clarinetist Artie Shaw (né Arthur Jacob Arshawsky; 1910–2004) and His Orchestra, with Helen Forrest (née Helen Fogel; 1917–1999) singing, were the first to help popularize the lush and complex "All the Things You Are" at *Artie Shaw Orchestra Helen Forrest All the Things You Are. Stephen Sondheim analyzes Kern's construction of the song with British American jazz pianist and composer Marian McPartland (1918–2013) on her NPR show *Piano Jazz* at *Sondheim Deconstructs All the Things You Are, while "All in Fun," simple on the surface, is given the wry Elaine Stritch treatment during her 2002 *Elaine Stritch: At Liberty* show at *Elaine Stritch All in Fun.

The next month, Cole Porter's *DuBarry Was a Lady* (December 6, 1939) opened starring Bert Lahr (né Irving Lahrheim; 1895–1967)—fresh off his turn as the Cowardly Lion in August's incomparable *The Wizard of Oz*—and Ethel Merman and Betty Grable. It was the story of a washroom attendant named Louis who dreams he's King Louis XV, in love with Madame Du Barry. (Jeanne Bécu, Comtesse du Barry [1743–1793] was indeed Louis's mistress, his last before being beheaded in 1793.) In the 1943 film version, Gene Kelly yearningly sings "Do I Love You?" to a gorgeous Lucille Ball as she leans upon his piano at *Gene Kelly Do I Love You? A fun follow-up shows Gene tapping up a storm to an orchestrated version of the song, with 18 lovely MGM dancers, at *Gene Kelly in Du Barry was a Lady. The fun "Give Him the Ooh-La-La" is a treat to hear at *Blossom Dearie Give Him the Ooh-La-La, as sung in her signature coquettish voice by Blossom Dearie (née Margret Blossom Dearie; 1924–2009), from her 1958 album of the same name. And Bing Crosby and Frank Sinatra nail "Did You Evah?" from the show, nicely transposed into the 1956 film *High Society* at *Bing and Frank Did You Evah.

FOUR

The 1940s

Two for the Show (February 8, 1940), the middle Broadway Revue to 1939's *One for the Money* and 1946's *Three to Make Ready*, featured a variety of sketches and songs written by and with lyrics by another female lyricist as rare as Dorothy Fields—in this case, actress, playwright, producer and director Nancy Hamilton (1908–1985). Her big hit, "How High the Moon," had music by Morgan Lewis (1906–1968) and was smoothly sung by Helen Forrest (1917–1999), backed by Benny Goodman and His Orchestra, at *How High the Moon Benny Goodman.

On February 9, 1940, Fred Astaire teamed up with a new female partner (for just one film, sadly), the great tap dancer Eleanor Powell, and his first male partner, song-and-dance man and future California senator George Murphy (1902–1992), in the Cole Porter–composed film musical *Broadway Melody of 1940*. Their tap duet, "Begin the Beguine," at *Begin the Beguine Astaire Powell, is justly famous, but two other numbers are equally noteworthy: "I've Got My Eyes on You" begins with an Astaire piano solo that segues into a tour de force tap number on and around chairs at *I've Got My Eyes on You Fred Astaire; and the "Juke-Box Dance," showcasing Fred and Ellie's skills with seeming improvisation, can be viewed at *Fred Astaire Eleanor Powell Jukebox Dance. According to Astaire himself—high praise, indeed—Powell "really knocked out a tap dance in a class by herself" (Astaire, 1959, p. 242).

Walt Disney's second feature-length animated film, *Pinocchio* (February 23, 1940), a story about a wooden puppet that wants to become a real human boy, was based on Italian author and journalist Carlo Collodi's (né Carlo Lorenzini; 1826–1890) 1883 children's novel *The Adventures of Pinocchio*. Over its opening credits, our old friend Cliff "Ukulele Ike" Edwards sings the dreamy "When You Wish upon a Star," with music by Leigh Harline and lyrics by Ned Washington, in the guise of Jiminy Cricket at *Disney's Pinocchio When You Wish upon a Star. The tune has since become the Theme Song of the Walt Disney Company.

Rhythm on the River (September 6, 1940) was a Paramount Pictures film musical starring Bing Crosby, Mary Martin, Basil Rathbone and Oscar Levant, a story about a fake composer who takes credit for other people's songs. With music by James V. Monaco and lyrics by Johnny Burke, several of the songs stand out, including the title tune, an upbeat and catchy jazz number sung by Bing and accompanied by a Dixieland band filled with hot percussion at *Bing Crosby Rhythm on the River. And it is great fun to see Levant's fingers fly on the piano as he accompanies Martin on "That's for Me" at *Mary Martin Oscar Levant That's for Me.

On October 11, 1940, 20th Century–Fox studios produced the first of several films that ostensibly took place in exotic locations, usually south of the border, providing audiences with escapist fare from the rumblings of World War II—in much the same way thirties musicals supplied respite from the travails of the Great Depression. In fact, these early forties films, many of which took place in Latin America, were partly created in response to President Roosevelt's "Good Neighbor Policy," intended to counter a burgeoning Nazi influence in the area. *Down Argentine Way* starred Portuguese-born samba singer Carmen Miranda (née Maria do Carmo Miranda da Cunha; 1909–1955), Betty Grable (with legs insured for $1 million, by Lloyd's of London), and the Nicholas Brothers, singing (in Spanish) and then tap dancing to the title song, composed by Harry Warren and with lyrics by Mack Gordon, at *Down Argentine Way Nicholas Brothers.

The all-black Broadway musical *Cabin in the Sky* (October 25, 1940) was a story about a compulsive gambler who is killed but then given a second chance to reform himself. If that sounds familiar to musical aficionados, it should, as it was partly based on Hungarian dramatist Ferenc Molnár's (1878–1952) 1909 play *Liliom*, itself the source material for Rodgers and Hammerstein's upcoming 1945 Broadway show *Carousel*. *Cabin in the Sky* boasted choreography shared between Katherine Dunham and George Balanchine, music by Vernon Duke, and lyrics by John Latouche (1914–1956) and Ted Fetter (1907–1996). The big hit was "Taking a Chance on Love," sung by Ethel Waters in the April 1943 film of the same name, with Eddie "Rochester" Anderson (né Edmund Lincoln Anderson; 1905–1977) and John W. Bubbles as delightful dance accompanists at *Taking a Chance on Love Ethel Waters.

Disney's *Fantasia* (November 13, 1940) was their third full-length animated film and second musical of the year, and included eight segments performed to classical music conducted by Leopold Stowkowski (1882–1977). Two memorable sequences featured the world famous Mickey Mouse as "The Sorcerer's Apprentice," set to French composer Paul Dukas's (1865–1935) 1897 symphonic poem of the same name, at *Fantasia Sorcerer's Apprentice, and hippos and alligators and ostriches and elephants prancing around to Italian opera composer Amilcare Ponchielli's (1834–1886) 1876 "Dance of the Hours," the finale from his opera *La Giaconda*, at *Fantasia Dance of the Hours. The animators used dancers from the Ballets Russes de Monte Carlo as models for their animals, and its story was inspired by George Balanchine's "Water Nymph Ballet" in 1938's *Goldwyn Follies*.

Based on the 1914 novel *Love Insurance* written by Charlie Chan's creator, Earl Derr Biggers (1884–1933), *One Night in the Tropics* (November 15, 1940) starred Burlesque comedians Bud Abbott (né William Alexander Abbott; 1897–1974) and Lou Costello (né Louis Francis Cristillo; 1906–1959) in their first film. The movie featured a number of the duo's funniest routines, including an early version of "Who's on First?" at the 31-minute mark at *One Night in the Tropics Abbott and Costello, *"Jonah and the Whale" at the 42-minute mark, *"Mustard" at the 1-hour, 3-minute mark, and the classic sleight-of-hand, double-talk *"Two Tens for a Five" at the 18-minute mark.

Tin Pan Alley (November 29, 1940), the story of Vaudeville sisters and their beau songwriters before World War I, was a 20th Century–Fox film musical starring Betty Grable and Alice Faye. The Nicholas Brothers, in yet another specialty act that this time dressed them up in near-naked attire, stole the show again in "The Sheik of Araby," a 1921 song with music by Ted Snyder (1881–1965) and lyrics by Harry B. Smith (1860–1936) and Francis Wheeler, at *Tin Pan Alley Nicholas Brothers. Belgian-born French guitarist Django Reinhardt's (né Jean Reinhardt; 1910–1953) 1937 version, with the Quintet du Hot Club de France (1934–1948) he founded with French violinist Stéphane Grappelli (1908–1997), moves the tune into overdrive at *Django Reinhardt Sheik of Araby.

Second Chorus (December 3, 1940), an unfairly overlooked film musical starring Fred Astaire, Burgess Meredith (1907–1997), and Artie Shaw and His Orchestra, is the story of perpetual college students (and rival trumpeters) Astaire and Meredith who keep failing to graduate. Astaire gets to "partner" with Shaw's orchestra as both conductor and tapper supreme on "Hoe Down the Bayou/Poor Mr. Chisholm," with music by Bernie Hanighen (1908–1976) and lyrics by Johnny Mercer, at *Astaire Two Magic Moments Second Chorus. And in the only known duet between Astaire and his longtime "silent" partner and co-choreographer (and stand-in for Ginger Rogers, when she was making other films), Hermes Pan—dressed up as a female ghost in high heels, no less—the two dance together while Pan lifts Astaire several times in the out-take number "Me and the Ghost Upstairs," also by Hanighen and Mercer, at *Me and the Ghost Second Chorus Out-Take.

Christmas Day 1940 provided Broadway with perhaps the greatest of all Rodgers and Hart's shows, *Pal Joey*, a musical that investigated the facts of life in all its tawdriness and emotional entanglements. No longer in the realm of musical comedy, the show had an unhappy ending, too, with the leads walking off stage in opposite directions.

[Rodgers and Hart] sailed into the thirties ... leaving behind a number of songs that blended Rodgers' ear-caressing music with Hart's witty, often rueful lyrics.... Not only did the book [of *Pal Joey*] involve blatant seductions, infidelity, and blackmail, mostly in a tacky nightclub setting, but some of the songs ... were bold in their sexual implications. Small wonder that many failed to notice, until years later, that the score was brilliant—one of their best—and that the show moved American musical theater into a new, more adult direction [Sennett, 2001, pp. 33–34].

Among the many melodic tunes, the alliterative "Bewitched, Bothered and Bewildered" became a standard for dozens if not hundreds of performers over the years. Have a listen to Ella Fitzgerald's impeccable intonation of the tune from her 1956 album *Ella Fitzgerald Sings the Rodgers & Hart Songbook*, at *Ella Fitzgerald Bewitched, Bothered, and Bewildered. Ella's take fortunately includes many of Hart's sexually overt lines, all too often censored out of so many versions. Enjoy the word play!

With a story about an unhappy female editor of a fashion magazine who undergoes psychoanalysis, the Broadway show *Lady in the Dark* (January 23, 1941) featured music by Kurt Weill and lyrics by Ira Gershwin. All songs but the longing "My Ship" were performed in the editor's dreamy imaginings, and that tune can be heard on piano and vocals by the 20-something polymath Clark Baxtresser at *Clark Baxtresser My Ship.

Buck Privates (January 31, 1941) was Burlesque comedians Bud Abbott and Lou Costello's 2nd of 36 films together and the one that made them famous. The story of two sidewalk peddlers who accidentally enlist in the army—it was still peacetime in the States at the time—the film was packed with more of their classic comedy routines ("Dice Game" and "40-Year-Old/10-Year-Old" were the strongest) and, courtesy of a contract with Universal Pictures, four fabulous songs by the Andrews Sisters. Written by Hughie Prince (1906–1960) and Don Raye (né Donald MacRaie Wilhoite, Jr.; 1909–1985), "Boogie Woogie Bugle Boy," their biggest hit, can be seen and heard at *Andrews Sisters Boogie Woogie Bugle Boy." It includes some cool choreography for the gals by Nick Castle, Sr. (1910–1968).

The Great American Broadcast (May 9, 1941), a film musical about the buildup to a coast-to-coast radio program after World War I, showcased the Nicholas Brothers in yet another specialty act, "Railroad Station Dance Specialty." They tap up a storm all over and around pieces of luggage, lampposts, and guardrails, finally ending up diving through a train's windows, at *Great American Broadcast Nicholas Brothers.

The Big Store (June 20, 1941), a story about a certain Wolf J. Flywheel who is hired by a big department store as both floorwalker and bodyguard, was the fifth and final film that the Marx Brothers performed in for MGM. Chico and Harpo play piano together this time, on the 1937 tune "Mamãe Eu Quero (Mom, I Want It)," penned by Vicente Paiva and Brazilian guitarist/

composer Jararaca (né José Luis Rodrigues Calazans; 1896–1977), at *The Big Store Piano Scene. Look for Harpo partnering himself in triplicate on violin, harp and cello at *Harpo Marx Playing Classics.

Sun Valley Serenade (August 21, 1941) was yet another of 20th Century–Fox's productions that "took place" in an exotic locale—this time, it was at Sun Valley, Idaho. The Glenn Miller (1904–1944) Orchestra (formed 1938) is featured, in their first of only two film musicals, gently swinging through the showcase number, "Chattanooga Choo-Choo," by composer Harry Warren and lyricist Mack Gordon, at *Glenn Miller Chattanooga Choo-Choo Sun Valley Serenade. Vocal group the Modernaires (1934–1960s) harmonize partway through the tune, followed by the rarely recorded Dorothy Dandridge (1922–1965) singing it and briefly dancing with the Nicholas Brothers until they tap it out to an ecstatic conclusion. The orchestra also blasts away on their biggest hit, "In the Mood," at *Glenn Miller In the Mood, and elsewhere backs up the velvet-voiced Pat Friday (née Helen Patricia Freiday; 1921–2016), singing for the lip-synching actress Lynn Bari, on the elegiac "I Know Why (And So Do You)" at *I Know Why Glenn Miller. The pop-jazz four-part harmony group the Manhattan Transfer (formed 1969) do fabulous justice to the same tune on their 1997 *Swing* album at *Manhattan Transfer I Know Why.

Lady Be Good (September 1, 1941), an MGM film musical that took its title and hit song from the 1924 Broadway Revue of the same name, told the story of a married songwriting team with its fair share of ups and downs. Several songs and dances are featured, including: Eleanor Powell furiously tap dancing a sweet duet with a dog that she trained herself, to an instrumental of the title Gershwin number at *Eleanor Powell Lady Be Good; Powell again furiously tap dancing with over a dozen mobile grand pianos, in a Busby Berkeley–choreographed number, to a boogie-woogie version of "Fascinatin' Rhythm" (also from the Broadway show), at *Eleanor Powell Fascinatin' Rhythm; and "The Last Time I Saw Paris," the Academy Award–winning song written by composer Jerome Kern and lyricist Oscar Hammerstein, as sung by newcomer Ann Sothern (née Harriet Arlene Lake; 1909–2001) to the city that was under siege at the time, at *The Last Time I Saw Paris Lady Be Good.

On September 25, 1941, Fred Astaire was teamed up with yet another new partner (for the first of two films), Rita Hayworth (née Margarita Carmen Cansino; 1919–1987), in a wartime case of mistaken identity, *You'll Never Get Rich*, a lavish black and white Columbia musical with songs by Cole Porter. A highlight was "March Milastaire (A-stairable Rag)," a solo tap dance in the barracks guardhouse at *Fred Astaire You'll Never Get Rich March Milastaire. If you can take your eyes off Astaire for a split second, watch how intensely the rest of the jailbirds watch him perform. Another outstanding number, "So Near and So Far," brings Rita and Fred together in a Latin-tinged song and dance full of off-beat syncopations, back-to-the-camera stop actions, and multiple romantic flourishes without much touching, at *Fred and Rita So Near and Yet So Far. "Boogie Barcarolle," at *Boogie Barcarolle, features a hot tap duet before a high-energy ensemble number, with Fred at the front, and "Since I Kissed My Baby Goodbye," at *Astaire Since I Kissed My Baby Goodbye, brings Fred back to the guardhouse in another cool solo tap (full of percussion sounds with props like a matchbox) after a bluesy rendition of the tune sung by the four-part harmony Four Tones (1930s–1950s).

Best Foot Forward (October 1, 1941) was a Broadway musical about a college kid who invites a celebrity to be his prom night date, and she accepts. With songs by Hugh Martin (1914–2011) and Ralph Blane (né Ralph Uriah Hunsecker; 1914–1995), and choreography by Gene Kelly (his last work on Broadway before heading to Hollywood), popular tunes included "Ev'ry Time," "Buckle Down, Winsocki," and "Just a Little Joint with a Jukebox." The latter was performed in the 1963 Off broadway revival by 17-year-old first-timer Liza Minnelli (b. 1946), re-created that same year on *The Ed Sullivan Show* (1948–1971; season 15, episode 29; April 1, 1963) with Bob Fosse-esque choreography by Danny Daniels (1924–2017), at *Liza Minnelli Sings Just a Little Joint.

Let's Face It! (October 9, 1941) was a Broadway musical based on the 1925 Russell Medcraft (1897–1962) and Norma Mitchell (1884–1967) play *The Cradle Snatchers*, a story about three suspicious wives who decide to give their husbands a run for their money. The songs, by Cole Porter, included the list-filled patter tune "Let's Not Talk about Love," sung by David Garrison (b. 1952; Steve Rhoades on *Married … with Children*), on the 2001 soundtrack album *Cole Porter's You Never Know*, at *Let's Not Talk Love David Garrison. Nancy Walker (née Anna Myrtle Swoyer; 1922–1992; Mildred on *McMillan and Wife*, Ida on *Rhoda*) sings the sweetly irritating "You Irritate Me So" on her 1959 album *I Hate Men* at *Nancy Walker You Irritate Me So.

Dumbo (October 31, 1941), Disney's fourth animated feature film, starred the titular flying elephant whose best friend, Timothy Q. Mouse, nudges him towards self-confidence. Two distinctly different tunes became hits: the hallucinogenic "Pink Elephants on Parade," with music by Oliver Wallace (1887–1963) and lyrics by Ned Washington (1901–1976), can be seen at *Dumbo Pink Elephants on Parade, while the ballad lullaby "Baby Mine," with lyrics by Washington and music by Frank Churchill, is given the blues treatment by singer-songwriter Bonnie Raitt (b. 1949) and the pop group Was (Not Was) (formed 1979) on the wonderful 1988 tribute album *Stay Awake: Various Interpretations of Music from Vintage Disney Films* at *Bonnie Raitt Was (Not Was) Baby Mine.

Sheet music for "The Memphis Blues" (1912), one of the first songs to embody the blues style in America, written by songwriter William Christopher (W. C.) Handy (1873–1958).

The heart of a film noir story about the search for an authentic bluesy sound, the "Blues in the Night" tune, with music by Harold Arlen and lyrics by Johnny Mercer, appeared in the November 15, 1941, film of the same name. Reminiscent of Paul Robeson and William Warfield, baritone William Gillespie (1908–1968) can be seen singing the song at *Blues in the Night.

The St. Louis Blues hockey team (formed 1967) was indeed named after the song "St. Louis Blues," written in 1914 by the "Father of the Blues," W. C. Handy (1873–1958). The tune also inspired the development of a ballroom dance style known as the fox-trot. The song was featured in the November 7, 1941, film musical *Birth of the Blues*, about the origins of the Original Dixieland Jass Band (1917–1936; "jazz" was spelled "jass" until the 1920s), with Louis Armstrong and His Orchestra's 1929 version heard at *Louis Armstrong St. Louis Blues (1929). And "The Memphis Blues," also written by Handy in 1912, was sung in the film by Bing Crosby at *Bing Sings Memphis Blues.

Babes on Broadway (December 31, 1941), one of a number of backyard musical films in which the participants invariably say to each other, "Hey, why don't we put on a show?" starred Judy Garland and Mickey Rooney and was directed by Busby Berkeley. Composer Burton Lane and lyricist Ralph Freed's (1907–1973) "How About You?" led the tunes, lovingly put over by Garland in the film at *Babes on Broadway How About You. Rosemary Clooney and the four-part harmony Hi-Los do a jazzy version of the tune on her 1956 television show at *The Hi-Lo's How About You Rosemary Clooney.

A tribute to actor-singer-dancer-playwright-producer-director-lyricist George M. Cohan, Warner Brothers' musical biopic *Yankee Doodle Dandy*, opened on May 29, 1942. James Cagney (1899–1986) portrayed the polymath entertainer, uncannily capturing his quirky, stiff-legged tap dynamics in "The Yankee Doodle Boy" at *Yankee Doodle Dandy James Cagney; the song was originally written by Cohan for his November 1904 show *Little Johnny Jones*. For slightly better Cagney tapping, see him with the song "Give My Regards to Broadway" at *James Cagney Give My Regards to Broadway. The film was colorized in 1986, but if you do not watch it in the original black and white, you'll have to return this book to where you bought it (just kidding … but barely).

"Wait Till You See Her," the best-known song from composer Richard Rodgers and Lorenz Hart's Broadway show *By Jupiter* (June 3, 1942), was inextricably cut one month after the show opened, but you can hear it silkily performed by Vic Damone (né Vito Rocco Farinola; b. 1928) on his 1956 album *That Towering Feeling!* at *Wait Till You See Her Damone. Set in the land of the Amazons, where women rule, do all the work, and men stay home to mind the kids and buy hats, "Nobody's Heart Belongs to Me" was a quiet little tune hidden deep within the farce. Breathily sung by jazz and pop singer Peggy Lee (née Norma Deloris Egstrom; 1920–2002), with British jazz musician George Shearing (1919–2011) at the piano, from their shared 1959 album *Beauty and the Beat!*, it can be heard at *Nobody's Heart Belongs to Me Peggy Lee George Shearing.

Footlight Serenade (August 1, 1942), about a boxer hired to lead a singing and dancing stage act, starred Betty Grable in an underrated film musical full of songs by composer Ralph Rainger and lyrics by Leo Robin. "I Heard the Birdies Sing," at *Betty Grable I Heard the Birdies Sing," features Betty (and a bevy of beauties) wearing boxing gloves and dancing and jabbing with a large silhouette of herself behind them on a screen, which at one point jumps down to dance and box alongside her, in a variation of the same kind of scene choreographer Hermes Pan dreamed up for Fred Astaire in the "Bojangles of Harlem" number from RKO's *Swing Time* six years earlier. Looking not unlike Astaire in style and body type, Pan himself, in a rare screen appearance, partners Grable in the Rainger instrumental "Land on Your Feet," at *Betty Grable and Hermes Pan Land on Your Feet. Pan looks like he's particularly relaxed and having a blast, and Grable, given the chance with strong choreography, was no slouch, either.

Paramount Pictures' *Holiday Inn* (August 4, 1942), a song-packed movie with Irving Berlin tunes starring Bing Crosby and Fred Astaire in the first of two films together, is reminiscent of the songwriter's 1933 Revue *As Thousands Cheer*, with the numbers ripped from newspaper headlines—except this show actually has a loose story revolving around a holiday inn that opens only on American holidays. A positive review—with brief clips from many of the numbers, including the big hit, "White Christmas"—was put up on the *New York Times* "Critics' Picks" video log of December 29, 2008, by their chief film critic, A. O. Scott (né Anthony Oliver Scott; b. 1966), at *Critic's Picks Holiday Inn.

Pardon My Sarong (August 7, 1942), Bud Abbott and Lou Costello's eighth film together, had the good fortune of including four-part harmony vocalists the Ink Spots (1934–1954) in two separate numbers: the first, the pre–Doo Wop ballad "Do I Worry?" with music by Stanley Cowan (1918–1991) and lyrics by Bobby Worth (1912–2002), can be enjoyed at the eight-minute mark of the film at *Abbott and Costello Pardon My Sarong; the second, "Shout, Brother, Shout," written by Herman Fairbanks and Harry Watson, followed by the tapping trio Tip, Tap, and Toe (1920s—1940s), is at the 21-minute mark. Just for fun, Abbott and Costello's absurd comic routine "Half a Bean" can be spotted at the 36-minute mark.

Orchestra Wives (September 4, 1942), a story about flirtations and upsets among an orchestra's wives, was a 20th Century–Fox film musical with music by Harry Warren and lyrics by Mack Gordon. As with *Sun Valley Serenade* the year before, Glenn Miller and his orchestra, the Modernaires, and the Nicholas brothers stole the show, this time with "I've Got a Gal in Kalamazoo" at *Orchestra Wives Got a Gal in Kalamazoo. This is the number that, along with typically fabulous taps including a double tour (two full jump turns in the air) into a floor split, Harold Nicholas was supposed to be wired up for safety as he literally runs up and backflips from a vertical wall, but the wire hadn't been hooked up yet, and he did it anyway. (Donald O'Connor does the same trick ten years later during his tour de force "Make 'Em Laugh" number in *Singin' in the Rain*, but if you look closely, that wall is sloped at a slight angle away from him, making his run and backflip somewhat easier.)

November 19, 1942, brought the second of two Astaire-Hayworth pictures to the screen, *You Were Never Lovelier*, with music by Jerome Kern and lyrics by Johnny Mercer. The film included Columbia Pictures' resident band, Xavier Cugat (né Francisco de Asis Javier Cugat Mingall de Bru y Deulofeu; 1900–1990) and his orchestra, but if you look fast, you can see none other than Fidel Castro—yes, *that* Fidel Castro (1926–2016), the long-term dictator of Cuba—as an extra hovering around in the picture. (Castro was a budding film actor early in his career.) Fred and Rita shone brightest in their song-and-dance number "The Shorty George," a tribute to the (supposed) inventor of the Lindy Hop, Savoy Ballroom dancer George "Shorty" Snowdon (1904–1982), at *Fred Astaire Rita Hayworth Shorty George.

Gene Kelly's big break on Broadway was the aforementioned 1940 *Pal Joey*, but in Hollywood it was the November 26, 1942, film musical *For Me and My Gal*, with co-star Judy Garland. The story was inspired by a real-life Vaudeville duo, Harry Palmer (c. 1889–1962) and Jo Hayden, working just before World War I. Discreetly directed for perhaps the first and only time by Busby Berkeley, with not one over-the-top extravagant number in the film, the title song, written in 1917 by George W. Meyer (1884–1959), Edgar Leslie (1885–1976), and E. Ray Goetz (1886–1954), is charmingly rendered in vocals and soft-shoe by the stars at *Judy Garland & Gene Kelly For Me and My Gal. "Ballin' the Jack," a popular 1913 song written by composer Chris Smith and lyricist Jim Burris—the phrase was used by railroad workers to mean "going at full speed"—is sung and danced to with ever-increasing speed at *Garland Kelly Ballin' the Jack.

Speaking of Garland, Johnny Mercer wrote the lyrics to "That Old Black Magic" (composed by Harold Arlen) in 1942 as a love letter to her, which she recorded earlier that year at *Judy Garland That Old Black Magic. The song was showcased later that same year in the film musical Revue *Star Spangled Rhythm* (December 30, 1942).

On Broadway and in Hollywood, the year 1943 brought some exceptional musicals to the planet, starting with perhaps the most seminal: *Oklahoma!* (March 31, 1943). The first of nine Broadway shows composer Richard Rodgers and librettist-lyricist Oscar Hammerstein wrote together (which included seven movies), the "production not only fused story, songs, and dances, but introduced the dream ballet to reveal hidden fears and desires of the principal characters" (Green and Ginell, 2014, p. 119).

The show was based on Lynn Riggs's 1931 play *Green Grow the Lilacs*, and the story was set in Indian Territory soon after the turn of the 20th century. Focused on Claremore (in northeast Oklahoma, near Tulsa), other towns mentioned were Catoosa, Bushy Head, and Quapaw, which was also the name of a Native American tribe. Surrounding a joyous celebration of Oklahoma's impending statehood (as the 46th), which occurred on November 16, 1907, Oklahoma had a booming cattle industry in the late 1800s, which ushered in the era of the cowboy (Hammerstein called them "cowmen"). Land runs from 1889–1895 occurred when the area was opened for white settlements on April 22, 1889, but the people known as Sooners snuck into the state early to wait for legalization. Oil was discovered in the state, so the Indians were screwed pretty badly over that issue, too. The Quapaw in particular, who sold 45 million acres of land for $18,000 before 1820, had it subsequently taken away— as so many tribes did.

People are often killed or die in Rodgers and Hammerstein shows: Jud Fry is accidentally killed in *Oklahoma!*, Billy Bigelow commits suicide in *Carousel*, Lieutenant Cable is killed in *South Pacific*, and the king dies in *The King and I*. All of their shows share a strong sense of community, but the reality of life is that characters must strive for happiness and overcome obstacles in order to reach their goals. This was a new idea in the development of musical theatre. Many of their shows also included a lengthy psychological, metaphorical ballet, and they were heavily weighted in a longer first act and a lighter, shorter second act. There was often a main romantic couple with a secondary subplot built around a humorous couple; and always, an earth mother.

Still, Rodgers and Hammerstein believed in the essential humanity of all their characters. They respected their villains and romantic leads alike, loving them for their mistakes as well as their triumphs and allowing their characters an unusual depth and three-dimensionality. The king is at once a barbarian (by our standards) *and* an intelligent ruler who cares about his country and his people. Billy Bigelow goes down the wrong road *because* he cares so much for his wife and unborn child. The audience can even empathize with poor Jud, isolated in his lonely room with his girlie pictures.

In fact, "Pore Jud Is Daid"—sung by Hugh Jackman and Shuler Hensley (b. 1967) during the 1998 West End revival at *Oklahoma Original London Cast—is a rather nasty little black comedy song sung by Curley about Jud's (impending) death. The song leads into Laurey drinking the Elixir of Egypt, sold to her by the traveling medicine man, which takes her into de Mille's "Dream Ballet"—seen in the 1955 film version with the original choreography at *Oklahoma Dream Ballet—presenting good versus bad in stark terms. While it is a very romantic story, Aunt Eller states Hammerstein's credo after Jud is accidentally killed on his own knife: "You got to get used to having all kinds of things happenin' to yer. You got to look at all the good on one side and all the bad on the other and say, 'Well, all right, then,' to both of them."

New York City's Stage Door Canteen was a real place of entertainment for troops on leave, and a Hollywood version of it by the same name, with over 80 celebrities making appearances large and small, was released on June 24, 1943. Some of the more curious featured numbers include violinist Yehudi Menuhin (1916–1999) playing "Ave Maria" (1825), by Franz Schubert (1797–1828), and "Flight of the Bumblebee" (1900) by Russian composer Nikolai Rimsky-Korsakov (1844–1908), at *Yehudi Menuhin Ave Maria Flight of the Bumblebee. Peggy Lee joins Benny Goodman and His Orchestra on the heartbreaker "Why Don't You Do Right?" (1936; originally "The Weed Smoker's Dream"), by Delta blues musician and composer Joseph "Kansas Joe" McCoy (1905–1950), at *Why Don't You Do Right Peggy Lee. The version that inspired Lee was performed in 1941 by Lil Green (née Lillian Green or Lillie May Johnson; 1919–1954), with William "Big Bill" Broonzy (né Lee Conley Bradley; 1903–1958) on guitar, at *Lil Green Why Don't You Do Right.

July 21, 1943, saw another all-black film musical released, *Stormy Weather*, with even more famous stars on display than in the April 1943 film version of *Cabin in the Sky*. Jazz pioneer Fats Waller (né Thomas Wright Waller; 1904–1943) performed his classic, Harlem-stride-style "Ain't Misbehavin'" (1929) on piano and vocals, which his band turns into a double-time Dixieland tune midway through at *Fats Waller Ain't Misbehavin' Stormy Weather. Singer/actress/civil rights activist Lena Horne sings one of her signature aching ballads, the title tune, written in 1933 for Ethel Waters to sing at the Cotton Club, with music by Harold Arlen and lyrics by Ted Koehler, at *Lena Horne Stormy Weather. It is immediately followed by Katherine Dunham and her dancers performing to an orchestration of the song at *Katherine Dunham—Stormy Weather. Cab Calloway and His Orchestra blast through the super-scat tune "Jumpin' Jive" (1939), written by Calloway, Frank Froeba (1907–1981), and Jack Palmer (1899–1976), with the Nicholas Brothers tapping up their super-athletic response to it afterwards at *Jumpin Jive Cab Calloway and the Nicholas Brothers. It was this dance that inspired no less a luminary than Fred Astaire to claim they were the greatest dancers of all time.

The Sky's the Limit (September 2, 1943), an RKO film starring Fred Astaire as a Flying Tiger pilot on leave, had music by Harold Arlen and lyrics by Johnny Mercer. Its big hit features Fred drunk at a bar singing the bluesy "One for My Baby (And One More for the Road)," then tapping up a storm and breaking all the glasses at *Astaire One for My Baby.

Thousands Cheer (September 13, 1943)—no relation to the 1933 Broadway musical, *As Thousands Cheer*—was a film about an aerialist who is drafted into the army but would rather be in the air force. It features Gene Kelly in a lovely duet with a mop, set to the 1910 song "Let Me Call You Sweetheart," with music by Leo Friedman (1869–1927) and lyrics by Beth Slater Whitson (1879–1930), at *Gene Kelly Let Me Call You Sweetheart.

Thank Your Lucky Stars (September 25, 1943) was one of the more consistently entertaining, Revue-type war movies, with songs composed by Arthur Schwartz and lyrics by a young, 33-year-old Frank Loesser (1910–1969), a full seven years before his big hit on Broadway, *Guys and Dolls*. What made the film so much fun was the uncharacteristic singing of several stars not known for their Polyhymnian chops: for example, the oft-dramatic Bette Davis (1908–1989), of all people, does a pretty darn good job with "They're Either Too Young or Too Old," at *Bette Davis They're Either Too Young or Too Old, while the oft-swashbuckler Errol Flynn (1909–1959) has a blast with the ditty "That's What You Jolly Well Get," at *Errol Flynn Thank Your Lucky Stars.

One Touch of Venus (October 7, 1943), a satire of American suburban values, fads, and sexual mores, had music by Kurt Weill and lyrics by poet Ogden Nash (1902–1971). In and around the Broadway show's humor, it featured the poignant love ballad, and eventual standard, "Speak Low." Backed by a percussive string quartet, the tune is sung by Italian Katyna Ranieri (b. 1927) on her 2000 album *The Fabulous Kurt Weill from America*, at *War and Love in 1943 Speak Low. The original Venus, Mary Martin, nearly seventy, sings a rich and heartfelt "That's Him" from the show in 1983 at the White House at *Mary Martin That's Him White House, while Kurt Weill himself, on piano and vocals, performs "Very, Very, Very" on his posthumous 1953 album *Tryout*, at *Kurt Weill Very Very Very.

I Dood It (November 10, 1043), a film musical starring Red Skelton (1913–1997) and Eleanor Powell, is the story about an average guy married to a big Broadway star who thinks he's wealthy. It opens with Jimmy Dorsey (1904–1957) and His Orchestra blasting away over the credits to Count Basie's 1937 classic "One O'Clock Jump" at *Jimmy Dorsey One O'Clock Jump. Director Vincente Minnelli (1903–1986), in only his second film, also featured Trinidad-born classical and jazz pianist Hazel Scott (1920–1981) deftly pounding the ivories on "Taking a Chance on Love," at *Taking a Chance Hazel Scott, followed by Lena Horne singing "Jericho" (the tune's origins go back to 19th-century slaves), at *Jericho Hazel Scott Lena Horne. Eleanor Powell trained hard for her complex dance routine with lariats and cowboys—including some fabulous rope jumping—on "So Long, Sarah Jane," written by Ralph Freed, Lew Brown, and Sammy Fain, at *Eleanor Powell Western Rope Tap So Long Sarah Jane.

Lyricist Alan Jay Lerner (1918–1986) and composer Frederick Loewe's (1901–1988) first Broadway musical, *What's Up?* (November 11, 1943), was a wartime show about aviators stuck at a girls' boarding school. A hidden gem, "My Last Love," is lovingly rendered on piano and vocals by the self-proclaimed Crown Prince of New York Cabaret, Steve Ross, on his 2009 album *I Remember Him Well: The Songs of Alan Jay Lerner*, at *My Last Love Steve Ross.

The all-black *Carmen Jones*, Oscar Hammerstein's World War II updating of Georges Bizet's fiery 1875 opera *Carmen*, opened on Broadway on December 2, 1943. In "Beat Out Dat Rhythm on a Drum," enjoy Tony Award–winner Pearl Bailey (1918–1990) singing the high-octane tune in the 1954 movie version of the show, at *Pearl Bailey The Star She Would Become, with percussionist extraordinaire Max Roach (1924–2007) on drums and a host of wasted dancers in director Otto Preminger's (1905–1986) dull and static filming of the scene. Look fast for the still-performing-in-2018 dancer Carmen De Lavallade (b. 1931) and modern dancer Alvin Ailey (1931–1989), before he created his world-famous Alvin Ailey American Dance Theater (formed 1959), in the rather frenetic Herbert Ross (1927–2001) choreography.

Busby Berkeley finally got his kaleidoscopic shot at Technicolor movies with *The Gang's All Here* (December 24, 1943), a story about complicated relationships between dancers and singers. In his phantasmagoric "Lady in the Tutti Frutti Hat," with music by Harry Warren and lyrics by Leo Robin, you may think you're hallucinating as you watch Carmen Miranda sing and dance with hundreds of huge bananas used in all sorts of (obviously sexual) ways at *The Lady in the Tutti Frutti Hat.

Up in Arms (February 17, 1944) starred Danny Kaye (né David Daniel Kaminsky; 1911–1987) in his first film musical, a story about a hypochondriac drafted into the army. It was loosely based on the 1923 Owen Davis (1874–1956) play *The Nervous Wreck*, itself the basis for Florenz Ziegfeld's 1928 musical *Whoopee*. "Tess's Torch Song," with music by Harold Arlen and scat-infused lyrics by Ted Koehler, showcased Kaye's goofy musical talents alongside Dinah Shore (née Fannye Rose Shore; 1916–1994) and the Goldwyn Girls in a surreal number choreographed by Danny Dare (1905–1996) at *Danny Kaye Up in Arms Tess Torch Song.

March 20, 1944, saw Gene Kelly not at his usual home, MGM, but on loan to producer Harry Cohn at Columbia Pictures.

> *Cover Girl* was the first of Kelly's three films (the others were *Singin' in the Rain* and *It's Always Fair Weather*) to feature a solo street dance. Here it was the "alter-ego" number, a purely cinematic creation in which Kelly moodily dances with his own image to reveal two sides of his personality [Green and Ginell, 2014, p. 128].

It was a tour de force number—with music by Jerome Kern—and Kelly had quite the challenge dancing with a superimposed image of himself that only we can see at *Gene Kelly Cover Girl Alter-Ego Dance. Elsewhere, "Put Me to the Test" featured both Kelly and Rita Hayworth in a fun duet, with lyrics by Ira Gershwin, at *Gene Kelly Rita Hayworth Put Me to the Test.

Going My Way (May 3, 1944), a film musical about a young priest taking over a parish from a veteran, starred Bing Crosby humorously singing (along with others) the pop classic "Swinging on a Star," with music by Jimmy Van Heusen and lyrics by Johnny Burke, at *Bing Sings Swinging on a Star. All the performers' tongues are firmly in cheek.

Bathing Beauty (June 27, 1944) was the third full-length film musical to feature competitive swimmer and actress Esther Williams (1921–2013). Its grand finale, at *A Escola de Sereias Esther Williams, was a spectacular water ballet choreographed by screenwriter, dancer, and director John Murray Anderson (1886–1954) in the Busby Berkeley style of extravagant geometric patterns and excess.

Canadian-born actress and soprano singer Deanna Durbin (née Edna Mae Durbin; 1921–2013) often sang arias from operas and operettas in her 20-plus films, most of which were also romantic comedies. But in the bleak film noir *Christmas Holiday* (July 31, 1944), directed by Robert Siodmak (1900–1973), based on the 1939 W. Somerset Maugham novel of the same name and starring Durbin as a woman married to an unstable and violent Southern aristocrat—uncharacteristically played by Gene Kelly, of all people—she sings the lilting "Spring Will Be a Little Late This Year," a lovely torch song by Frank Loesser, at *Deanna Durbin Spring Will Be a Little Late This Year.

In Society (August 15, 1944) was another wartime Abbott and Costello film which also starred Marion Hutton (1919–1987) singing with the Glenn Miller Orchestra. But the funniest scene straight out of a 1918 Vaudeville routine called "Floogle Street" (sometimes spelled "Flugel Street") is "Bagel Street," an absurdist and surreal comedy act about the fictional Susquehanna Hat Company, at *In Society Susquehanna Hat.

Lights of Old Santa Fe (November 6, 1944), a Western film about a rodeo owner and her struggles, starred King of the Cowboys Roy Rogers (né Leonard Franklin Slye; 1911–1998) and his wife and actress, singer-songwriter Dale Evans (née Lucille Wood Smith; 1912–2001). The title song, written by film composer and TV producer Jack Elliott (né Irwin Elliott Zucker; 1927–2001), is lovingly sung by Roy, Dale, and George "Gabby" Hayes (1885–1969) at *Roy Rogers Dale Evans Lights of Old Santa Fe.

In the tenth-greatest movie musical of all time (according to the American Film Institute; formed 1965), *Meet Me in St. Louis* (November 22, 1944), a story starting in 1903 and leading up to the 1904 Louisiana Purchase Exposition (World's Fair), featured music by Nacio Herb Brown and lyrics by Arthur Freed, especially their big hits "The Trolley Song" and "Have Yourself a Merry Little Christmas." You can see these two most famous numbers at *Judy Garland Trolley Song and *Judy Garland Have Yourself a Merry Little Christmas. I have a special fondness for the heartfelt little number, "You and I," which is mimed by exasperated father figure Leon Ames (1902–1993) and often melodramatic actress Mary Astor (née Lucile Vasconcellos Langhanke;

1906–1987), but dubbed by the lyricist himself and a (mysterious) D. Markas, at *You and I (Duet) Meet Me in St. Louis.

The Broadway musical *On the Town* (December 28, 1944), a story of three sailors on 24-hour leave in New York City, boasted the collaborative work of lyric and book writers Betty Comden and Adolph Green, composer Leonard Bernstein, and choreographer Jerome Robbins. The show was an expansion of the Robbins-Bernstein 30-minute ballet *Fancy Free* from earlier that year, created for American Ballet Theatre (formed 1937), which can be seen in a 1986 New York City Ballet PBS performance at *Fancy Free Ballet.

The only song to make the transition from stage to screen, "New York, New York"—not to be confused with John Kander and Fred Ebb's 1977 song "New York, New York," performed by the songwriters themselves in a 1997 PBS Great Performances special at *Kander and Ebb Perform New York, New York—explosively opens the December 30, 1949, film with Gene Kelly, Frank Sinatra, and Jules Munshin on location in some of the scenes at *New York, New York On the Town.

Tonight and Every Night (January 9, 1945), a film musical about wartime romance (and tragedy) in a London musical (loosely based on the Windmill Theater, which never missed a show during the Blitz), had songs by Marlin Skiles (1906–1981) and George Duning (1908–2000) and featured some fabulous jazz dances with Rita Hayworth, Jack Cole, and his dancers. Take a special look at "What Does an English Girl Think of a Yank?" at *Rita Hayworth What Does an English Girl, with Rita's vocals dubbed by Martha Mears (1910–1986), and "You Excite Me," at *Rita Hayworth You Excite Me, with Hayworth contracting her abdomen all over the place (that just sounds wrong, but it's true).

Rodgers and Hammerstein's second Broadway collaboration, *Carousel* (April 19, 1945), was based on the 1909 Ferenc Molnár's (1878–1952) play *Liliom*, a story of a carousel barker who dies but is given a second chance (he blows that opportunity, too). The justly seminal "If I Loved You," as sung by Gordon MacRae (1921–1986) and Shirley Jones (b. 1934) in the 1956 film version at *If I Loved You Carousel, was a tune about adults exploring the conditional possibilities of love rather than typical musical comedy lightning-strike infatuations. The song "You'll Never Walk Alone," that ends the show, was Hammerstein's credo in life, and it allowed a character called the Starkeeper to speak the eternally relevant lines of optimism, which lead into the film version of the song at *R & H Carousel You'll Never Walk Alone. Elsewhere, the original Billy Bigelow, baritone singer-actor John Raitt (1917–2005), performed the fourth-wall breaking "Soliloquy" for a 1958 television special at *John Raitt Soliloquy.

The Naughty Nineties (June 20, 1945), a film that takes place on a showboat along the Mississippi River during the 1890s, was Burlesque comedians'

Bud Abbott and Lou Costello's 15th of 36 films together. It is most notable for featuring the only full-length version of their classic "Who's on First?" routine, at *Abbott and Costello Who's on First. If you listen carefully, you can hear the cameramen trying to cover their laughs. And if you've never seen this number before (or even if you have), I dare you not to laugh.

MGM's musical *Anchors Aweigh* (July 19, 1945), the first of three films with Gene Kelly and Frank Sinatra together, was most famous for another of Kelly's cinematic innovations, complex live action dancing with animation, in "The Worry Song," with music by Sammy Fain (1902–1989) and words by Arthur Freed. If you haven't seen this number before, enjoy Gene's dancing and singing with Jerry the Mouse (sung by Sara Berner; 1912–1969), originally from Hanna Barbera cartoons, at *The King Who Couldn't Dance/Worry Song. If you're interested in *how* Gene "danced" with an animated mouse, Bill Taylor, from the Visual Effects Society (formed 1997), explains the process step by step at *How Gene Kelly Danced with Jerry. Tom and Jerry would swim underwater in another full-length film eight years later with Esther Williams in *Dangerous When Wet* (July 3, 1953) at *Dangerous When Wet Tom and Jerry.

The only Rodgers and Hammerstein show written just for film, *State Fair*'s (August 29, 1945) big hit, "It Might as Well Be Spring," as sung by Louanne Hogan (1919–2006) dubbing actress Jeanne Crain (1925–2003) at *It Might as Well Be Spring, is reminiscent of "A Cockeyed Optimist," except the latter wasn't written until four years later, for *South Pacific*, so "Cockeyed Optimist" is really derivative of "It Might as Well Be Spring." A jazzed-up version by singer Stacey Kent (b. 1965), with husband Jim Tomlinson (b. 1966) on saxophone, from her 2002 album *In Love Again: The Music of Richard Rodgers*, at *Stacey Kent It Might as Well Be Spring, has a great bossa nova rhythm.

A loose, very loose, biopic about George Gershwin, *Rhapsody in Blue* (September 22, 1945) featured a number of important milestone tunes by the composer, including the title tone poem (1924) conducted by its first conductor, Paul Whiteman, and mimed on piano (to Oscar Levant's playing) by Robert Alda (né Alphonso Giuseppi Giovanni Roberto D'Abruzzo; 1914–1986) at *Rhapsody in Blue Debut Film.

Yolanda and the Thief (November 20, 1945), Fred Astaire's one truly surreal film musical in his career, is the story of a thief who cons his way into a woman's life by getting her to believe he is an angel. It was directed by Vincente Minnelli and had songs composed by Harry Warren and lyrics by Arthur Freed. The truly bizarre 15-minute "Dream Ballet," starring Astaire and Lucille Bremer (1917–1996) and choreographed by Eugene Loring (né Le Roy Kerpestein; 1911–1982), has to be seen to be believed at *Yolanda and the Thief This Heart of Mine—complete with reverse rhythm film footage. But the genuine highlight of the film is the innovative "Coffee Time," at *Coffee Time Yolanda and the Thief, with the dancing performed in 5/4 time set to music in 4/4 time! It may be Astaire's most rhythmically complex, spellbinding dance ever. (The Dali-like black and white wavy lines on the floor help sustain the number's off-kilter, vertiginous vibe.)

A "lost" Alan Jay Lerner and Frederick Loewe Broadway musical, *The Day Before Spring* (November 22, 1945) was the story of a married woman who, at a college reunion, considers leaving her husband to reunite with an old flame. As sung by pianist and singer Todd Schroeder and cabaret crooner Barbara Brussell, from her 2005 album *Lerner in Love: The Lyrics of Alan Jay Lerner*, the sweet "You Haven't Changed at All" recounts that very encounter at *You Haven't Changed at All Barbara Brussell.

The new year ushered in a nostalgic look back at the Revues of Ziegfeld with *Ziegfeld Follies* (January 1946), the third of three films on the 20th-century impresario. Structured similarly to a typical production, it was filmed over three years (1944–1946) and required seven different directors. Gene Kelly and Fred Astaire danced and sang together for the first and only time in a musical to the Gershwins' "Babbitt and the Bromide," from 1927's *Funny Face*, at *Fred Astaire Gene Kelly Babbitt and the Bromide. Fanny Brice, the only cast member in the film who had actually performed in a Follies, does her unpleasant-in-the-21st-century exaggerated Jew in *The Sweepstakes Ticket, and Astaire introduces a bevy of Ziegfeld beauties—with a young Cyd Charisse on pointe and a younger Lucille Ball cracking a whip—in the opening number, "Here's to the Girls," an obvious homage to Irving Berlin's theme song for the *Ziegfeld Follies of 1919*, "A Pretty Girl Is Like a Melody," at *Here's to the Girls—Ziegfeld Follies. For our rarefied 21st-century sensibilities, the nearly two-hour film is hard to sit through—not a narrative thread to be found—but if one partakes of the occasional song or dance or comedy number, it's a fair approximation of the Revue format from a hundred years ago.

March 30, 1946, brought the show *St. Louis Woman*, about a jockey on a winning streak, to Broadway starring the Nicholas Brothers and Pearl Bailey. Ruby Hill and Rex Ingram sang composer Harold Arlen and lyricist Johnny Mercer's blues tune "Come Rain or Come Shine" in the show, but here's Ray Charles on the classic tune from his 1959 album *The Genius of Ray Charles* at *Ray Charles—Come Rain or Come Shine.

Thirty-one years before the Depression-era cartoon character Little Orphan Annie (1924–2010) got herself a Broadway show, another Annie, Buffalo Bill Cody's Wild West Show sharpshooter Annie Oakley (née Phoebe Ann Mosey; 1860–1926), inspired the Rodgers and Hammerstein-produced *Annie Get Your Gun*, which opened on May 16, 1946. Starring Ethel Merman in one of her most famous roles, Jerome Kern was the intended composer but, just as he was beginning the assignment, he died of a cerebral hemorrhage. Famed librettist Dorothy Fields suggested Irving Berlin take over, and Berlin wrote one of his best scores, including the gorgeous ballad "They Say It's Wonderful," rendered by Bernadette Peters (b. 1948) and Tom Wopat (b. 1951) for the 1999 revival at *Annie Get Your Gun (1999 Broadway Revival Cast).

January 10, 1947, saw the Broadway musical *Finian's Rainbow* arrive. Composer Burton Lane (né Morris Hyman Kushner; 1912–1997) and lyricist E. Y. Harburg's most renowned score includes gorgeous tunes like "Look to the Rainbow," "How Are Things in Glocca Morra?" and "That Old Devil Moon," all nicely contrasted with typical pun-filled Harburg ditties like "Something Sort of Grandish" and "When the Idle Poor Become the Idle Rich." The latter is sardonically rendered by Fred Astaire and Petula Clark (b. 1932) in the 1968 film version at *When the Idle Poor Become the Idle Rich.

A 1946 musical called *Annie Get Your Gun*, with songs by Irving Berlin, was loosely based on the life of 19th-century sharpshooter Annie Oakley (née Phoebe Ann Mosey; 1860–1926). This photo was taken sometime in the 1880s.

E. Y. "Yip" Harburg got the idea for the show because he wanted to satirize an economic system that required gold reserves to be buried at Fort Knox. In this show, Harburg continues his punny work from *The Wizard of Oz* (the leprechaun's name is Og, just one letter different from …), particularly in the songs "The Begat" and "When I'm Not Near the Girl I Love." George Gershwin mentored Burton Lane, and a lush depth of melody and strong sense of rhythm characterize much of his compositional work. One of the three wishes that the legendary crock of gold allowed was to turn bigoted Southern senator Billboard Rawkins black, but one of the problems of reviving the show over the years is its blackface requirements in the second act, making it difficult to produce in our 21st century.

Lyricist Alan Jay Lerner and composer Frederick Loewe's first big hit, *Brigadoon*, the story of an invisible Scottish town that reappears once every hundred years, hit the stage on March 13, 1947.

By dealing with themes of substance, by their adherence to the concept of the integrated musical, and by their ability to make the past come vividly alive to modern audiences, Lerner and Loewe established their special niche in the musical theatre while still laying claim to being the stylistic heirs of Rodgers and Hammerstein [Green and Ginell, 2014, p. 134].

Lovely ballads such as the title tune, "Heather on the Hill," "I'll Go Home with Bonnie Jean," "Come to Me, Bend to Me," and "Almost like Being in Love" fill out the score. As a couple of sheep look querulously on, that last song is treated as a cool and easy soft-shoe by Gene Kelly in the 1954 film version at *Almost Like Being in Love 1954 Gene Kelly. Baritone George Dvorsky renders the tune rich on a 2005 soundtrack album at *Almost Like Being in Love Brigadoon Original Studio Cast Recording.

It Happened in Brooklyn (April 7, 1947) is a feel-good movie that takes place just after World War II. It's got six songs with music by Jule Styne and lyrics by Sammy Kahn, including "Time After Time," gorgeously rendered by Frank Sinatra at *Frank Sinatra Time After Time. Inspired by the title of the 1979 science fiction movie of the same name, pop singer, songwriter, and LGBTQ activist Cyndi Lauper (b. 1953) wrote and sang a tune with the same title on her 1983 *She's So Unusual* album, heard and seen here from her official video at *Cyndi Lauper Time After Time.

New Orleans (April 18, 1947) was a film musical that starred Billie Holiday (in her only feature film) and Louis Armstrong falling in love during the birth of the blues in the title town. The powerful "Do You Know What It Mean to Miss New Orleans?" with music by Louis Alter (1902–1980) and lyrics by Eddie DeLange (1904–1949), "Farewell to Storyville" (written by Holiday and Armstrong), and "The Blues Are Brewin'" (also by Alter and DeLange) can all be seen at *Billie Holiday All Her Songs in New Orleans.

Living in a Big Way (June 10, 1947) was a sweet little Gene Kelly black and white film about two people who barely know each other after World War II but marry anyway. With songs by Lennie Hayton (1903–1971), Kelly does a neat duet with a dog in "Fido and Me" at *Living in a Big Way Fido and Me, and with a host of kids on and around a construction site—at one point, clearly without a safety net or body double, he works some parallel bar action high atop the unfinished building—at *Gene Kelly Living in a Big Way.

Down to Earth (August 21, 1947), a film musical starring Rita Hayworth, had a story about the muse Terpsichore upset with a producer who misrepresents all nine muses. Loose basis for the 1980 film *Xanadu*, Hayworth is featured in several numbers with music by rare female composer, the Queen of the Jukebox Doris Fisher (1915–2003), lyricist Allan Roberts (1905–1966), and choreography by Jack Cole, including "Let's Stay Young Forever," at *Let's Stay Young Forever Down to Earth.

Are You with It? (March 20, 1948), starring Donald O'Connor (1925–2003), was a film musical about a young insurance agent who quits his job to take up with a carnival. Best-known for his role as Cosmo Brown in the 1952 film *Singin' in the Rain*, O'Connor appeared in many unheralded movies tapping and singing his heart out throughout the late 1930s and 1940s before that most famous picture came along. Have a look at him at his athletic best alongside co-stars Lew Parker (1910–1972) and Louis DaPron (1913–1987) in "Applied Mathematics" at *Donald O'Connor Tap Solo Are You with It.

With songs by Cole Porter and directed by Vincente Minnelli, Judy Garland's husband, Gene Kelly appeared in his second of third pictures with Garland in *The Pirate* (May 20, 1948). Listen carefully to the words and music of "Be a Clown," at *Be a Clown Gene Kelly The Pirate, and then compare them to "Make 'Em Laugh" four years later from *Singin' in the Rain* at *Make 'Em Laugh Singin' in the Rain, ostensibly composed by Nacio Herb Brown and lyrics by Arthur Freed. Besides the fact that Gene Kelly sings the first tune and dances it with the fabulous Nicholas Brothers and that Donald O'Connor sings the second and performs classic Vaudeville pratfalls in it, do you notice any difference between the two? It is reported that none other than Irving Berlin, while visiting the set when "Make 'Em Laugh" was being recorded, exclaimed that he had just seen that number ["Be a Clown"] in *The Pirate*. Even Stanley Donen (b. 1924), co-director with Kelly on *Singin' in the Rain*, said Brown and Freed's song was total plagiarism; but apparently, by 1952, Porter remained thankful (after two Broadway flops) for the job given him on *The Pirate* by producer Freed, and so he didn't sue—but certainly could have.

The film musical *Romance on the High Seas* (June 25, 1948) made Doris Day (née Doris Mary Ann Kappelhoff; 1922–2019) a star in her debut movie, singing songs by composer Jule Styne and lyricist Sammy Kahn. The slow ballad "It's Magic" was the tune nominated for an Academy Award, but "It's You or No One" and "Put 'Em in a Box, Tie 'Em with a Ribbon, and Throw 'Em in the Deep Blue Sea," both performed with the Page Cavanaugh (1922–2008) Trio, that had the jazz juice at *It's You or No One Doris Day and *Put 'Em in a Box Doris Day, respectively.

After *The Pirate* earlier in the year, Kelly and Garland and Minnelli were immediately rehired for producer Arthur Freed's next picture at MGM, *Easter Parade* (June 30, 1948), this time with a host of Irving Berlin songs, but Minnelli and Garland were having marital troubles, and Kelly broke his ankle. His recommendation? Some guy who had retired in 1946 after his second of two films with Bing Crosby. (That would be Fred Astaire, in *Blue Skies*.) Fred jumped (probably literally) at the chance to work with Garland, for the first and only time, and *Easter Parade* became as perennial a springtime hit as *The Wizard of Oz* had become for autumn.

The hits of "Steppin' Out with My Baby" (with an impeccably timed slow-motion dance by Astaire), "Drum Crazy" (Astaire's second of three film percussion solos, the first 11 years earlier in *A Damsel in Distress*, and the third 9 years later, in *Daddy Long Legs*), "Shaking the Blues Away" (a gangbusters tap solo for Ann Miller), and the title song are all worth their weight in gold—at *Fred Astaire Steppin' Out with My Baby, *Easter Parade Drum Crazy, and *Shakin' the Blues Away Ann Miller, respectively—but the low-key tune sung by Garland (as a reprise) to Astaire at a piano, "It Only Happens When I Dance with You," is the most charming of all the film's hits at *Easter Parade It Only Happens When I Dance with You.

On the second-to-last day of 1948, Cole Porter's biggest hit *Kiss Me, Kate*—turned into a 1953 film without the comma in its title—opened at the New Century Theatre. Porter's hysterical, censor-beating lyrics were never more proudly on display than in "Brush Up Your Shakespeare," seen from the film at *Brush Up Your Shakespeare, as performed by James Whitmore and Keenan Wynn. (I wonder which Roman general's name from the fifth century BCE rhymes with "heinous"?) Also, have a listen to the elegiac "So in Love," gorgeously rendered for the 1990 AIDS charity album *Red Hot + Blue: A Tribute to Cole Porter*, by Canadian pop-country singer/songwriter k. d. lang (née Kathryn Dawn Lang; b. 1961) at *So in Love KD Lang.

Fortunately for us, Bob Fosse (1927–1987) was given permission by choreographer Hermes Pan to create and perform his first recorded piece of choreography in the film—all 65 seconds of it—midway through the "From This Moment On" number. Look for his signature asymmetrical and athletic jazz steps kick into high gear when they transform the song at the 2:10 spot of *From This Moment On. He is partnered with Jack Cole and Gene Kelly assistant Carol Haney (1924–1964) in the number.

On the very last day of 1948, *Words and Music*, a biopic about composer Richard Rodgers and lyricist Lorenz Hart opened in Hollywood, filled to the brim with the songwriters' tunes put over by a host of celebrity performers. After ten pictures together, "I Wish I Were in Love Again," from 1937's Broadway show *Babes in Arms*, was the final duet for Mickey Rooney and Judy Garland onscreen, at *I Wish I Were in Love Again. Lena Horne performs the classic "The Lady Is a Tramp," from the same show, at *Lena Horne Lady Is a Tramp. And, as noted earlier in the discussion about the 1936 show *On Your Toes*, Gene Kelly and Vera-Ellen perform their version of the tragic "Slaughter on 10th Avenue" at *Words and Music Slaughter on Tenth Avenue.

South Pacific, a Broadway show with music by Richard Rodgers, lyrics by Oscar Hammerstein, and a story based on James Michener's 1947 book *Tales of the South Pacific*, opened at the Majestic Theatre on April 7, 1949. Controversy over its centerpiece, "You've Got to Be Carefully Taught," a song describing how racism is a nurtured habit, not genetic, was rampant, especially in the South.

In 1953, with the tour in Atlanta, there was controversy over "You've Got to Be Carefully Taught." Two Georgia state legislators, Senator John D. Shepard and Representative David C. Jones, objected to the song, stating that though *South Pacific* was a fine piece of entertainment, that song "contained an underlying philosophy inspired by Moscow," and explained, "Intermarriage produces half-breeds. And half-breeds are not conducive to the higher type of society.... In the South, we have pure blood lines and we intend to keep it that way." They stated that they planned to introduce legislation to outlaw such communist-inspired works. The Northern press had a field day; Hammerstein, when asked for comment, responded that he did not think the legislators were representing their constituents very well, and that he was surprised at the suggestion that anything kind and decent must necessarily originate in Moscow. In part because of the song, touring companies of *South Pacific* had difficulty getting bookings in the Deep South ["*South Pacific* (Musical)"; https://en.wikipedia.org/wiki/South_Pacific_(musical)#Race; retrieved October 1, 2015].

Hammerstein insisted the song stay, and stay it did, poignantly sung at a pivotal moment in the production by the character of Lieutenant Cable—played by John Kerr (1931–2013) but dubbed by Bill Lee (1916–1980)—in the 1958 film version at *You've Got to Be Taught South Pacific. The tune is sung, with accompanying video, in lovely three-part, a cappella harmony, by British musician-songwriter Ian Matthews (né Iain Matthew McDonald; b. 1946) on his 1978 *Stealin' Home* album at *Carefully Taught Ian Matthews.

Take Me Out to the Ball Game (April 13, 1949) was the second of three film musicals starring Gene Kelly and Frank Sinatra together, a story about two Vaudevillians who also play for a fictional 1908 baseball team. The original song with the same title as the film was written by Jack Norworth (1879–1959) and Albert Von Tilzer (1878–1956) in 1908, and Frank and Gene's soft-shoe version of it can be seen at *Take Me Out to the Ballgame Frank Sinatra Gene Kelly.

The Barkleys of Broadway, Fred and Ginger's tenth and final film musical together, opened on May 4, 1949. Originally intended to capitalize on Astaire and Garland's *Easter Parade* chemistry from the previous year, Miss Rogers came to the rescue when Judy turned up sick. "Bouncin' the Blues," at *Ginger & Fred in Bouncing the Blues, an instrumental from a score by composer Harry Warren and lyricist Ira Gershwin, recaptured if for just two minutes the duo's magical dance and song chemistry from their RKO years. Another fab duet, "Swing Trot," normally shown over the film's opening credits, is performed sans titles in the 1997 film *That's Entertainment III*, so we can see it without distraction, at *Astaire and Rogers Swing Trot. The couple also made amends for not dancing to "They Can't Take That Away from Me," the Academy Award–winning George and Ira Gershwin song Fred sang to Ginger in the 1937 film musical *Shall We Dance*, by doing just that in this film at *They Can't Take That Away from Me Barkleys of Broadway. See if you can spot a few references to earlier moves in the number from, say, "Cheek to Cheek"

(*Top Hat*, 1935), "Let's Face the Music and Dance" (*Follow the Fleet*, 1936) or "Never Gonna Dance" (*Swing Time*, 1936).

Neptune's Daughter (June 9, 1949), a film musical about the hijinks at the Neptune swim suit company, featured Frank Loesser's award-winning 1944 song "Baby It's Cold Outside," as sung by Ricardo Montalbán (1920–2009) and Esther Williams, at *Baby It's Cold Outside Neptune's Daughter. Loesser's bouncy tune "(I'd Like to Get You on a) Slow Boat to China" was supposed to be in the film, but the censors deemed it too risqué, so here it is sung by Bette Midler and Barry Manilow (he's also on piano) in their duet from his 2011 album *My Dream Duets* at *Slow Boat to China Bette Midler Barry Manilow.

A biopic about Ziegfeld star Marilyn Miller, *Look for the Silver Lining* (July 30, 1949) starred June Haver (née June Stovenour; 1926–2005) as Miller and Ray Bolger as Jack Donahue (1908–1984), a favored partner of hers in the late 1920s. While most people think of Bolger solely as the Scarecrow in 1939's *The Wizard of Oz*, he was one heck of an athletic and polyrhythmic tap dancer, too, and was featured in two numbers from the film: "Who?" at *Ray Bolger Who, and "Can't You Hear Me Callin' Caroline?" at *Ray Bolger June Haver Look for the Silver Lining. The songs are by Dave Buttolph (1902–1983).

On December 8, 1949, the Broadway show *Gentlemen Prefer Blondes* opened, appropriately, at the Ziegfeld Theatre. With music by Jule Styne (né Julius Kerwin Styne; 1905–1994) and lyrics by Leo Robin (1900–1984), its biggest hit, "Diamonds Are a Girl's Best Friend," achieved nearly sublime status with Marilyn Monroe's version in the July 1953 film version of the show at *Marilyn Monroe—Diamonds Are a Girl's Best Friend. The half-naked women in this filmed number, posing as giant candelabra and clad in nothing but all-black lingerie, were as over-the-top stunning as the yards and yards of wholly saturated pink and red Technicolor gowns and sets created by William Travilla (1920–1990) and Claude E. Carpenter (1904–1976), respectively. One can easily imagine where choreographer Jack Cole had Monroe time her hand placement during certain lyrics such as "pear-shaped" or "rocks." It becomes clear as the number progresses that Monroe's gown stayed put on her torso through sheer willpower.

Equally risqué, and a primer in Cole's modern dance technique, is "Ain't There Anyone Here for Love?," with music by Hoagy Carmichael and Harold Adamson (1906–1980) lyrics, featuring Jane Russell shamelessly, gleefully flirting with dozens of bathing-suited men, at *Ain't There Anyone Here for Love?

On the same day—December 8, 1949—the film version of 1944's groundbreaking Broadway show *On the Town* opened in Hollywood. "New York, New York" was filmed partly on location, and remains an apt, high-energy celebration of the city by composer Leonard Bernstein and lyricists Betty

Comden and Adolph Green, at *New York, New York On the Town. The "Miss Turnstiles Ballet," featuring Vera-Ellen in a star dance turn at *On the Town Miss Turnstiles Ballet, was one of the first non-singing, all-instrumental ballet numbers featured in a film musical. In the 2014 Broadway revival of the original Broadway show, with choreography by Joshua Bergasse, American Ballet Theatre principal Misty Copeland (b. 1982) scintillates in another version of that seminal ballet at *Miss Copeland Performs the Miss Turnstiles Ballet.

FIVE

The 1950s

The film version of Broadway's *Annie Get Your Gun* (1946) opened on May 17, 1950, and was the biggest box office musical that year. Miraculously, two-thirds of Irving Berlin's score was kept in the stage-to-screen transference, including the unofficial anthem to the art form, "There's No Business like Show Business," at *There's No Business Like Show Business—Annie Get Your Gun.

Three Little Words (July 12, 1950) was a biopic loosely based on the collaboration between failed professional baseball player and early Vaudeville pianist-composer Harry Ruby (1895–1974) and Vaudeville comedian, magician, dancer and lyricist Bert Kalmar (1884–1947), played, respectively, by Red Skelton (né Richard Skelton; 1913–1997) and Fred Astaire. Their 1931 song "Nevertheless (I'm in Love with You)," at *Vera Ellen Come on Papa Nevertheless, gives us a sense of the typically sweet charm of their early 20th-century tunes. Dubbed by the original boop-boop-a-doop girl, Helen Kane, a 17-year-old Debbie Reynolds (1932–2016) performs their 1928 "I Wanna Be Loved by You" alongside Carleton Carpenter (b. 1926) at *Three Little Words I Wanna Be Loved by You.

The movie *Summer Stock* (August 31, 1950) was Judy Garland's final musical for MGM and the last of her three films with Gene Kelly. Her solo showstopper "Get Happy," at *Get Happy, with music by Harold Arlen and lyrics by Ted Koehler, was the highlight for her in the film (and recorded two months after filming had stopped), while Gene's solo, "Newspaper Dance," at *Gene Kelly Summer Stock Dance, was his.

The film musical *Tea for Two* (September 2, 1950), inspired by the 1925 Broadway show *No, No, Nanette*, featured Doris Day as both singer and pretty darn good tapper alongside dancer Gene Nelson (né Leander Eugene Berg; 1920–1996) in "I Know That You Know," a 1926 song written by composer Vincent Youmans and lyricist Anne Caldwell, at *Tea for Two 1950 I Know That You Know.

The Toast of New Orleans (September 9, 1950), a film musical with tunes by Nicholas Brodszky (1905–1958) and Johnny Green, was about a bayou fisherman in 1905 with a natural singing talent. Starring tenor Mario Lanza (né Alfredo Arnold Cocozza; 1921–1959) in his second of only eight films, the film's "Tina Lina" featured a singing Lanza, dancer James Mitchell (1920–2010) and 18-year-old dancer Rita Moreno (née Rosa Dolores Alverío Marcano; b. 1931) in rhythmically complex choreography by Eugene Loring (né Le Roy Kerpestein; 1911–1982) at *Mario Lanza Tina Lina Rita Moreno.

The Broadway musical *Call Me Madam* (October 12, 1950), with songs by Irving Berlin, was a political spoof about an American socialite who becomes ambassador to the fictional European country of Lichtenburg. Starring Ethel Merman, who was the only actor from the original show to make it into the 1953 film version, Berlin wrote her a duet to sing which was, in fact, separate lyrics and melodies brought together in harmonic and rhythmic counterpoint—two parts of "You're Just in Love"—which can be seen with Donald O'Connor in the film at *You're Just in Love Donald and Ethel. (The song's double structure is similar to "Play a Simple Melody," one he wrote for his first stage musical, *Watch Your Step*, back in 1914.) Also in the film, O'Connor and Vera-Ellen perform a wonderfully polyrhythmic, complex dance throughout an architecturally fantastic wine cellar full of props, wall corners, archways, and step levels, set to "Something to Dance About" at *Vera and Donald Something to Dance About. O'Connor said his dances in this film were his best ever, and it's hard to disagree with him.

Guys and Dolls, based on several Damon Runyon (né Alfred Damon Runyon; 1880–1946) short stories about gamblers, gangsters, and n'er-do-wells in the New York underworld, opened on Broadway on November 24, 1950, and turned out to be songwriter Frank Loesser's biggest show full of hits. "I'll Know," "Luck Be a Lady," "Sit Down, You're Rockin' the Boat," "Adelaide's Lament," and "Sue Me" were but half of its wonderful tunes. Frank Sinatra as Nathan Detroit and the original Adelaide, Vivian Blaine (née Vivian Stapleton; 1921–1995), plaintively sing that last tune in the 1955 film version at *Guys and Dolls Sue Me. Later in the same film, Marlon Brando himself, as Sky Masterson, holds his own singing "I'll Know" at *Marlon Brando I'll Know. Some of choreographer Michael Kidd's best ensemble dances can be seen set to an orchestration of "Luck Be a Lady" at *Guys and Dolls 1955 Gambler Dance.

The Broadway musical *Out of This World* (December 21, 1950), with songs by Cole Porter, was based on the Roman playwright Plautus's play from the third century BCE *Amphytrion*, a mythological story about the gods Jupiter and Mercury in search of human entertainment. William Redfield (1927–1976) as Mercury runs through the Porter patter list song "They Couldn't Compare to You," full of typically riotous double entendres, on the soundtrack album at *They Couldn't Compare to You.

At War with the Army (December 30, 1950), the 2nd (of 17) films starring the comedy duo of Jerry Lewis (né Joseph Levitch; 1926–2017) and Dean Martin (né Dino Paul Crocetti; 1917–1995), takes place on a U.S. Army base in Kentucky at the end of World War II. Jerry sings and hams his way through the silly ditty "Beans," written by Jerry Livingston (1909–1987) and Mack David (1912–1993), at *Martin and Lewis Beans, complete with repetitive harmonies around the word "beans" by his army buddies. Monty Python fans will be able to relate, as similar repetitions of another food word appear in their 1970 TV sketch at *Monty Python Spam.

Fred Astaire and Jane Powell starred in *Royal Wedding* (March 23, 1951), a film musical set in 1947 London just before the wedding of Princess Elizabeth (b. 1926). With music by Burton Lane and lyrics by Alan Jay Lerner, Fred's famous dance-on-the-ceiling number, "You're All the World to Me," appears at *You're All the World to Me. How did they do that? For the answer, watch the TV show *Glee*'s season 4, episode 15 (March 4, 2013) behind-the-scenes homage to Astaire and MGM, recapitulated by Jayma Mays (b. 1979) and Matthew Morrison (b. 1978), at *Rando Productions Glee Rolling Room.

Back in the film, Fred and Jane go at it in mock fury in a hysterical Vaudevillian number "How Could You Believe Me When I Said I Love You When You Know I've Been a Liar All My Life," one of the longest song titles ever written, at *How Could You Believe Me Royal Wedding. And Astaire's fabulous "duet" with a hat rack is in this one at *Sunday Jumps Astaire. Check out those oh-so-cool red socks.

Based on Margaret Landon's 1944 novel *Anna and the King of Siam*, itself derived from governess Anna Leonowens' (1831–1915) memoirs, *The English Governess at the Siamese Court* (1870), about her work in the 1860s for Thailand's (then known as Siam) King Mongkut and his children, composer Richard Rodgers and lyricist-book writer Oscar Hammerstein's *The King and I* (March 29, 1951) opened on Broadway starring Gertrude Lawrence and Russian-born Yul Brynner (né Yuliy Borisovich Briner; 1920–1985). Like the later "Spoonful of Sugar" in *The Sound of Music* (1959), "I Whistle a Happy Tune" helped calm the anxieties of both Anna and her son Louis upon their arrival in a new world, as sung by Lawrence on the Original Cast Album at *Lawrence Whistle a Happy Tune.

Meet Me after the Show (August 15, 1951), a story about relationships put into turmoil over a Broadway show, starred Betty Grable and Macdonald Carey (1913–1994) as the troubled couple. With music by Jule Styne and lyrics by Leo Robin, the testosterone-fueled, Jack Cole–choreographed "No-Talent Joe" featured Grable, an uncredited Gwen Verdon (née Gwyneth Evelyn Verdon; 1925–2000) as Sappho, and Arthur Walge (b. 1924), a 6' 6" weightlifter in the title role, at *Betty Grable Gwen Verdon No Talent Joe.

The 17-minute ballet "An American in Paris," from the film musical *An American in Paris* (November 11, 1951), is justifiably famous for Gene Kelly's choreography and dancing, with Leslie Caron (b. 1931) and ensemble, as set to Gershwin's 1928 jazz-inflected tone poem. With excerpts at *An American in Paris Ballet, the number also honors six late 19th-century French Impressionist painters (Dufy, Renoir, Utrillo, Rousseau, Van Gogh, Toulouse-Lautrec) via huge painted sets. But it is the charming *Girl Crazy* (1930) melody "Embraceable You," also treated in six distinct musical ways (Romantic, blues, waltz, brassy jazz, symphonic idyll, full-throated symphonic) by the inestimable MGM Orchestra and danced in six vignettes by the 20-year old Caron at *Leslie Caron An American in Paris Embraceable You, that wows us. Elsewhere and often overlooked, the simple opening of the film is a delight as it showcases Gene's choreographic chops with props as he wakes up to prepare breakfast in his little room at *Gene Kelly Opening American in Paris.

A story about the lives and loves of families during the California Gold Rush in the mid–1850s, the Broadway musical *Paint Your Wagon* (November 12, 1951) had music by Frederick Loewe and lyrics by Alan Jay Lerner. Baritone Harve Presnell (né George Harvey Presnell; 1933–2009), as Rotten Luck Willie, sings the restless "They Call the Wind Maria," in the 1969 film version of the show at *They Call the Wind Maria Presnell. In the same film, Clint Eastwood (b. 1930) did his own singing on the lovely "I Talk to the Trees" at *Clint Eastwood Talk to the Trees. Some of us of a certain age heard (translation: memorized) the tune as performed (translation: playfully tampered with) by the comedy/singing duo the Smothers Brothers on their 1966 album *Golden Hits of the Smothers Brothers, Vol. 2*, at *I Talk to the Trees Smothers Brothers.

The Belle of New York (February 22, 1952), a film musical that takes place in turn-of-the-20th-century New York, starred Fred Astaire and Vera-Ellen, had choreography by Robert Alton and Astaire, and songs by composer Harry Warren and lyricist Johnny Burke. Vera-Ellen's strong dancing pushed Astaire and Alton to create even more dance-heavy numbers than usual, including a routine set to "A Bride's Wedding Day Song," at *Belle of New York Bride's Wedding Day, similar in virtuosity to Fred and Ginger's "Waltz in Swing Time" duet from 1936's *Swing Time*. "I Wanna Be a Dancin' Man" features Astaire in a solo sand dance at *I Wanna Be a Dancin' Man, which is fun to compare to Bob Fosse's partial homage ensemble version, at *I Wanna Be a Dancin' Man Fosse, from his 1978 Broadway show *Dancin',* as filmed for PBS in 1999.

If it was possible, Gene Kelly topped himself in *An American in Paris* half a year later on April 11, 1952, with composer Nacio Herb Brown and lyricist Arthur Freed's songbook *Singin' in the Rain*, the story of the stranger-than-fiction silent film's transition into sound. (Although it's best not to compare two great films for different reasons.) Standouts include the title number, of course, at *Singin' in the Rain Gene Kelly, and "Good Morning," with the trio of Kelly, Donald O'Connor, and Debbie Reynolds singing, tapping, and goofing around, at *Good Morning—Singin' in the Rain. "Moses Supposes" and "Make 'Em Laugh" were also fabulous—the latter song a total rip-off of Cole Porter's "Be a Clown" from *The Pirate* (1948)—at *Gene Kelly Moses Supposes and *Make 'Em Laugh Donald O'Connor, respectively.

Lovely to Look At, the July 4, 1952, film version of the 1933 Broadway show and 1935 Hollywood film *Roberta*, re-used many of Jerome Kern and Dorothy Fields' tunes, especially "I'll Be Hard to Handle" (with lyrics by Bernard Dougall), a dynamite tap dance and song by Ann Miller, who bats away a half-dozen howling "dogs" with her purple, arm-length gloves, at *Ann Miller—I'll Be Hard to Handle.

Million Dollar Mermaid (December 4, 1952) was a biographical musical film about Australian swimmer Annette Kellerman (1886–1975) that starred Esther Williams in water ballet choreography by Busby Berkeley. Two of several spectacles with Berkeley's typical kaleidoscopic patterns can be seen at *From Million Dollar Mermaid and *Underwater Ballet Million Dollar Mermaid, the latter set to the "Waltz of the Flowers" excerpt from composer Peter Tchaikovsky's 1892 *The Nutcracker*. Producer-directors Joel (b. 1954) and Ethan Coen's (b. 1957) film *Hail, Caesar!* (2016) seems to honor Berkeley's work in *Million Dollar Mermaid*—for a few minutes, at least, at *Hail Caesar the Mermaid Ballet Scene.

The I Don't Care Girl (January 20, 1953) was a loose biopic about Canadian-born Eva Tanguay (1878–1947), who billed herself as the Queen of Vaudeville. Starring Mitzi Gaynor in the title role, several numbers filmed in brightly lit, saturated colors evoke the extravagance of Tanguay's showbiz life, including her biggest hit song, the 1905 "I Don't Care," with music by Harry O. Sutton and lyrics by Jean Lenox (a rare female songwriter), in the powerful jazz-inflected choreography by Jack Cole, at *Mitzi Gaynor the I Don't Care Girl. (Look fast for a funny Oscar Levant in drag!) Tanguay herself, embodying the emancipated woman of her time, can be heard suggestively singing the tune in a 1922 recording at *Vaudeville Star Eva Tanguay I Don't Care. You can also see her briefly onstage and in film in an undated and untitled Quebec television show at *L'Artiste de Vaudeville Eva Tanguay.

Peter Pan (February 5, 1953), based on the 1904 James M. Barrie (1860–1937) play *Peter Pan; or, the Boy Who Wouldn't Grow Up*, was Disney's 14th animated film. It featured several songs by Sammy Fain, including the Disney favorite, "Second Star to the Right," sung by the Mellomen quartet (formed 1948) and the Jud Conlon (né Justin Conlon; 1910–1966) Chorus (formed 1947) at *Peter Pan Main Title Music. James Taylor and the three-sister singing group the Roches (formed 1973) also do a lovely version of the song on the 1988 compilation album *Stay Awake: Various Interpretations of Music from Vintage Disney Films* at *Second Star to the Right James Taylor.

Small Town Girl (April 10, 1953), a film musical about mixed-up relationships in a small town, featured songs by composer Nicholas Brodszky and lyricist Leo Robin and starred Ann Miller, Bobby Van, Jane Powell, and Nat King Cole, and a few numbers choreographed by Busby Berkeley. Miller sings and taps up a storm in and around an entire mostly underground orchestra, just their arms and instruments visible through holes cut out of the surreally slanted floor, in the wacky "I've Gotta Hear That Beat" at *I've Gotta Hear That Beat Small Town Girl. "Take Me to Broadway" showcases Van's tapping and athletic skills all over a music store at *Take Me to Broadway Small Town Girl, while elsewhere, all he does is hop on two feet around an entire town in *Bobby Van Take Me to Broadway.

Vaudeville star, film actress, writer and Australian swimmer Annette Kellerman (1887–1975), the subject of the 1952 film musical *Million Dollar Mermaid*, is seen here in a 1900 photograph wearing her famous one-piece bathing suit.

The Broadway show *Can-Can*, a story about showgirls in the Montmartre area of Paris in 1890s, opened on May 7, 1953, and made it to the silver screen seven years later (March 1960). A compendium of Cole Porter hits such as "Just One of Those Things," "Let's Do It," "It's All Right with Me," "You Do Something to Me," and "C'est Magnifique," that last song can be heard with Porter himself on both piano and vocals at *Cole Porter Sings and Plays C'est Magnifique. If you listen carefully to the raw 1952 demo recording, you can hear him occasionally hand turn the score's pages.

The Band Wagon (August 7, 1953) started out as a Broadway Revue in June 1931, but the film version threw out the original story and used just the title, the same star (Fred Astaire), and composer Arthur Schwartz and lyricist Howard Dietz's songs. The one new song, "That's Entertainment," at *That's Entertainment—The Band Wagon, nearly took over the role of signature theatre tune from Irving Berlin's "There's No Business like Show Business," presented six years earlier in *Annie Get Your Gun*. Choreographer Michael Kidd helped Astaire through *The Girl Hunt Ballet, which may look familiar to fans of another Michael, Jackson (1958–2009), as the latter borrowed both the outfit and narrative structure of the number for his "Smooth Criminal" video on his 1987 album *Bad*, at *Michael Jackson—Smooth Criminal. (Look fast for Jackson's wink at Kidd's other gangster number, "Luck Be a Lady," from the 1955 film *Guys and Dolls*, and an even shorter nod to Jerome Robbins's 1961 *West Side Story*.) The Vaudevillian patter tune and dance "Triplets," introduced in Schwartz and Dietz's 1938 Broadway show *Between the Devil*, is available for your pleasure at *Band Wagon Triplets. "Dancing in the Dark," the lush Schwartz and Dietz song from the original Broadway Revue, was transformed in the film into a transcendent pas de deux by Astaire and Cyd Charisse at *Dancing in the Dark, also choreographed by Kidd (with Astaire uncredited). It requires no commentary.

Based on the Dobie Gillis short stories by Max Schulman (1919–1988), which also became a 1959–1963 TV series, *The Affairs of Dobie Gillis* (August 14, 1953) was a film musical about the hijinks of a Midwestern college freshman and his pal. Starring Bobby Van (né Robert Jack Stein; 1928–1980) as Gillis and Bob Fosse as his friend, the two perform the boisterous "You Can't Do Wrong Doing Right," written by Al Rinker (1907–1982) and Floyd Huddleston (1918–1991); it is full of typical Fosse asymmetries and his quirky athleticism, with Barbara Ruick (1930–1974) and Debbie Reynolds performing, too, at *Fosse Reynolds Van Ruick Song and Dance.

October 1953 saw *Kiss Me Kate* (without the comma in the title) open, which was the film version of Broadway's *Kiss Me, Kate* (December 1948; with the comma). Incredible for a film version, almost all of Cole Porter's songs transferred to the screen, although the censors typically had to fiddle (translation: censor) with some of his words. Filmed in 3-D but rarely shown in that format today, nevertheless look for gloves, scarves, jewelry, and a fan flung directly at the camera during Ann Miller's song and taps in "Too Darn Hot" at *Too Darn Hot—Kiss Me Kate.

Based on the 1911 play of the same name by the American-born British playwright and novelist Edward Knobloch (né Edward Gustav Knoblauch; 1874–1945), the December 3, 1953, Broadway show *Kismet* (the word means "fate" or "destiny" in the Turkish and Urdu languages) was the story of a poet in a fictional Baghdad who talks himself out of all sorts of problems. With music and lyrics by Robert Wright (1914–2005) and George Forrest (1915–1999), pop crooner Vic Damone (né Vito Rocco Farinola; 1928–2018) and actress Ann Blyth (b. 1928) sing the lovely "Stranger in Paradise" in the 1955 film version at *Stranger in Paradise Kismet. All the tunes in the show were adaptations of nearly a dozen from the opera *Prince Igor* (1887), composed by Alexander Borodin (1833–1887). Original show choreographer Jack Cole's classic jazz arms are on display in the "Not Since Ninevah" film dance at *Jack Cole Choreography Ninevah.

With music and lyrics by Richard Adler (1921–2012) and Jerry Ross (né Jerold Rosenberg; 1926–1955), *The Pajama Game* opened on Broadway on May 13, 1954. One of its big hits, "Hey There," can be heard as a duet by the lyric baritone John Raitt (1917–2005) with himself, recorded later that year at *Hey There The Pajama Game. Raitt was the father of blues singer Bonnie Raitt (b. 1949), and his only leading role in a film was in the August 1957 version of *The Pajama Game*, with almost everyone else and most of the songs from the Broadway show also transferred intact. One of Bob Fosse's classic numbers, "Steam Heat," full of his signature body isolations and athleticism, appeared in both the show and the movie, at *The Pajama Game—Steam Heat.

Based on Plutarch's (46–120 CE) story *Rape of the Sabine Women* (the Latin word for "rape," *raptio*, meant "abduction" back then, rather than its current meaning), *Seven Brides for Seven Brothers* (July 22, 1954), with music by composer Gene de Paul (1919–1988) and lyrics by Johnny Mercer, was a high-energy film full of Michael Kidd's athletic choreography. Set on professional dancers such as Jacques D'Amboise (né Joseph Jacques Ahearn; b. 1934), Russ Tamblyn (b. 1934), Tommy Rall (b. 1929), and Matt Mattox (1921–2013), the acrobatic "Barn-Raising Number" is rightly famous in musical theatre history at *Barn Raising Dance. But the often overlooked "Lonesome Polecat" demonstrates Kidd's typical character-driven dances in an uncharacteristically restrained, even poignant, way at *Seven Brides for Seven Brothers—Lonesome Polecat.

Certainly "The Man That Got Away" and "Gotta Have Me Go with You" are two of the highlights of Judy Garland's comeback film masterpiece, *A Star Is Born* (September 29, 1954), but the singer-actress always had a special fondness for songs in which she could dress down rather than up (see "Be a Clown" from *The Pirate* and "A Couple of Swells" from *Easter Parade*, both from 1948). In this film, it was "Lose That Long Face," a lost number found for the 1983 restoration, with Judy in her favored element—ripped pants, overlong overcoat, straw hat, and heavy boots—not only singing the tune but hamming and tapping it up quite a bit, at *A Star Is Born Lose That Long Face. With tunes by Harold Arlen and Ira Gershwin, the film was a real tour de force for Garland.

The Kidnapping of the Sabine Women, a 1582 masterpiece carved from a single block of marble by 16th-century Italian Flemish sculptor Giambologna (1529– 1608), stands in the outdoor Loggia dei Lanzi in Florence. It depicts the ancient Roman myth upon which the 1954 film musical *Seven Brides for Seven Brothers* was originally inspired.

On October 14, 1954, a film named after the uber-famous winter season song in *Holiday Inn* (August 1942) opened in Hollywood, *White Christmas*. It was really just a pastiche of classic Irving Berlin tunes, with a story loosely based on that previous decade's musical, but this time it starred Danny Kaye in the Fred Astaire part, and playing the Bing Crosby part was Bing Crosby again. In *"The Best Things Happen When You're Dancing," written for the film by Berlin and choreographed by an unbilled Bob Fosse (but staged by Robert Alton), it's a pleasure to see Kaye not only holding his own dancing with Vera-Ellen but playing it straight, a rare sight. In the number "Choreography," seen in *White Christmas Choreography Alton (and Fosse again, it seems clear), we see a gentle parody of "Modern Dance," especially the Martha Graham–Isamu Noguchi dance-sculpture collaborations via Kaye, Ellen, and six women in purple stretch fabric à la Graham's 1930 solo "Lamentation" (see *Martha Graham Lamentation).

Six days later, on October 20, 1954, the fourth and most famous Broadway version of *Peter Pan* opened—out of now over a dozen stage and screen adaptations, including the recent September 2015 film *Pan*—starring eternal pixie Mary Martin (1913–1990). Children of a certain age (including yours truly, six years old by a week) saw the third and most famous television version of this show in living color on NBC on December 8, 1960. We glowingly remember (and believed in) the magic as Peter and the children flew for the first time during the song "I'm Flying," penned by Mark Charlap (né Morris Isaac Charlip; 1928–1974) and Carolyn Leigh (1926–1983), seen at *I'm Flying—Peter Pan.

The underrated film musical *Athena* (November 4, 1954) starred Debbie Reynolds and Jane Powell singing and dancing their way through a story about a conservative lawyer in love with the daughter of a fitness fanatic. The high-octane patterns of "I Never Felt Better," with manic movements of six women, two hunks, and furniture choreographed by Valerie Bettis (1919–1982), was set to composer Hugh Martin (1914–2011) and lyricist Ralph Blane's (1914–1995) catchy song at *I Never Felt Better Athena.

Deep in My Heart, the December 9, 1954, biopic about operetta composer Sigmund Romberg (1887–1951), was a flop when it came out but, for fans of the MGM stable of singers and dancers, it was packed with cameos. Two include "One Alone" (from Romberg's music for 1926's *The Desert Song*), a balletic duet full of contemporary lifts on and around stairs by James Mitchell and Cyd Charisse, at *Cyd Charisse James Mitchell Deep in my Heart One Alone; and, in their only filmed work together, younger brother Fred Kelly (1916–2000), who taught his older Gene brother how to tap, perform "I Love to Go Swimmin' with Women" (from 1921's *Love Birds*) at *I Love to Go Swimmin with Women.

Twentieth Century–Fox studio producer Darryl Zanuck (1902–1979) was so pleased with Ethel Merman's success in the 1953 film musical *Call Me*

Madam that he signed her to a second all–Irving Berlin film, *There's No Business like Show Business* (December 16, 1954)—which was the title of the biggest hit song from another Merman show, Broadway's *Annie Get Your Gun* (May 1946). However, Marilyn Monroe (née Norma Jean Mortenson; 1926–1962) stole the movie from Merman in the ultra-steamy "Heat Wave"—taken from a weather report headline, it was originally written for Berlin's 1933 Revue, *As Thousands Cheer*—and was set to body titillations perfectly timed with the sexual innuendo lyrics by choreographer Jack Cole, at *Marilyn Monroe Performing "Heat Wave."

The last score Cole Porter wrote for a Broadway musical, *Silk Stockings* had adapted the wonderful Greta Garbo 1939 film *Ninotchka* ("Garbo laughs!") to the stage on February 24, 1955, and then back to the movies in July 1957. Some of the composer-lyricist's greatest songs appear in both show and film, including "Paris Loves Lovers," "Satin and Silk," "It's a Chemical Reaction, That's All," and the censor-busting "All of You," the latter two seen as a medley at *All of You—Fred Astaire & Cyd Charisse. As in "Dancing in the Dark" from *The Band Wagon* four years earlier, Cyd and Fred dance a gorgeous duet together, Fred even partnering her in a couple of classical finger turns.

Composers and lyricists Richard Adler and Jerry Ross's second Broadway show, *Damn Yankees*, opened on May 5, 1955, and was, sadly, their final one, after the untimely death of Ross at the tender age of 29 later that year. The show and film version (September 1958) were both choreographed by Bob Fosse, who also worked on the songwriters' previous show and film, *The Pajama Game*. Fosse can be seen for the first and only time performing a duet with his soon-to-be wife Gwen Verdon (1925–2000) in a silly number written just for the film, "Who's Got the Pain?" at *Fosse and Verdon in Damn Yankees Who's Got the Pain. And the goofy "Heart," at *You Gotta Have Heart," hits charmingly dissonant high notes.

On the same day *Damn Yankees* opened on Broadway—May 5, 1955— the charming, rarely seen, and underappreciated film musical *Daddy Long Legs*, starring Fred Astaire and Leslie Caron, opened in Hollywood. Just short of his 56th birthday, Astaire more than holds his own with the young kids of the day in the upbeat, jazzy, pre-rock-and-roll Johnny Mercer number "Sluefoot" at *Daddy Long Legs—Sluefoot.

Having choreographed a number of film musicals in the early 1950s, Michael Kidd finally acted and danced in one—along with Gene Kelly and Dan Dailey—in *It's Always Fair Weather* (September 1, 1955), a kind of sequel to Gene Kelly and Frank Sinatra's December 1949 film *On the Town*. As underrated as Astaire's *Daddy Long Legs* from three months earlier, *Fair Weather* had three wonderful numbers happily strewn about: the split-screen song-and-then-garbage-can-lid dance "Once upon a Time," at *Gene Kelly Once

Upon a Time; Kelly's solo roller skating number "I Like Myself," at *I Like Myself (It's Always Fair Weather); and Cyd Charisse's knock-out number with a bunch of boxers, "Baby, You Knock Me Out," at *Baby, You Knock Me Out— Cyd Charisse.

It's fun to compare Kelly's roller skating in this film to Fred and Ginger's in the April 1937 *Shall We Dance*, set to the Gershwins' "Let's Call the Whole Thing Off," at *Fred Astaire and Ginger Rogers—Let's Call the Whole Thing Off, and then compare both to Charlie Chaplin's blindfolded backwards skating in his mostly silent 1936 film *Modern Times* at *Charlie Chaplin Roller Skating. For good measure, compare all three to Donald O'Connor's dance skating in the 1953 film *I Love Melvin*, in the song "Life Has Its Funny Ups and Downs," at *Donald O'Connor Taps on Roller Skates.

Two months later, on October 11, 1955, the film version of Broadway's 1943 groundbreaker *Oklahoma!* finally made it to the screen. Many a hit moved from stage to screen, including the title song, "Oh, What a Beautiful Mornin'" and "Surrey with the Fringe on Top," "I Cain't Say No," "People Will Say We're in Love," and "Out of My Dreams." Even though he almost kills Curley out of a jealous fury late in the story, the villain of the piece, Jud Fry, is softened just enough by Rodgers and Hammerstein that we almost feel sorry for him during the tongue-in-cheek "Pore Jud Is Dead," here sung by the Aussie Wolverine himself, Hugh Jackman (b. 1968) and Shuler Hensley (b. 1967), in the 1999 PBS version of the 1998 London revival at *The Original London Cast Pore Jud Is Dead.

The next month, the 1950 Broadway show *Guys and Dolls*, with music and lyrics by Frank Loesser, made it to the screen (November 3, 1955). In addition to producer Samuel Goldwyn surprisingly hiring Marlon Brando (1924–2004) as Sky Masterson, who sang and danced to his own songs *and* did justice to them, Goldwyn asked Broadway scenic designer Oliver Smith (1918–1994) to create "purposely stylized, two-dimensional sets that emphasized the artificiality of the hard-shell but soft-centered characters who populate the very special world of Damon Runyon [the author of the original stories]" (Green and Ginell, 2014, p. 200). You can see some of Smith's multicolored, surreal sets in the background of the song "Guys and Dolls," sung by Frank Sinatra, Stubby Kaye, and others, at *Frank Sinatra—Guys and Dolls.

March 15, 1956, saw *My Fair Lady* open, a show that would turn out to be the longest-running musical on Broadway in the 1950s and 1960s (until 1964's *Hello, Dolly!*), lasting over nine years and 2717 performances. (The 1983 Eddie Murphy/Dan Aykroyd film *Trading Places* also takes on the timeworn concept of an experiment with a bet attached.) Librettist and lyricist Alan Jay Lerner had English stage and screen actor, comedian, singer and monologist Stanley Holloway (1890–1982) in mind for Eliza's father, the carousing Cockney Alfred P. Doolittle, even before the show was written, and he was the only other actor besides Rex Harrison (as Henry Higgins) to perform in the film version eight years later (October 1964). One of the songs he made famous, "With a Little Bit of Luck" (he named his 1967 autobiography after the song), from the film version is at *My Fair Lady—With a Little Bit of Luck.

Broadway's *The Most Happy Fella* (May 3, 1956), composer/lyricist/librettist Frank Loesser's vehicle, had a big hit with "Standing on the Corner," which has been remade by dozens of crooners as a standard lounge song (especially Dean Martin's version, from his 1964 album, *Hey, Brother, Pour the Wine*, at *Dean Martin Standing on the Corner). But producer/screenwriter Seth Mac-Farlane (b. 1973)—yes, *that* Seth MacFarlane, of TV's *Family Guy* (b. 1999) and the two *Ted* movies (2012, 2015)—is a heck of a crooner himself, and styles his sweet baritone after hero Frank Sinatra. He sings the show's "Joey, Joey, Joey" from a 2012 BBC program at *Seth MacFarlane Joey, Joey, Joey. If you haven't seen MacFarlane sing yet, prepare to be knocked out.

Full of mock drunkenness, Cole Porter's playful "Well, Did You Evah?" is done up right by Bing Crosby and Frank Sinatra in *High Society* (July 17, 1956), the film musical adaptation of Philip Barry's (1896–1949) 1939 play *The Philadelphia Story*, at *Bing Crosby & Frank Sinatra—Well, Did You Evah. One of Porter's last great ballads also appears in the film, "True Love," a perfectly simple love duet sung by Bing and, with her own heartfelt voice, Grace Kelly, of all people, at *High Society—True Love.

November 15, 1956, saw Michael Kidd's choreography onstage again in composer Gene de Paul and lyricist Johnny Mercer's *Li'l Abner*, a satirical musical fantasy in the style of *Finian's Rainbow* set in a rural Southern community. Based on Al Capp's (né Alfred Gerald Caplin; 1909–1979) Depression-era comic strip (1934–1977) of the same name, Kidd's madcap energy was never on better display than during the "Sadie Hawkins' Day" dance, re-created in the December 1959 film version at *Fifties Cheesecake Dance.

November 29, 1956, saw composer Jule Styne and lyricist-librettists Betty Comden and Adolph Green's Broadway show *Bells Are Ringing* arrive. Shooting star Judy Holliday (née Judith Tuvim; 1921–1965), who won a Tony Award for her touching portrayal of chatty telephone operator Ella Peterson, sings the bittersweet "The Party's Over" at *Judy Holliday—The Party's Over, from the June 1960 film version.

Based on the 1759 Voltaire novel of the same name, which was a story about the disillusionment of its lead character, the comic opera *Candide* (December 1, 1956) is suffused with Leonard Bernstein's music (and, mostly, poet Richard Wilbur's lyrics). Lyric soprano Barbara Cook (1927–2017) became famous singing "Glitter and Be Gay"—and its famously notorious high C notes—at *Barbara Cook Glitter and Be Gay, while Seth Rudetsky deconstructs the score, and this tune in particular, online in the Masterworks

Broadway Podcast Theatre project at *Seth Rudetsky Deconstructs Glitter and Be Gay.

A musical with the title of the Gershwins' November 1927 Broadway Revue, *Funny Face* made it to the screen nearly 30 years later on February 13, 1957, but it had a wholly different story and only five numbers from the original. It did have Fred Astaire again, fortunately, but instead of his sister, Adele, Audrey Hepburn took her place, and besides singing all her own songs, she does excellent justice to Eugene Loring's bebop-inspired choreography in the quirky "Basal Metabolism" number set in a Beatnik club at *Audrey Hepburn's Crazy Dance—Basal Metabolism.

Four months later, Astaire's second musical of 1957, *Silk Stockings* (July 18), which also takes place in Paris, had music and lyrics by Cole Porter. The dancer was 58 years old and the composer 63, but rather than showing their age (much), they chose to spoof both the recent emergence of rock and roll with "The Ritz Roll and Rock," at *Fred Astaire—The Ritz Roll and Rock, and big screen innovations such as VistaVision and CinemaScope, which the film itself used in the clever "Stereophonic Sound," at *Stereophonic Sound— Silk Stockings, with Janis Paige (née Donna Mae Tjaden; b. 1922), as she dances and sings alongside Fred. Ironically, many television rebroadcasts of the film cut off the wide-screen format parodied in the number, proving Porter's point.

West Side Story opened on Broadway on September 26, 1957, and it was met with lukewarm interest, running just 732 performances. (*The Music Man*, from December later that year, ran almost twice as long and won the best musical Tony.) Not until the film version four years later (September 1961) did the team of composer Leonard Bernstein, budding lyricist Stephen Sondheim, director/choreographer Jerome Robbins, librettist Arthur Laurents, and producer Harold Prince make the history books take notice.

> Robbins was not content simply to cast the finest dancers on Broadway [and in the film]. He wanted each dancer to embody a different character, knowing the motivation behind every step. Because these dancers could truly act, they exhibited the kinetic energy necessary to keep hurtling the momentum of the show to its inevitable conclusion. To help his cause, Robbins kept the actors playing the Sharks and Jets separate during rehearsals, naturally forming cliques in their own groups, with a real animosity developing between the onstage gangs (which the ruthless Robbins exploited to the hilt). The director also had each dancer write his or her character's autobiography, giving each role a singular personality with a specific dance vocabulary that could be identified by the audience, whether consciously or not. By understanding their roles in the drama, the dancers … had a deep purpose in the dramatic action, and this sense of identity helped *West Side Story* maintain a consistent tone [Bloom and Vlastnik, 2008, pp. 316–317].

Almost every song in *West Side* is hummable, and many lovers of the show can sing at least some of the words and tunes to "Something's Coming,"

"Maria," "Tonight," "America," "Cool," and "I Feel Pretty." The film's prologue was shot on location on West 65th Street, at that time mostly back alleys and basketball courts (and where opened the following year Lincoln Center for the Performing Arts); its street energy is palpably present at *West Side Story—Prologue. Elsewhere, the song and dance "America" embodied the challenges Puerto Ricans had in trying to assimilate into the country at *West Side Story—America. The entire movie is, arguably, the greatest musical ever filmed.

The December 19, 1957, Broadway show *The Music Man* is the story of a con man who finds love with a town's librarian. The Beatles' very own Paul McCartney sang a bang-up version of Iowa-born-and-bred composer/lyricist/librettist Meredith Willson's (1902–1984) gorgeous ballad "Till There Was You," with George Harrison nailing the guitar part, six short years later in November 1963, at the Prince of Wales Theatre in London, at *The Beatles— Till There Was You (Live). Other tunes in the show include "Seventy-Six Trombones," "Trouble," "Shipoopi," "Iowa Stubborn," and "Gary, Indiana." In the April 1962 film, one can spot little Ronnie Howard on hand as Winthrop Paroo midway through his third season as Opie on *The Andy Griffith Show*.

Based on mime, actress and journalist Sidonie-Gabrielle Colette's (1873– 1954) 1944 novella of the same name, and with a screenplay and lyrics by Alan Jay Lerner, music by Frederick Loewe, and direction by Vincente Minnelli, *Gigi*, one of the last great film musicals from Hollywood's Golden Age, opened on May 15, 1958. Starring Maurice Chevalier, Louis Jourdan, and Leslie Caron, highlights include Chevalier's charming "Thank Heaven for Little Girls," at *Thank Heaven for Little Girls, and the wonderfully contradictory "I Remember It Well," at *I Remember It Well, between Chevalier and fellow vintage performer Hermione Gingold (1897–1987).

Flower Drum Song, Rodgers and Hammerstein's penultimate show, opened on the Great White Way on December 1, 1958, and was directed by Gene Kelly (with Carol Haney as choreographer). The November 1961 film was choreographed by Hermes Pan, Fred Astaire's old collaborator, in a style reminiscent of Jerome Robbins on *West Side*—street-wise cool with knees and elbows bent, and full of jazz chassés (slides)—most noticeably in "Grant Avenue" at *Grant Avenue Flower Drum Song.

In an 1880s murder mystery in and around a London wax museum, Gwen Verdon stole the Tony Award–winning show *Redhead* (February 5, 1959). Her soon-to-be husband Bob Fosse was at the helm in his first double-duty job as director and choreographer, particularly with the tongue-and-body-twisting "Erbie Fitch's Twitch," a riotous number by composer Albert Hague (1920–2001) and lyricist Dorothy Fields, fortuitously engraved on television celluloid the same year at *Gwen Verdon Erbie Fitch's Twitch.

Speaking of stealing the show, whichever one Ethel Merman was in—

from her first, 1930's *Girl Crazy*, to her last, *Gypsy* (May 21, 1959), as Mama Rose, the ultimate ruthless helicopter mother of stripper Gypsy Rose Lee—stealing the show was a given. Other notable Roses include Rosalind Russell (September 1962 film), Angela Lansbury (1973 London production and 1974 Broadway revival), Tyne Daly (1989 revival), Bette Midler (1993 television movie), Bernadette Peters (2003), and Patti LuPone (2008). LuPone inhabits one of the many hits, composer Jule Styne and lyricist Stephen Sondheim's "Together (Wherever We Go)," along with her co-stars Boyd Gaines and Laura Benanti, at *Gypsy (2008 revival)—Together Wherever We Go.

The hills—and Broadway's Lunt-Fontanne Theatre seats—were alive with *The Sound of Music* for over 1400 performances beginning on November 16, 1959, Rodgers and Hammerstein's last show before Oscar died nine months later from cancer. Like *West Side Story* two years earlier, the Broadway *Sound*, as difficult as it is for 21st-century audiences to believe, received lukewarm support from the critics but gained its biggest following when the film came out in March 1965. Even more so than *West Side's*, *Sound's* tunes were not only hummable but delightedly memorized by suburban kids like me growing up in sixties Long Island, New York (and, frankly, all over the planet).

> Truly, *The Sound of Music* was a show better suited to the movies than the stage. As the curtain rose in the stage version, Maria was seen in a tree with a backdrop of the Alps behind her. No matter what they did to make it look real, it was still a chicken wire and papier-mâché tree in the Lunt-Fontanne Theatre. In the movie version, Julie Andrews twirled in a meadow, amid the real Alps, as captured by a magnificent helicopter shot. A song like "Do Re Mi" that came across as slightly insipid on stage became a rouser on the screen, what with the quick cutting of travelogue shots of Salzburg. The final chase and escape over the mountains was more vivid in the film, and *The Sound of Music*, a show that on Broadway was a hit, took on mammoth proportions after the film version was embraced by the public [Bloom and Vlastnik, 2004, p. 297].

See a part of that film's song at *Do Re Mi, and a 2009 flash mob version with dozens of dancers in Antwerp, Belgium, at *Historic Flashmob in Antwerp Train Station, viewed by over 22 million people as of late November 2015. I'd like to think Dick and Oscar would have loved it.

The third Broadway musical that was awarded the Pulitzer Prize for drama (after 1930's *Of Thee I Sing* and 1949's *South Pacific*), *Fiorello!* (November 23, 1959) was about New York City's favorite mayor (its 99th), the progressive Republican Fiorello La Guardia (1882–1947). With Jerry Bock composing and Sheldon Harnick writing the words, the wry waltz "Politics and Poker," sung mainly by Tom Bosley (1927–2000; Mr. Cunningham on TV's *Happy Days*) as La Guardia, and Howard Da Silva (1909–1986) as Ben Marino, can be heard at *Fiorello—Politics and Poker—Original Broadway Version.

Mary Rodgers (1931–2014), daughter of some Broadway guy with the same last name, composed the music for *Once upon a Mattress* (November 25, 1959). With lyrics by Marshall Barer (1923–1998), who is most famous for his work on the theme song to *Mighty Mouse* (c. 1955), of all things, the musical is based on the 1835 Hans Christian Andersen fairy-tale *The Princess and the Pea* and was the show that made Carol Burnett (b. 1933) a major star. Two versions of the hit "Happily Ever After," sung by Burnett and Sarah Jessica Parker (b. 1965; in the 1996 revival), over 35 years apart, are fun to compare at *Happily Ever After and *Sarah Jessica Parker—Happily Ever After, from the Original Soundtrack Recording and New Broadway Cast Recording respectively.

Six

The 1960s

On April 14, 1960, *Bye Bye Birdie* opened and was the

launching pad for the Broadway careers of songwriters Charles Strouse and Lee Adams [Strouse would become most famous for *Annie* 17 years later], librettist Michael Stewart, and director-choreographer Gower Champion (his first of nine book musicals). It was also the earliest musical about the rock and roll phenomenon and the effect of its idols on impressionable teenagers [Green and Ginell, 2014, p. 188].

Canadian-born Broadway and Hollywood choreographer Onna White (1922–2005), along with Academy Award–winning cinematographer Joseph Biroc (1903–1996), created their own mini-musical for the song "The Telephone Hour," exploiting film's split-screen and quick-cut editing techniques during the high-energy April 1963 movie version at *Musical Number: Bye Bye Birdie—Telephone Hour.

The Fantasticks, with music by Harvey Schmidt (b. 1929) and lyrics by Tom Jones (b. 1928), remains the longest-running musical ever—42 years and 17,162 performances—beginning on May 3, 1960, and playing continuously Off Broadway until January 13, 2002. (Its revival began four years later, on August 23, 2006, and is playing yet again to this day.) Its major hit about yearning love, "Try to Remember," sung by the original El Gallo/Narrator, musical theatre and *Law and Order* star Jerry Orbach (1935–2004), is performed in a 1982 TV special at *Jerry Orbach—Try to Remember (1982).

On December 3, 1960, librettist-lyricist Alan Jay Lerner and composer Frederick Loewe's *Camelot*—originally, a French romantic fictional story about a 12th-century castle and court of King Arthur—tread the boards with Richard Burton (né Richard Jenkins; 1925–1984) as King Arthur and Julie Andrews as Guinevere. Burton's at least as good a singer as Brando was in the film version of *Guys and Dolls* five years earlier, and you can hear his mellifluous baritone for yourself on the original soundtrack as he romps through the title song at *Camelot 03: Camelot.

147

Producer David Merrick's version of *Carnival!*—originally a 1950 short story called "The Man Who Hated People," by Paul Gallico (1897–1976)—opened on Broadway on April 12, 1961. The big hit, "Love Makes the World Go Round," was performed with a throaty sexiness by Swedish American actress and singer Ann-Margret (née Ann-Margret Olsson; b. 1941) on Merrick's 1964 album *David Merrick Presents Hits from His Broadway Hits* at *Love Makes the World Go Round.

Frank Loesser's second-biggest hit (after *Guys and Dolls*) was the Broadway show *How to Succeed in Business without Really Trying*, which opened on October 14, 1961. Boston-born Robert Morse (b. 1931) played J. Pierpont Finch and sings the hit song "I Believe in You" directly into the mirror with equal parts seriousness and self-mocking irony, as seen in the March 1967 movie version at *I Believe in You—Robert Morse.

Loesser's eight-word-titled show of 1961 was bested by two words the next year on May 8, 1962, in Stephen Sondheim's *A Funny Thing Happened on the Way to the Forum*. Produced by George Abbott, directed by Harold Prince and choreographed by Jack Cole, an uncredited Jerome Robbins also staged and choreographed some numbers, especially the first, "Comedy Tonight." The exuberantly irreverent Zero Mostel (né Samuel Joel Mostel; 1915–1977), reprising his Broadway role as Pseudolus for director Richard Lester's (b. 1932) October 1966 film version (edited in the rapid-cut style of his work on the August 1964 Beatles' film debut, *A Hard Day's Night*), introduces the pun-filled, alliterative opener at *Comedy Tonight.

"Who Will Buy?" at *Who Will Buy—Oliver, is one of the many highlights in the December 1968 film version of British composer/lyricist/librettist Lionel Bart's (né Lionel Begleiter; 1930–1999) June 1960 West End and January 1963 Broadway *Oliver!* The number, choreographed by Onna White, starts out with a quiet version of the tune sung by on-location street vendors in London and builds in intensity via dancing and singing bodies that eventually fill the screen. Along with just Gene Kelly, Fred Astaire, Michael Kidd, Jerome Robbins, and Stanley Donen—very rare company indeed—White received an Honorary Academy Award for her work on film. Other hits from the show and film that many sixties kids like me know by heart include "Consider Yourself," "Food, Glorious Food," "Where Is Love?," and "I'd Do Anything."

Complete with banjo accompaniment and Dixieland swing energy, Louis Armstrong's version of the title song, at *Hello Dolly Louis Armstrong, of composer/lyricist Jerry Herman's *Hello, Dolly!* knocked "I Want to Hold Your Hand" by the Beatles out of the number one pop chart position when the Broadway show opened on January 16, 1964. Originally titled *Dolly, A Damned Exasperating Woman*, the December 1969 film version, starring Barbra Streisand and Walter Matthau, was the last movie musical directed by Gene Kelly (it was choreographed by Michael Kidd).

Mezzo-soprano and polymath Barbra Streisand (b. 1942) began her sixties-decade reign on Broadway and in Hollywood with composer Jule Styne and lyricist Bob Merrill's stage hit about Ziegfeld's funny girl Fanny Brice (1891–1951) in *Funny Girl* (March 26, 1964). "People," the biggest hit, among others like "Don't Rain on My Parade" and "The Music That Makes Me Dance," can be heard belted out by Streisand with her typical velvety robustness in the September 1968 film version at *People from Funny Girl.

Closing after just nine shows but quickly becoming a cult favorite, the Arthur Laurents–penned zany, absurdist *Anyone Can Whistle* (April 4, 1964), with music and lyrics by Stephen Sondheim, was Angela Lansbury's (b. 1925) first Broadway musical. (After a blackout, act 1 ends with the whole cast sitting out in the house clapping at the audience.) Broadway.com has a wonderful eight-minute excerpt of several numbers from and interviews about the fabled April 10, 2010, one-night revival of the show (through the New York City Center Encores! Series; formed 1994), starring Sutton Foster (b. 1975), Raúl Esparza (b. 1970), and Donna Murphy (b. 1959) at *On the Scene: Anyone Can Whistle at Encores! As a treat, have a listen to Sondheim's own demo for the title song at *Stephen Sondheim Anyone Can Whistle (Demo).

Precursor by nearly two decades to the fast-cut editing of MTV's first years on TV (formed 1981), director Richard Lester's breakneck film about the Beatles, *A Hard Day's Night*, opened on July 6, 1964, a mere six months after they performed for the first time in America on the *Ed Sullivan Show*. Just a bit of the group's frenetic cinema verité energy from their first U.S. visit can be felt watching the trailer for the film's remastered 2014 release at *A Hard Day's Night Official Remastered Trailer.

August 27, 1964, saw the blockbuster film musical *Mary Poppins* open with hummable songs as varied and popular as those from *West Side Story*, *South Pacific* and *A Hard Day's Night*. Composer-lyricist brothers Richard and Robert Sherman's "Chim Chim Cheree," "A Spoonful of Sugar," "Feed the Birds," "Let's Go Fly a Kite," and "Supercalifragilisticexpialidocious" knocked out pre-teen and early-teen kids like me over and over again; we couldn't watch the film often enough. However, if you do not succumb to the sentimentality of "Feed the Birds" and begin to cry (or at least get a lump in your throat) when you watch and listen to Julie Andrews sing it at *Feed the Birds, you're not human.

As if the tunes in the August release of *Mary Poppins* weren't wonderful enough to memorize when kids like me were ten years old, "Tradition," "Matchmaker, Matchmaker," "If I Were a Rich Man," "To Life," and "Sunrise, Sunset" made our cups runneth over the next month (September 22, 1964) with the opening of composer Jerry Bock and lyricist Sheldon Harnick's greatest hit, *Fiddler on the Roof*. The first number of the show (and the film, seven years later, in November 1971) was stunning, performed here by Topol (né Chaim Topol; b. 1935) in the film at *Fiddler on the Roof—Tradition.

With direction by Arthur Penn (1922–2010; *Bonnie and Clyde, Little Big Man*) and music by Charles Strouse and lyrics by Lee Adams—both of whom wrote the tunes for the more famous *Bye Bye Birdie* (1960) and *Annie* (1977)—and a book by socially conscious provocateur Clifford Odets (and William Gibson, after Odets died in 1963), written specifically for Sammy Davis, Jr.—*Golden Boy* (October 20, 1964) was the story about the personal and civil rights challenges and interracial romance (and their controversial-for-its-time kiss onstage) between a boxer and his manager's girlfriend. "Don't Forget 127th Street," a song and dance (with choreography by modern dance icon Donald McKayle; 1930–2018) taking place in character Joe Wellington's hometown of Harlem, is re-created in Davis's own 1966 television special, *The Swinging World of Sammy Davis, Jr.*, at *Don't Forget 127th Street—Sammy Davis, Jr.

The poignant ballad "Who Can I Turn To?" was one of several hits (including "The Joker" and "Feeling Good") in book, music and lyric writers Anthony Newley and Lesley Bricusse's *The Roar of the Greasepaint—The Smell of the Crowd* (May 16, 1965), the allegorical story of 1960s class struggles between Sir, Cocky, the Kid, and the Negro. Have a look at (and compare) two distinct approaches to the tune: first, Anthony Newley himself, on the *Ed Sullivan Show*, fully inhabiting his own song at *Anthony Newley—Who Can I Turn To, and Sammy Davis, Jr., in a somewhat bombastic but no less moving version at *Sammy Davis, Jr.—Who Can I Turn To.

The Beatles' second film (directed, as with their first one, by Richard Lester), *Help!*, came out on July 29, 1965. Packed once again with great hits such as the title song, "You're Gonna Lose That Girl," "You've Got to Hide Your Love Away," and "Ticket to Ride," the group previewed the latter tune during their Wembley Stadium performance earlier that year (on April 11, 1965) at *Beatles—Ticket to Ride (Live at Wembley Stadium 1965).

Loosely based (originally) on Henry James' posthumously published 1917 novel *The Sense of the Past*, composer Burton Lane and librettist-lyricist Alan Jay Lerner wrote the songs for *On a Clear Day You Can See Forever* (October 17, 1965), the story about a reincarnated woman with ESP (extra-sensory perception). With the same title as the show, its big hit, lovingly harmonized by Nancy Wilson and Andy Williams at *Andy Williams and Nancy Wilson—On a Clear Day, is fittingly complemented by Liza Minnelli on the *Late Show with David Letterman* singing another lush melody from the show, "What Did I Have That I Don't Have?" at *Liza Minnelli—What Did I Have.

Broadway really did try to ignore the sixties, deliberately falling out of sync with pop culture, counter-culture, and the civil rights turmoil of the times. Based on Miguel de Cervantes's 1605 and 1615 two-part novel *Don Quixote*, about a man fighting to revive chivalry and bring justice to the world, *Man of La Mancha* (Off-Broadway, November 22, 1965; Broadway,

Broadway's *Man of La Mancha* (1968) was inspired by the 17th-century novel *Don Quixote* by Spanish author Miguel de Cervantes (1547–1616), embellished in the 19th century by illustrations such as this one by French printmaker Gustave Doré (1832–1883).

March 20, 1968) is proof of that; and yet maybe it embodies some of the idealistic hopes of the era after all. If you did not know that the actor who played Gomer Pyle in the sixties TV show (1964–1969), *Gomer Pyle, U.S.M.C.*, Jim Nabors (b. 1930), was an extraordinary baritone (or even if you did), here is your chance to marvel at the power of his voice as he sings the big hit from the show, "The Impossible Dream," in the 99th episode of the fourth season, "The Show Must Go On" (November 3, 1967), at *Gomer Pyle The Impossible Dream. The stirringly resonant hit tune was written by composer Mitch Leigh and lyricist Joe Darion. Turns out it was the favorite song of both Bobby and Teddy Kennedy and was sung at the latter's 2009 funeral by Brian Stokes Mitchell, who played the lead in the 2002 Broadway revival.

On January 29, 1966, director-choreographer Bob Fosse starred his wife Gwen Verdon in composer Cy Coleman and lyricist Dorothy Fields's (the same Dorothy Fields of the 1930s Astaire-Rogers films *Roberta* and *Swing Time*) Broadway show *Sweet Charity*. Fosse also helmed the January 1969 film version, with Shirley MacLaine in the lead role, two highlights of which included the sexually charged, typically minimalist "Hey, Big Spender" and the boisterous "There's Gotta Be Something Better Than This" (both co-starring Chita Rivera, b. 1933, who as of 2018 was still performing on Broadway) at *Big Spender and *There's Gotta Be Something Better Than This, respectively.

Angela Lansbury starred in the Broadway show *Mame* (May 24, 1966), with music and lyrics by Jerry Herman, while Lucille Ball, not to confuse the issue, starred in the March 1974 non-musical Broadway comedy *Auntie Mame*, itself based on the film of the same name from December 1958, starring Rosalind Russell. The perky and bombastic *"We Need a Little Christmas" cheered up the proceedings.

November 20, 1966, brought composer John Kander and lyricist Fred Ebb's *Cabaret* to Broadway. Kurt Weill–type tunes such as "Wilkommen," "The Money Song," "If You Could See Her," and the title number ironically comment on the story of sleazy nightclub denizens struggling for their lives in pre-Hitler Germany. Written just for the Bob Fosse–directed January 1972 film version, "Tomorrow Belongs to Me," at *Tomorrow Belongs to Me Cabaret, is boldly performed as a love song by a young, blond and deliberately androgynous Nazi teenager. Just over 20 years after World War II had ended, the song encapsulates the coming horrors in Germany and the world. At both the 1:40 and 2:25 points of the song, look fast for an old man in the crowd thinking, "Oh no, not again," real fear etched deep into the lines of his face. Fosse brilliantly alternates cuts between this gentleman and actor Joel Grey, master of ceremonies in the story, as he raises his head knowingly to look directly at us in nodding assent, "Yes, sir, it's happening again"—a chilling moment.

Starring Catherine Deneuve, Michel Legrand's music, and Jacques Demy's lyrics again, *The Young Girls of Rochefort* (March 6, 1967), sort of a sequel to *The Umbrellas of Cherbourg* from the previous year, featured Gene Kelly in a couple of cameos, reminiscent of *On the Town* and *An American in Paris*, this time singing (in French) and dancing, especially at *Gene Kelly Young Girls of Rochefort.

Richard and Robert Sherman's songs appeared in Disney's 19th animated film, *The Jungle Book* (October 18, 1967), which was based on the 1894 Rudyard Kipling book of the same name. "I Wanna Be Like You," performed by orangutan King Louie—jazzily sung by famed Italian American singer and bandleader Louis Prima (1910–1978)—can be enjoyed at *The Jungle Book I Wanna Be Like You, while Italian singer and composer Raphael Gualazzi (b. 1981) jazzes up the tune even more on the 2016 CD *Jazz Loves Disney*, at *Raphael Gualazzi I Wanna Be Like You.

Hair: The American Tribal Love-Rock Musical opened on Broadway on April 29, 1968, and reached the screen 11 years later in the Milos Forman–directed March 1979 film. No less than four songs from the Galt MacDermot, Gerome Ragni and James Rado–scored show became huge 1969 AM radio hits: the title song (number two), by the Cowsills (formed 1965), at *The Cowsills—Hair in Color; "Aquarius/Let the Sunshine In" (number one), by the 5th Dimension (formed 1966) at *Aquarius (Let the Sunshine In); "Easy to Be Hard" (number four), by Three Dog Night (formed 1967) at *Easy to Be Hard—Three Dog Night; and "Good Morning Starshine" (number three), by Oliver (né William Oliver Swofford; 1945–2000), at *Oliver—Good Morning Starshine. For 14-year-olds like me at the time, singing along to such easy-on-the-ears tunes belied the intensity of the emotional turmoil of the same era for teens barely four years older who were drafted into the Vietnam War. Flower-power alums of the Summer of Love, many of them were anti-establishment youth fighting for race and gender equality. The show and film also included more realistic, deliberately provocative songs such as "Hashish," "Going Down," "Prisoners in Niggertown," and "Black Boys/White Boys," the latter rendered on film at *Black Boys/White Boys—Hair, 1979 (choreographed by modern dance icon Twyla Tharp).

After seven failed attempts, Broadway's 1947 *Finian's Rainbow* finally made it to the silver screen 21 years later on October 9, 1968. Starring in his 35th and final film musical, Fred Astaire played Finian McLonergan and was dully directed by—if you can believe it—the same creator of the three Godfather films beginning four years later, Francis Ford Coppola (b. 1939). Fortunately, the spry Astaire, at 68 years young, steals the movie every time he's onscreen, and most of composer Burton Lane and lyricist E. Y. "Yip" Harburg's lovely songs from the Broadway show transferred nicely, including the typically pun-filled and class conscious Harburg ditty, "When the Idle Poor

Become the Idle Rich," here at *Fred Astaire—Quando os pobres ociosos tornam se ricos ociosos (complete with Portuguese subtitles).

The Broadway show *1776* opened on March 16, 1969, and in Hollywood in November 1972. Composer and lyricist Sherman Edwards's (1919–1981) only, sadly, musical, its catchy tunes such as "Sit Down, John," "The Lees of Old Virginia," "But Mr. Adams," "Molasses to Rum," and "The Egg" moved the actual events surrounding the signing of the Declaration of Independence winningly forward. President Richard Nixon (1913–1994) saw the song "Cool, Cool Considerate Men," a major centerpiece of the story, as a slur on conservatives and demanded it be excised from the film version (much as Southern critics wanted Rodgers and Hammerstein's "Carefully Taught" ripped out of their 1949 *South Pacific*). The edit was refused by director Peter Hunt (1925–2002) but subsequently perpetrated by producer Jack Warner (a friend of Nixon's) in post-production while Hunt was on vacation.

Thirty years later, in the 2002 DVD version, the lost song (set as a minuet!) was finally reinserted, and can be seen at *1776 the 1972 Complete Movie in English, at the 1-hour, 29-minute mark. Embedded in the spliced-up performance is the telling truth that perhaps irked conservatives the most, spoken by actor Donald Madden (1933–1983) as Senator John Dickinson of Pennsylvania: "Don't forget that most men with nothing would rather protect the possibility of becoming rich than face the reality of being poor."

SEVEN

The 1970s

On April 26, 1970, *Company*, the first of six-in-a-row Stephen Sondheim–scored, Hal Prince–directed shows, opened on Broadway.

Every decade seems to give birth to a musical that propels the art form to a new level or at least sends it in a new direction. In the 1900s, George M. Cohan's *Little Johnny Jones* (1904) ushered in an all-American sound and soul for the musical comedy. Jerome Kern's Princess Theatre shows, with their intimate, American-based locales, marked the 1910s. The 1920s began with the *Ziegfeld Follies of 1919* and the ascendancy of Irving Berlin and ended with the groundbreaking *Show Boat*, the best attempt thus far at merging song and story. The 1930s brought *The Band Wagon*, the ultimate Broadway revue featuring a new sophistication of writing, stagecraft, and staging. The 1940s saw Rodgers and Hammerstein's *Oklahoma!* and a whole new formula for the musical comedy. In the 1950s, the musical reached its peak with *My Fair Lady*. The 1960s were ushered in with *The Fantasticks* and the birth of the Off broadway musical. And the 1970s had *Company* [Bloom and Vlastnik, 2008, p. 74].

It had Jonathan Tunick's incomparable, metallic orchestrations; Boris Aronson's antiseptically urban set (a youth spent in Russia and Germany in the constructivist 1920s contributed to an artistry involving projected scenery and cutting edge experimentation); George Furth's (1932–2008) cagey and revealing book; and Hal Prince's sparse, knowing staging.

Sondheim's musicals demand more of theatergoers than they are sometimes willing to give, but his shows are almost always worth the effort…. Many of his songs deal with subjects outside the usual range of popular music: the need for human connection, coupled, ironically, with the fragility of most human relationships; the quirks and obsessions of romantic love; the pleasures and pains of the married state. He had moved a distance from his mentor, Oscar Hammerstein. Hammerstein searched for "Bali Ha'i"; Sondheim goes into the woods and finds predatory giants and wolves. It may be that playgoers are reluctant to follow him there…. By the eighties and nineties, of course, musical theater had been taken over by spectacle rather than content [Sennett, 2001, p. 125]

The melodic abrasiveness of tunes such as the title song, "The Little Things You Do Together," and "You Could Drive a Person Crazy," "Getting

155

Married Today," "The Ladies Who Lunch" (compare the definitive sardonic show-stopper by Elaine Stritch at *Elaine Stritch Sings "Here's to the Ladies Who Lunch" to, say, Patti LuPone's version during Stephen Sondheim's 80th birthday celebration at *Patti LuPone—Ladies Who Lunch), and "Being Alive" helped this show thoroughly break tradition. Actor and singer Dean Jones (1931–2015), of Disney's sixties fame with *That Darn Cat!* (1965), *The Ugly Dachshund* (1966), and *The Love Bug* (1968), knocks that last tune out of the park during Donn Alan (D. A.) Pennebaker's (b. 1925) documentary film of the original cast album (May 3, 1970) at *Being Alive—Company OBC, 1970—Dean Jones.

Silently one evening in the fall of 1970, my not-so-devout Jewish grand-father nobly suffered through part of the double-record *Jesus Christ Superstar* (September 1970) that I had provocatively foisted on his ears. "Blasphemous," was all he could utter, while his wife, my grandmother, looked on bemusedly but equally disapproving. Unable to fully appreciate what *Hair* had done for the sixties, I was finally beginning, at almost 17 years old and a senior in high school, to rebel enough (against most anything even vaguely authoritarian) to embrace the contemporary fervor *JC* proffered to me, and boy, did I flaunt it. Neither the Broadway show in October 1971 nor the August 1973 film could have appealed to me more than the album hits buzzing around in my head such as "What's the Buzz?" "Heaven on Their Minds," the two lovely ballads "Everything's Alright" and "I Don't Know How to Love Him," and "King Herod's Song," the latter done in classic honky tonk style as sung by Mike d'Abo (b. 1944) at *King Herod's Song—Mike D'Abo. Any subsequent work by composer Andrew Lloyd Webber and lyricist Tim Rice would never hold a candle to the influence their 1970 epic had on my impressionable young mind. Oh heck, if you've got the time, you might as well listen to the whole thing at *Jesus Christ Superstar (1970 Original London Concept Recording).

The story of the highs and lows during a Ziegfeld Follies–type reunion at a soon-to-be-demolished theatre, *Follies*, with a book by James Goldman, music and lyrics by Stephen Sondheim, and direction by Harold Prince, opened on April 4, 1971. As of July 2018, Jeremy Jordan's (b. 1984; *The Flash*, *Supergirl*) 2015 version of *"Losing My Mind" at Feinstein's/54 Below New York nightclub had been seen 1.5 million times on YouTube, while Elaine Stritch's "I'm Still Here," from Sondheim's 80th birthday party celebration at Avery Fisher Hall in 2010 at *I'm Still Here Elaine Stritch, remains unparal-leled.

Happily, a second welcome controversy for "Rebel Me," again dealing with religion, came out with the soundtrack to the May 1971 Off broadway production of *Godspell*. Again, it was the album from July 1971—not the film (March 1973) or the Broadway show (June 1976)—that turned on this budding hippie wannabe when it arrived in record stores that summer. Composer/lyricist Stephen Schwartz's (b. 1948) "Prepare Ye the Way of the Lord," "Save the People," the AM radio hit "Day by Day," "All for the Best" (its Vaudeville sound reminiscent of "King Herod's Song," from the previous year's *Jesus Christ Superstar*), "Light of the World," "Turn Back, O Man," "We Beseech Thee," and the heartrending "On the Willows" all swayed me into believing that *this* was the true path to spiritual ecstasy. (I still feel that way.) Have a listen to the whole album at *Godspell (Full Album)—Stephen Schwartz. I certainly did, many, many times, and still do.

Starring polymath actor-director-screenwriter Gene Wilder (né Jerome Silberman; 1933–2016) in a truly offbeat, magical role, the beloved *Willy Wonka and the Chocolate Factory* film opened on June 30, 1971. With songs written by English actor, singer, and songwriter Anthony Newley (1931–1999) and composer, lyricist, and playwright Lesley Bricusse (b. 1931), the story about a selfless boy (and four other not-so-pleasant children) who is invited to visit a factory filled with all things chocolate was based on a 1964 novel by Welsh-born poet, author and fighter pilot Roald Dahl (1916–1990). Wilder's lovely and, yes, somewhat unsettling version of "Pure Imagination," at *Willy Wonka Pure Imagination, still transports kids young and old to a dreamlike world. "The Candy Man," at *The Candy Man, became an unexpected number one *Billboard Hit 100* hit for singer-tap dancer-actor Sammy Davis, Jr—his only number one hit in his entire career—and was recorded for his April 1972 album *Sammy Davis, Jr. Now*. Made into a July 2005 film starring Johnny Depp, the film was adapted into a Broadway show in April 2017; both versions hew to the original novel's title, *Charlie and the Chocolate Factory*.

Because of the late hard rock era that was still dominant in the early 1970s, nostalgia for the *early* rock and roll fifties, with the opening of *Grease* in February 14, 1972, felt much more distant than the 15 years since Elvis Presley's relative innocence in the film *Jailhouse Rock* (October 1957). Composers and lyricists Jim Jacobs (b. 1942) and Warren Casey's (1935–1988) infectious "Summer Nights," "Freddy, My Love," "Hopelessly Devoted to You," "Greased Lightnin'," and the title song continue to work their peppy magic on so many of us to this day. But it was the deeply poignant contrast of "There Are Worse Things I Could Do," sung by Stockard Channing (née Susan Antonia Williams Stockard; b. 1944) in the role of Rizzo from the June 1978 film version at *Grease—There Are Worse Things I Could Do, that stuns the heart in its barely two-and-a-half minute length. A rash of TV musicals, highlighted by the March 7, 1955, live broadcast of *Peter Pan* on NBC and pumped into overdrive by the series of *High School Musicals* beginning in January 2006, Fox's *Grease* on January 31, 2016, followed in the footsteps of the spectacle-over-story *Sound of Music Live!* (December 2013) and *Wiz Live!* (December 2015). (*Hairspray, Dirty Dancing*, and *Rocky Horror Picture Show* are also in the live TV pipeline.)

Scored by Stephen Schwartz, of *Godspell* fame, *Pippin* opened on Broadway on October 23, 1972, starring Ben Vereen (né Benjamin Augustus Middleton; b. 1946) as Leading Player. A television version was made in 1981 also starring Vereen. A Broadway revival that turned the show into a big top circus production, with extravagant direction by Diana Paulus, knocked the roof off the joint in 2013, but the essence of Bob Fosse's original direction and choreography can be seen in the 1981 version via Vereen's polyrhythmic soft shoe and hip minimalism halfway through "Glory" at *Glory—Pippin—Ben Vereen.

A Little Night Music (February 25, 1973), all composed in ¾ time by Stephen Sondheim, has the songwriter's one true and great hit embedded within it, "Send In the Clowns."

> "Send In the Clowns" is performed in two completely different styles: dramatic and lyric. The dramatic style is the theatrical performance by Desirée, and this style emphasizes Desirée's feelings of anger and regret [which] acts as a cohesive part of the play. The lyric style is the concert performance, and this style emphasizes the sweetness of the melody and the poetry of the lyrics. Most performances are in concert, so they emphasize the beauty of the melody and lyrics. Sondheim teaches both dramatic and lyric performers several important elements for an accurate rendition: "The dramatic performer must take on the character of Desirée: a woman who finally realizes that she has misspent her youth on the shallow life. She is both angry and sad, and both must be seen in the performance. Two important examples are the contrast between the lines, 'Quick, send in the clowns' and 'Well, maybe next year.' Sondheim teaches that the former should be steeped in self-loathing, while the latter should emphasize regret. Thus, the former is clipped, with a break between 'quick' and 'send,' while the latter 'well' is held pensively" [*Stephen Sondheim Teaches at Guildhall School of Music, Part 2* (Video Class); Guildhall School of Music, London: Guildhall School of Music; 2006].

The two approaches to the song can best be compared by listening to its original interpreter from the Broadway show, Glynis Johns (b. 1923), at *Glynis Johns—Send in the Clowns, and, of course, Judy Collins's (b. 1939) celestial pop version (Top Chart level number 19) on her 1975 record album *Judith* at *Judy Collins—Send in the Clowns.

Opening on Broadway on June 3, 1975, with music by John Kander, lyrics by Fred Ebb, and direction and choreography by Bob Fosse, *Chicago* used all that jazz to razzle dazzle audiences about a real-life 1920s murderer who gets off through hucksterism via songs like "All That Jazz," "Razzle Dazzle," "When You're Good to Mama," "Cell Block Tango," and "We Both Reached for the Gun." The latter two can be seen, respectively, in the Rob Marshall–directed and –choreographed December 2002 film version at *Cell Block Tango and *Chicago—We Both Reached for the Gun.

Winning nine Tony Awards and the Pulitzer Prize for drama, *A Chorus Line* (July 25, 1975) had a 19-year run, almost single-handedly changing

Broadway into the most desirable place in New York. The show had music by Marvin Hamlisch (1944–2012), lyrics by Edward Kleban (1939–1987), and direction/choreography by Michael Bennett (1943–1987).

> [Although] it dealt with the hopes, fears, frustrations, and insecurities of a specific group of dancers auditioning for a chorus line, the musical skillfully conveyed the universal experience of anyone who has ever stood in line in an effort to present his or her qualifications for a job. Since that means just about all of us, *A Chorus Line* managed to create such a strong empathetic bond with its audiences that it became far and away the longest running production—musical or dramatic—ever staged [until *Phantom of the Opera* topped it] on Broadway [Green and Ginell, 2014, p. 243].

"One," the ultimately ironic grand finale as seen at *A Chorus Line— One (Finale), from the December 1985 film version, summarizes the goals of all dancers who aspire for any job they can get in a Broadway show. This particular song and dance conflates them into an ensemble that must dance as one, not separate and individual stars. Polymath Broadway actor, pianist, and Sirius XM radio show host Seth Rudetsky brilliantly analyzes another song from the show, "At the Ballet," at *Seth Rudetsky—Deconstructs "At the Ballet" from A Chorus Line.

Tim Curry played a transvestite transsexual from Transylvania in *The Rocky Horror Picture Show*, which opened in Hollywood on August 14, 1975. The film quickly became a midnight cult experience for audiences who squirted water and threw pieces of toast at the screen while singing along to it all. With music and lyrics by Richard O'Brien, its big hit, "The Time Warp," involving the simplest of dance steps, can be seen and heard at *Time Warp— Rocky Horror Picture Show.

With Southern-tinged country music by Robert Waldman (b. 1936) and lyrics by playwright Alfred Uhry (b. 1936; *Driving Miss Daisy, Parade*), *The Robber Bridegroom* (October 7, 1975) was a musical based on the 1942 Eudora Welty (1909–2001) novella of the same name—itself loosely based on tale number 40 of the Brothers Grimm collection of fairy tales, c. 1812—which is set in 18th-century Mississippi about a Robin Hood–type hero. "Deeper in the Woods," sung by the ensemble from the 2016 revival soundtrack at *Deeper in the Woods, captures the folksy, mythological energy of the legend.

Annie, based on the newspaper comic strip *Little Orphan Annie* (1924– 2010), was created by American cartoonist Harold Gray (1894–1968) and opened on Broadway on April 21, 1977. As of 2015, it had been adapted into three film versions: in April 1982, November 1999, and December 2014. Interpretations of composer Charles Strouse (b. 1928) and lyricist Martin Charnin's (b. 1934) biggest hit from the show, "Tomorrow," is fun to compare among the three tykes who played the title role in those films at *Annie 1982 Tomorrow (Aileen Quinn; b. 1971), *Annie Tomorrow 1999 Movie (Alicia Morton; b. 1987) and *Tomorrow Annie 2014 (Quvenzhané Wallis; b. 2003).

Saturday Night Fever caught the entire world up on the power of disco music and dance when it opened in Hollywood on December 14, 1977. As with *Jesus Christ Superstar* and *Godspell*, the film's soundtrack was packed with hits and had even more legs than the film (which was no slouch itself). Enjoy the transcendent ballad "How Deep Is Your Love," written and sung by the Bee Gees, at *Bee Gees—How Deep Is Your Love.

Madeline Kahn (née Madeline Gail Wolfson; 1942–1999) is best known to non-musical aficionados for her roles in both of Mel Brooks' 1974 hit movies, *Blazing Saddles* (February) and *Young Frankenstein* (December), especially in the former when she sang the hysterical Brooks-penned "I'm Tired" (at *I'm Tired Madeline Kahn). But her operatic work in the Broadway show *On the Twentieth Century* (February 19, 1978; based on the 1934 John Barrymore and Carole Lombard screwball comedy film, *Twentieth Century*), with music by Cy Coleman and lyrics by Betty Comden and Adolph Green, performing alongside co-stars John Cullum, Imogene Coca, and a young Kevin Kline, particularly in the song "Never," at *Madeline Kahn—Never, stole that show.

Bob Fosse's *Dancin',* which opened on March 27, 1978, was a pure dance revue highlighting the choreographer's many hits over the years plus new material. Honoring Fred Astaire's sand-dance nonchalance in "I Wanna Be a Dancin' Man," seen at *Fred Astaire—I Wanna Be a Dancing Man (itself an homage to Astaire by lyricist Johnny Mercer, who wrote the song in 1952 with composer Harry Warren for the film *The Belle of New York*), Fosse closed act 1 with his typically quirky, rhythm-driven minimalism with over a dozen dancers in the same straw top hat and white jacket as Astaire at *I Wanna Be a Dancin' Man—Fosse, re-created in the 1999 video/DVD *Fosse*.

Stephen Sondheim's Grand Guignol tune, "The Worst Pies in London"— made up equally of priest and pauper parts—was sung by the original Mrs. Lovett, Angela Lansbury, when *Sweeney Todd: The Demon Barber of Fleet Street* opened on Broadway on March 1, 1979, seen at the Tony Awards at *Sweeney Todd OBC—The Worst Pies in London. With his origins in a serialized 1846 penny dreadful titled *The String of Pearls*—a penny dreadful was a popular, cheap, and highly dramatized Victorian-era form of weekly magazine story—Sweeney was a psychopathic barber hell bent on revenge, perfect fodder for musical treatment. The show won eight Tony Awards including Best Musical, Best Leading Actor (Len Cariou; b. 1939), Best Leading Actress (Angela Lansbury; b. 1925), Best Direction (Harold Prince; b. 1928), and Best Scenic Design (Eugene Lee; b. 1939; *Candide*, *Wicked*, *Saturday Night Live*).

On the stage of the Uris Theater in New York, this tale of horrors was transformed into a mountain of steel in motion. Prince's scenic metaphor for *Sweeney Todd* was a 19th-century iron foundry moved from Rhode Island and reassembled on the stage, which critic Jack Kroll aptly described as "part cathedral, part factory, part prison that dwarfed and degraded the swarming denizens of the lower orders" ["Sweeney Todd: The Demon Barber of Fleet Street"; https://en.wikipedia.org/wiki/Sweeney_Todd:_The_Demon_Barber_of_Fleet_Street; retrieved November 28, 2017].

John Doyle's (b. 1953) pared down direction of the 2004 London revival employed a cast that performed the score onstage with their own instruments; it transferred to Broadway the next year and won both Doyle and orchestrator Sarah Travis Tony Awards. (Similarly spare Doyle-directed Sondheim revivals such as *Company* and *Merrily We Roll Along* followed.) On *Sondheim! The Birthday Concert*—to celebrate his 80th, filmed live at Avery Fisher Hall in New York City on March 15–16, 2010—Patti LuPone (b. 1949) and Michael Cerveris (b. 1960) and George Hearn (b. 1934), all Sondheim alums from different shows, put over the darkly comic "A Little Priest" with longtime Sondheim collaborator Paul Gemignani conducting at *A Little Priest Sondheim 80th Birthday. December 2007 saw Johnny Depp (b. 1963), Helena Bonham Carter (b. 1966), and Alan Rickman (1946–2016) star in the popular film version.

Composer Andrew Lloyd Webber and lyricist Tim Rice's *Evita* began as a concept album in 1976, just as their *Jesus Christ Superstar* had in 1970, and the libretto-free opera-musical—entirely sung through—opened on Broadway on September 25, 1979, after a hugely successful year in London. Based on the brief life of controversial proto-feminist and champion of the poor Eva Perón (1919–1952), the Spanish-language version of the justly famous hit "Don't Cry for Me Argentina," can be heard at *No Llores Por Mi Argentina, as sung by Buenos Aires–born Elena Roger (b. 1974), star of the West End (2006) and Broadway (2012) revivals. It is illuminating to compare the charm of Roger's heartbreaking soprano to Patti LuPone's (b. 1949) soaring vocal—the original Evita on Broadway—at the 1980 Tony Awards at *Don't Cry for Me Argentina—Patti LuPone.

All That Jazz, Bob Fosse's semi-autobiographical take on open-heart surgery and the making of a musical, opened in Hollywood to rave reviews on December 20, 1979. The song and dance "Take Off with Us/Airotica" pushed the double-entendre tone of Cole Porter tunes into overt sexuality at *Bob Fosse—Take Off with Us. (Warning: R rated.)

EIGHT

The 1980s

Opening on April 30, 1980, *Barnum*, a story about businessman extraordinaire Phineas Taylor (P.T.) Barnum's (1810–1891) life, his American Museum, and eventual collaboration with James Anthony Bailey (1847–1906)—which led to the establishment of the Ringling Bros. and Barnum & Bailey Circus (1871–2017)—was both a traditional Broadway musical and an Extravaganza full of jugglers, trapeze performers, and clowns. "The Museum Song," a typical patter tune in the Cole Porter list tradition (with Cy Coleman music and Michael Stewart lyrics), was frenetically delivered by the original lead actor, Jim Dale (b. 1935), at *Barnum OST—The Museum Song. It recounts with ever-increasing rapidity the huge variety of spectacles Barnum put on display to overwhelm his audiences, all for the exorbitant price of a dollar. (Interestingly, 21st-century children of all ages are more familiar with Dale's pedigree than many adults, as it is his voice narrating all seven *Harry Potter* audiobooks!) Australian-born polymath Hugh Jackman (b. 1968) portrays the great showman in the recent *The Greatest Showman*, which opened a full year after it was scheduled, on Christmas Day, 2017, in order not to compete with fellow blockbuster musical *La La Land* (December 2016). (See below for discussions of both.)

Fame (May 12, 1980), an Alan Parker film musical based on four years of the lives of high-schoolers studying at the High School of Performing Arts in New York City, starred Irene Cara, Debbie Allen, and a host of actual students (mostly in cameos) singing and dancing their hearts out. Notably, the title tune, "Hot Lunch Jam," "I Sing the Body Electric," and "Red Light" were the most infectious, but the delicate "Out Here on My Own," sung and played by Irene Cara (b. 1959) accompanying herself on piano at *Irene Cara Out Here on My Own," and *"Is It Ok If I Call You Mine?" sung and played by Paul McCrane (b. 1961) accompanying himself on guitar, quietly stole the film.

Alongside cameos by blues legends such as Aretha Franklin, Ray Charles, and James Brown, Saturday Night Live comedian alums John Belushi (1949–

1982) and Dan Aykroyd (b. 1952) starred in *The Blues Brothers* (June 20, 1980), a film comedy musical filled to the brim with hits from the past. Blues composer and musician Robert Johnson's 1936 "Sweet Home Chicago" was nicely rendered at *The Blues Brothers Sweet Home Chicago, while famed Harlem Cotton Club conductor Cab Calloway revisited his big 1932 hit "Minnie the Moocher" at *Cab Calloway Minnie the Moocher.

Gene Kelly's last film musical visibly dancing and singing (he was choreographic consultant to the 1997 animated film *Cats Don't Dance*) was in the musical fantasy *Xanadu* (August 8, 1980), playing Danny McGuire, the name of his character in 1944's *Cover Girl*. Have a look at his pretty-darn-good dancing chops at the age of 68 (with Olivia Newton-John!) in "Whenever You're Away from Me" at *Whenever You're Away from Me.

Including hit songs from numerous thirties films such as *Dames*, *Gold Diggers of 1933*, *Gold Diggers of 1935*, *Footlight Parade*, and *42nd Street*, the Broadway version of *42nd Street* sadly opened on the same night its director-choreographer Gower Champion died: August 25, 1980. Always one to capitalize on any act, even one such as Champion's death, producer David Merrick—dubbed "The Abominable Showman"—announced the tragedy at the eleventh curtain call; needless to say, the gasp heard throughout the theatre did not hurt the box office. Composer Harry Warren and lyricist Al Dubin were well represented in a show that paid homage to backstage musicals (and Champion's legacy) with songs like "Young and Healthy," the title song, "Lullaby of Broadway," and "We're in the Money," the latter, with Ginger Rogers singing her heart out in pig-Latin, shown in its original Busby Berkeley glory at *Gold Diggers of 1933—We're in the Money.

While the contemporary world saw the inimitable American stage and screen character actor Christopher Walken (b. 1943) "fly," dance and tap a little in Fatboy Slim's riotous *"Weapon of Choice" 2001 video, the older generation already knew he had it in him as early as December 11, 1981, in the nostalgic film musical *Pennies from Heaven*, also starring Steve Martin (b. 1945) and Bernadette Peters (b. 1948). Here's Walken lip-synching and tearing up his taps during a strip tease to Cole Porter's "Let's Misbehave" at *Christopher Walken—Pennies from Heaven.

Nine (May 9, 1982) was a Broadway musical based on Federico Fellini's 1963 film *8½* (by then, the director had made six full-length features and three "half" films, hence the odd number for the title), a semi-autobiographical story of a film director facing a midlife crisis in Venice. Surrounded by over a dozen fawning women, "Guido's Song," as narcissistically performed by Antonio Banderas (b. 1960) during the 2003 Tony Awards at *Nine the Musical, features both music and lyrics by Maury Yeston.

The first of a number of British Invasion musicals on Broadway begun in the early 1980s, mega-musical producer Cameron Mackintosh's (b. 1946)

Cats opened on October 7, 1982, with music by Andrew Lloyd Webber and lyrics by poet T. S. Eliot (1888–1965). Audiences lapped up the show for 7,485 performances over a nearly eighteen year period. Betty Buckley (b. 1947) as Grizabella brought the house down during the 1983 Tony Awards singing the hit "Memory" (after "Jellicle Songs for Jellicle Cats") at *Betty Buckley 1983 Tony Awards Performing "Memory."

The first big film (number 3 ranking in 1983) to feature previously written pop songs not recorded by the performers onscreen, *Flashdance* (April 15, 1983) rode the coattails of a new MTV (Music Television) generation that had been launched on cable in August 1981. African Irish American actress Jennifer Beals (b. 1963) performed the close-ups for French dancer Marine Jahan (b. 1959) in many numbers, including the finale, "Flashdance…. What a Feeling" (written by Giorgio Moroder, Keith Forsey, and Irene Cara), as seen at *Flashdance What a Feeling.

The 1973 French play *La Cage aux Folles*, by Jean Poiret (1926–1992), led to the October 1978 opening of the French film of the same name, which in turn inspired composer/lyricist Jerry Herman to pen tunes for the first openly gay Broadway musical of the same name. Opening on August 21, 1983, its big hit "I Am What I Am" (not to be confused with Popeye's signature phrase), was sung and danced by the Chorus and the original Albin, George Hearn (b. 1934), at *La Cage aux Folles I Am What I Am. The story also spawned a popular American non-musical film starring Nathan Lane and Robin Williams in March 1996, called *The Birdcage.*

February 17, 1984, was the date of the Hollywood release of *Footloose*. The musical was based on a true story about Elmore City, Oklahoma, a town that forbade dancing, from the town's inception in 1861 until, if you can believe it, 1980! The film followed hard on the heels of the previous year's *Flashdance*, employing the same pop-music strategy of tunes not sung onscreen; in this case, all but the title song hadn't even been written prior to the film's editing. The star of the movie, Kevin Bacon (b. 1958), reprised his big dance number on TV to the title tune (composer/lyricist Kenny Loggins) and "Never" (Michael Gore/Dean Pitchford) during the film's 30-year anniversary after The Tonight Show television host Jimmy Fallon (b. 1974) humorously noted that dancing had been outlawed on his show. Bacon nailed the number at the age of 55 (by renting the film and practicing to his own image, with a little help from stunt doubles and gymnasts, obviously) at *Kevin Bacon's Footloose Entrance. Compare to the original at *Footloose Dancing Warehouse Scene (1984).

"Finishing the Hat" and "Move On," two artful songs about the challenging reality of making art from composer/lyricist Stephen Sondheim's Pulitzer Prize-winning Broadway musical *Sunday in the Park with George* (May 2, 1984), are poignantly reprised by the original George and Dot, tenor

Mandy Patinkin (né Mandel Bruce Patinkin; b. 1952) and soprano Bernadette Peters (née Bernadette Lazzara; b. 1948), during *Sondheim's 80th Birthday Concert* (PBS; November 2010) at *Finishing the Hat—Mandy Patinkin.

With music and lyrics by country/bluegrass composer Roger Miller (1936–1992), of 1964 hit song "King of the Road" fame (at *Roger Miller, King of the Road), *Big River*, based on Mark Twain's 1884 novel *The Adventures of Huckleberry Finn*, opened on Broadway on April 25, 1985. The tune "Worlds Apart," at *Worlds Apart (1985 Original Broadway Cast), simply and tenderly explains the meaninglessness of the racial differences between Jim and Huck as sung by operatic baritone Ron Richardson (1952–1995), whose great-grandparents were both slaves, and Daniel H. Jenkins (b. 1963), respectively.

With music by Andrew Lloyd Webber (b. 1948) and lyrics by Don Black (b. 1938), "Unexpected Song" became something of a hit for the multilingual English crossover soprano Sarah Brightman (b. 1960) … but here is the original performer in *Song and Dance* (September 18, 1985), Bernadette Peters, blasting it out in one of her many one-woman shows, this one in London's Royal Festival Hall on September 17, 1998, at *Unexpected Song by Bernadette Peters. The star briefly explains the story of the show, which was made up of all songs in Act I and all dancing (with choreography by currently-resigned New York City Ballet Dance Master Peter Martins, in the American version) in Act II.

The mystery of *The Mystery of Edwin Drood*, Charles Dickens' (1812–1870) final, unfinished novel at the time of his death, was that no one knew who killed who by the end. Several fun literary and radio and cinema and television efforts to finish the story ensued, including one by a Vermont printer claiming he was channeling Dickens' ghost, but it was British-American singer-songwriter-dramatist Rupert Holmes (né David Goldstein; b. 1947), of 1979's "Escape (The Piña Colada Song)" fame, who created the Music Hall and Panto-inflected musical comedy finally called, simply, *Drood* (December 2, 1985). Holmes cleverly wrote multiple denouements for each night's audience to vote on, keeping the living and breathing relationship between audience and performers particularly fresh. At breakneck speed, the patter song "Both Sides of the Coin" (sung by Will Chase and Jim Norton, from the 2012 Broadway revival, at *Both Sides of the Coin Mystery of Edwin Drood) encapsulates the madcap energy of this multi-Tony Award winning show.

Prepare to be knocked out, even by a poorly-recorded YouTube version of the act 1 finale, "Beat Me Daddy, Eight to the Bar," of Bob Fosse's final Broadway show, *Big Deal* (April 10, 1986). Danced by Wayne Cilento (b. 1949; *Wicked, Sweet Charity* revival) and Bruce Anthony Davis (b. 1959; *All That Jazz*), plus ensemble, at *Bob Fosse Big Deal, Fosse polyrhythms proliferate via multiple and simultaneous body isolations, gestures, and patterns in every

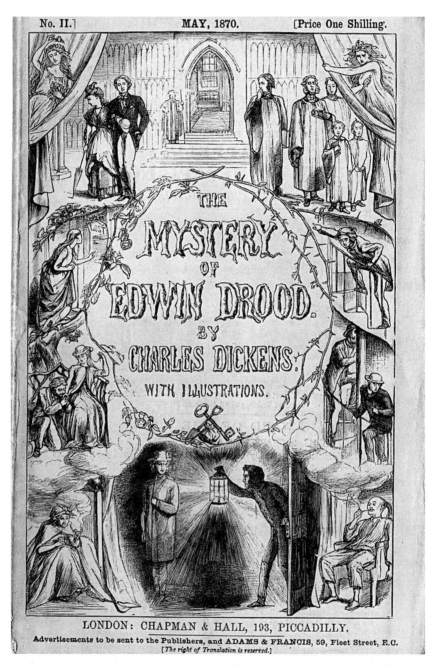

Charles Dickens's (1812–1870) final, unfinished novel, *The Mystery of Edwin Drood* (1870), was finished by songwriter and librettist Rupert Homes (b. 1947) as a mystery musical with several possible endings voted on by the audience.

body—four minutes of stunningly pure artistry on display. Based on Italian director Mario Monicelli's 1958 comic caper film, *Big Deal on Madonna Street*, the show also incorporated nearly thirty songs from the Great American Songbook.

Howard Ashman (1950–1991) wrote the book and lyrics and Marvin Hamlisch (1944–2012) the music for the Broadway version of the 1975 film *Smile* (November 24, 1986), a behind-the-scenes, lightly satirical look into an imaginary teen beauty pageant. Released posthumously in a 2008 double album, *Howard Sings Ashman*, the lyricist himself sings the simultaneously yearning and ironic "Disneyland" at *Disneyland (Composer Demo).

Les Misérables' (West End in October 1985; Broadway on March 12, 1987) heartbreaking lament, "I Dreamed a Dream," as sung by the out-of-nowhere Scottish singer Susan Boyle (b. 1961) on the third season of *Britain's Got Talent* (formed 2007), received over 100 million YouTube hits within five days of her audition (see *Susan Boyle First Audition—Britain's Got Talent). Based on the epic 1862 Victor Hugo (1802–1885) historical novel (2,783 pages!) of the same name about mercy, duty, grace and redemption, the story of *Les Misérables* is set during the tumultuous years of 1815 to 1832 in France, with music by Claude-Michel Schönberg (b. 1944) and lyrics by Alain Boublil (b. 1941; English translation by Herbert Kretzmer; b. 1925). "One Day More," a choral anthem comprised of 17 parts that stops the show at the end of Act I, is sung by The Dream Cast in Concert at the Royal Albert Hall on the 10th Anniversary of the British version at *One Day More, and epitomizes the grand scope and scale of the show. Broadway fans may faint (from happiness) watching stars Lin-Manuel Miranda, Audra McDonald, Jesse Tyler Ferguson, Jane Krakowski and James Corden blasting out the tune in the back of a mini-van during Corden's June 6, 2016, *Late, Late Show* Carpool Karaoke episode at *Tony Awards—Broadway Carpool Karaoke—One Day More.

On August 21, 1987, the hit film *Dirty Dancing* opened starring heart-throb Patrick Swayze (1952–2009) and Jennifer Grey (b. 1960; Joel Grey's daughter), who steamed up the screen dancing mildly, by 2018 standards, to the number one song "(I've Had) The Time of My Life" (songwriters John DeNicola, Donald Markowitz, Franke Previte) at *Dirty Dancing—Time of My Life.

Into the Woods, composer/lyricist Stephen Sondheim's dark look at fairy tales, opened on Broadway on November 5, 1987 (and Hollywood in December 2014), reaping a number of powerful Tony Award-winning tunes including the cautionary "Children Will Listen," sung here by original cast member Bernadette Peters in her September 1998 London concert at the Royal Festival Hall at *Children Will Listen by Bernadette Peters.

Still running on Broadway as of July 2018 (in its 30th year!), composer Andrew Lloyd Webber and lyricists Charles Hart and Richard Stilgoe's *The*

Phantom of the Opera opened on January 9, 1988. The original story, written in 1911 by French novelist Gaston Leroux (1868–1927), spawned six films— 1925, 1943, 1962, 1982, 1989, and 2004—and shows no signs of slowing down. The story is about a romantic triangle and demonstrates that love redeems all, but I find the show simplistic, maudlin, sappy, over-blown, bombastic, full of totally one-dimensional characters, and endlessly derivative; other than these minor concerns, I can see why people like it so much. But, as Kantor and Maslon say, megahits like producer Cameron Mackintosh's tap into a

> pop-rock synthesis of high-voltage ballads with ever-ascending key changes that required, first and foremost, singers who could belt the hell out of them. By June 2009, *Cats*, *Phantom*, *Les Misérables*, and *Miss Saigon* ... had run a combined total of [sixty-five] years on Broadway [2010, p. 393].

Regardless of my reservations, the truly lovely "All I Ask of You," sung by Americans Patrick Wilson (b. 1973) and Emmy Rossum (b. 1986), can be seen and heard from the December 2004 film at *The Phantom of the Opera—All I Ask of You.

"One Night in Bangkok" (sung by Murray Head, number 3 on the pop charts) and "I Know Him So Well" (sung by Elaine Paige and Barbra Dickson, number 1), with music by ABBA's Benny Andersson (b. 1946) and Bjorn Ulvaeus (b. 1945) and lyrics by Tim Rice (b. 1944), were the two big hits from *Chess* (April 28, 1988, on Broadway; 1984 concept album first), but tunes such as "Quartet (A Model of Decorum and Tranquility)" and "Endgame" were the more sophisticated (while still remaining hummable). The former can be seen performed by Josh Groban (b. 1981), Idina Menzel (b. 1971), David Bedella (b. 1962), and Marti Pellow (b. 1965) in a May 2008 performance at The Royal Albert Hall in London called *Chess in Concert* (June 2009 on PBS), at *Chess Quartet.

November 6, 1989, saw the opening of one of those rare Off broadway shows with legs—*Closer Than Ever*—a contemporary Revue with lyrics by theatre director, producer, and lyricist Richard Maltby, Jr. (b. 1937; *Ain't Misbehavin*,' *Fosse*, *Ring of Fire*) and music by film, television, and stage composer David Shire (b. 1937; *All the President's Men*, *Big*). A book musical with no book—as with opera, everything in the show is sung through—all of the self-contained "story" songs deal with everything from security to aging, mid-life crises to second marriages, working couples to unrequited love. The tune-filled show has a number of highlights, including the *"She Loves Me Not" duet between versatile baritone Richard Muenz (b. 1948) and soprano Lynne Wintersteller, the *"One of the Good Guys" solo for Brent Barrett (b. 1957), and the ensemble number *"There's Nothing Like It."

Performed during the 1990 Tony Awards, *"We'll Take a Glass Together"—with music and lyrics by Robert Wright (1914–2005) and George

Forrest (1915–1999)—is a rousing duet between bookkeeper Otto Kringelein (Michael Jeter; 1952–2003) and Baron Felix Von Gaigern (tenor Brent Barrett). Epitomizing the gaiety and grand opulence of *Grand Hotel* (November 12, 1989), the show was directed and choreographed by polymath Tommy Tune (b. 1939) and was based on the 1929 novel by Austrian Vicki Baum (1888–1960) and the 1932 MGM film of the same name. In 1992, the producers replaced then 60-year-old actress-dancer Liliane Montevecchi (b. 1932), in the role of about-to-retire (for the seventh time) Elizaveta Grushinskaya, with then 70-year-old Cyd Charisse, helping to ensure its run of over 1000 performances.

American film and theatre actor and singer Samuel E. Wright (b. 1946) remains best known for his vocals as Sebastian, the Jamaican red crab, on the Academy Award-winning tune "Under the Sea" in Disney's 28th animated film, *The Little Mermaid* (November 17, 1989), seen at *The Little Mermaid—Under the Sea. With music by Alan Menken and lyrics by Howard Ashman, it is a happy-ending version of Hans Christian Andersen's (1805–1875) 1837 fairy tale and, 25 years after its previous musical hit, *Mary Poppins*, the show put Disney Studios back on track both on and off screen.

NINE

The 1990s

Who's in love with whom, in what ways, and for how long? The Broadway musical *Aspects of Love* (April 8, 1990), with songs by composer Andrew Lloyd Webber (b. 1948) and lyricist Don Black (b. 1938), explores a variety of romantic and platonic trysts that seem to change at the drop of a hat. Hints of those relationships are on display in the cast performance of the hit tune "Love Changes Everything" at *Aspects of Love Tony Awards.

Based on Trinidad-born Rosa Guy's (1922–2012) 1985 novel, *My Love, My Love: Or, the Peasant Girl*—with elements of Shakespeare's *Romeo and Juliet* (1597) and Hans Christian Andersen's *The Little Mermaid* (1837) thrown in for good measure—the musical *Once on This Island* (October 18, 1990) is a story about sacrifice and the redeeming power of love embodied in the heart of a peasant girl called Ti Moune. As we all know, children and adolescents almost always leap before they look, especially in matters of the heart. (Never adults, no.) The poignant ballad "Ti Moune," at *Once on This Island Ti Moune, with lyrics by Lynn Ahrens (b. 1948) and music by Stephen Flaherty (b. 1960), is sung by adoptive parents Mama and Tonton—Sheila Gibbs (*The Lion King*) and Ellis Williams (b. 1951), respectively—as they reluctantly find their way forward to let her go. When LaChanze (née Rhonda LaChanze Sapp; b. 1961; *The Color Purple*) as Ti Moune in the original production joins in, she brings a yearning counterpoint to her parents' struggle via a gentle three-part harmony.

Composer Claude-Michel Schönberg (b. 1944) and lyricists Alain Boublil (b. 1941) and Richard Maltby's (b. 1937) *Miss Saigon* reached Broadway on April 11, 1991. Based on Giacomo Puccini's (1858–1924) opera *Madame Butterfly* (1904) but relocated to 1970s Vietnam, it starred Filipina Lea Salonga (née Maria Lea Carmen Imutan Salonga; b. 1971) as Vietnamese orphan Kim and controversially cast Welsh-born Jonathan Pryce (b. 1947) as the half-French, half-Vietnamese pimp Tran, the Engineer. In a 2000 touring production to her hometown of Manila, Ms. Salonga reprised her role alongside Will Chase (b. 1970) as Chris to sing their love duet "Sun and Moon" at *Sun and Moon—Miss Saigon, Manila. In the March 2017 Broadway revival, Fil-ipino Jon Jon Briones (b. 1965) plays the Engineer and sings "The American Dream" (at *The American Dream Live), ostensibly about what his life will be like after emigrating to the United States but also a dark commentary on American colonialism around the globe.

In the Broadway musical *The Secret Garden* (April 25, 1991), the ghosts haunting Misselthwaite manor entreat 10-year-old Mary to find the garden and help it grow—which in turn brings everyone closer to the beginnings of health, both physical and emotional. With mystical, folk-song tinged music by Lucy Simon (b. 1943; Carly Simon's older sister) and words by playwright Marsha Norman (b. 1947; *'Night, Mother*), tunes like "How Could I Ever Know," at *The Secret Garden How Could I Ever Know, convince Mary's uncle Archibald that there is hope after all. As sung by Mandy Patinkin (b. 1952; *The Princess Bride, Homeland, Sunday in the Park with George*) and soprano Rebecca Luker (b. 1961; *Passion*), it's a penetrating duet between Archibald and his dead wife Lily's ghost.

The collaboration among lyricists Betty Comden (1917–2006) and Adolph Green (1914–2002), composer Cy Coleman (1929–2004; *City of Angels*), and librettist Peter Stone (1930–2003; *Charade, 1776, Titanic*) brought *The Will Rogers Follies* to Broadway on May 1, 1991. A Revue about famed humorist, cowboy, vaudeville performer and social commentator Will Rogers (né William Penn Adair Rogers; 1879–1935), the show mimicked the Ziegfeld Follies themselves, where Rogers often performed. "Our Favorite Son," at *Our Favorite Son Happy indepenDANCE Day, showcased the precision of director Tommy Tune's (b. 1939) choreography as performed by Keith Car-radine (b. 1949; *Nashville, Deadwood*), playing Rogers alongside 16 Follies girls.

With songs by composer Alan Menken (b. 1949) and lyricist Howard Ashman (1950–1991), Disney's film *Beauty and the Beast* (November 22, 1991)—the original 1740 fairy tale was written by French novelist Gabrielle-Suzanne Barbot de Villeneuve (1685–1755)—built mightily on their 1989 *Little Mermaid* hit. This time, the Busby Berkeley–esque Extravaganza number "Be Our Guest," sung primarily by the character of Lumière—and Angela Lans-bury (b. 1925), as Mrs. Potts—was crooned by actor, dancer, and singer Jerry Orbach (1935–2004; *42nd Street, Dirty Dancing, Law and Order*) in the style of the French singer/actor Maurice Chevalier (1888–1972). Enjoy the com-parison between the animated and Broadway (April 1994) versions, both at *Beauty and the Beast—Be Our Guest.

Crazy for You (February 19, 1992), a Revue boasting 18 George and Ira Gershwin tunes, was drawn primarily from the original 1930 *Girl Crazy* musi-cal but with added songs from other shows. Highlighting typical Gershwin hits such as "Someone to Watch over Me," "I Got Rhythm," and "Nice Work

If You Can Get It" (which was a centerpiece of yet another Gershwin catalogue show of the same name, in 2012), an atypical Gershwin number, the slow-poke cowpoke tune "Bidin' My Time," demonstrated the brothers' versatility with genres. Have a listen to and compare three versions: one from the original 1930 show performed by a vocal quartet called the Foursome (*1931 Hits Archive Bidin' My Time the Foursome), Judy Garland's version from the 1943 movie *Girl Crazy* (with her cowboy cast and Mickey Rooney), at *Judy Garland Stereo Bidin' My Time 1943—look for some nifty clog dancing in cowboy boots near the end—and the short and sweet version from the 1992 show at *Crazy for You Bidin' My Time. Interestingly, suave cosmopolitan Cole Porter (1890–1964) tackled the country style in 1934's aborted film *Adios, Argentina*, with his easygoing giddy-up song "Don't Fence Me In," charmingly put over in a 1944 recording by Bing Crosby and the Andrew Sisters at *Bing Crosby & Andrew Sisters Don't Fence Me In.

Among other pop and rhythm and blues hits that he wrote and played with his mid-century Tympani Five Band, "Is You Is or Is You Ain't My Baby?" (1944) nicely represented "King of the Jukebox" composer Louis Jourdan (1908–1975; with lyricist Billy Austin, 1896–1964). The tune is specially featured in the Revue *Five Guys Named Moe*, which opened on Broadway on April 8, 1992. Hear the original tune at *Louis Jourdan Is You Is or Is You Ain't (My Baby), and watch the man himself, in all his pre-rock-and-roll glory, wailing away on his trademark sax and singing and dancing on another of his hits, "Caldonia" (1945), at *Louis Jourdan—Caldonia—1946.

Based on the actual Newsboys Strike of 1899, the film musical *Newsies* (music by Alan Menken, lyrics by Jack Feldman), opened on April 10, 1992. Initially a flop that became a cult favorite, it opened on Broadway twenty years later in March 2012. Catchy tunes led by the "King of New York" number highlight the upbeat musical. Choreographed by Kenny Ortega (b. 1950), the vocal-heavy-with-occasional-tap screen version at *Newsies: King of New York is worth comparing with the Christopher Gattelli–choreographed tap-heavy-with-vocals-secondary Broadway version at *King of New York—Newsies (Thanksgiving Day Parade 2012).

Jelly Roll Morton (né Ferdinand Joseph LaMothe; 1890–1941), self-proclaimed inventor of jazz, was paid the highest tribute by tap dancer/singer Gregory Hines in the starring role of *Jelly's Last Jam* when it opened on Broadway in April 26, 1992. "That's How You Jazz" (not to be confused with "Now You Has Jazz," written by Cole Porter for the Louis Armstrong and Bing Crosby duet in the 1956 film *High Society*) was featured in the show and can be seen with Hines and chorus at *Broadway's Jelly's Last Jam. As a related aside, actor Hugh Laurie (né James Hugh Calum Laurie; b. 1959), who most famously starred in the television series *House* for eight seasons (2004–2012) and also played Bertie Wooster on British television's charming *Jeeves and*

Wooster (1990–1993), remains a heck of a pianist/blues and jazz singer as of this writing, and does a truly bang-up job on another of Morton's tunes, "I Thought I Heard Buddy Bolden Say," on Laurie's own CD *Let Them Talk* (April 2011) at *Hugh Laurie—Buddy Bolden's Blues.

With book and direction by James Lapine (b. 1949) and music and lyrics by William Finn (b. 1952; *The 25th Annual Putnam County Spelling Bee*), *Falsettos* opened on Broadway on April 29, 1992. Super-fan Tommy (at MusicalTheatreMash on YouTube and @MusicalMash on Twitter) calls the show a "solid, important, human story [that is an] exploration of your chosen family ... with intimately three-dimensional characters." His comments are an honest and accurate way of saying it's about two gay couples set in the early and late 1980s, one male (sharing a son from an earlier heterosexual relationship) and one female, and all Jewish. During the 2016 revival, soprano belter Stephanie J. Block (b. 1972) as Trina sings a kind of ragtime tune about breaking down in spite of her efforts at keeping it together at *I'm Breaking Down.

The musical comedy film *Sister Act* (May 29, 1992), starring Whoopi Goldberg (née Caryn Elaine Johnson; b. 1955), is about a Reno lounge singer on the run from mobsters who hides out as a nun at a San Franciscan convent. "I Will Follow Him (Chariot)" (1961), a woman's love song to her man, became a number one Billboard 100 hit in 1963 for Little Peggy March (née Margaret Annemarie Battavio; b. 1948) at *Little Peggy March I Will Follow Him, but was cleverly adapted into a reverential hymn to God in the film, sung by all the actors in four-part harmony before modulating into an upbeat Doo Wop number, at *Sister Act I Will Follow Him. The movie was turned into an April 20, 2011, Broadway musical and re-set in late seventies Philadelphia, with original tunes by composer Alan Menken (b. 1949; *The Hunchback of Notre Dame, Enchanted*) and lyricist Glenn Slater (b. 1968; *Tangled, School of Rock*) added.

The Goodbye Girl (March 4, 1993) Broadway musical is based on the 1977 romantic comedy film of the same name written by Neil Simon (b. 1927) and starring Richard Dreyfuss (b. 1947) and Marsha Mason (b. 1942). "Good News, Bad News," at *Good News, Bad News, recounts the positives and negatives of three people unwillingly sharing an apartment—an out-of-work actor and a single mother with a ten-year-old daughter. Martin Short (b. 1950) and Bernadette Peters (b. 1948) play the odd couple and sing the tune to no one in particular—or maybe it's to each other, in the hopes of ...

Based on the highly cinematic 1976 novel, banned in Buenos Aires, by Argentine Manuel Puig (1932–1990)—it was also made into a popular 1985 film starring William Hurt (b. 1950), Raúl Juliá (1940–1994), and Sonia Braga (b. 1950)—*Kiss of the Spider Woman* opened on Broadway on May 3, 1993 (West End, October 1992) with typical, cynically tinged black comedy music and lyrics by John Kander and Fred Ebb respectively. Winning seven Tony Awards, including Best Musical, Original Score, and Featured Actress (Chita Rivera; b. 1933), the "Prologue," at *Kiss of the Spider Woman Prologue, sets the dreamlike, even nightmarish, tone for the already tortured prisoners, Marxist revolutionary Valentin and sex offender/homosexual window dresser Molina, as they slowly bond in jail.

Achieving semi-cult status for adults and kids alike owing to its mix of fun, fear, romance, German Expressionism, and stop-motion animation, Tim Burton's dark fantasy film musical *The Nightmare before Christmas* opened just before Halloween on October 29, 1993. With a score and lyrics written by Danny Elfman (b. 1953; *Beetlejuice, Hulk*), "Jack's Lament"—at *Jack's Lament, Nightmare Before Christmas—recounts the sad tale of Jack Skellington, the Pumpkin King (as sung by Elfman himself), as he bemoans his fate: the insufficiency of fulfillment in scaring people. Shortly, when Jack falls into Christmas Town and sings "What's This?" the black and white film transforms into a startling scene filled with bright colors (at *Nightmare Before Christmas, What's This?), just as when Dorothy opened her door after the cyclone dropped her house into the land of Oz in 1939's *The Wizard of Oz* (see *Dorothy Entering Technicolor).

Arguably his most intimate, richly evocative score, Stephen Sondheim's (b. 1930) *Passion*, with a book by James Lapine, opened on Broadway on May 9, 1994. Adapted from Ettore Scola's (1931–2016) film *Passione d'Amore* (1981), the story follows the obsessive love of Fosca, an ailing and homely woman, for Giorgio, a virile army captain. "Loving You," by Donna Murphy (b. 1959) as Fosca at *Loving You Sondheim Passion, encapsulates this woman's reason for living. On February 13, 2013, New York City radio station WQXR hosted "'Passion' in the Afternoon," a roundtable discussion and songfest of Sondheim's work coincident to director John Doyle's (b. 1953) minimalist revival of the show at the Classic Stage Company (formed 1967; 136 E. 13th Street). In order to perhaps better understand such driven feeling, add Judy Kuhn's (b. 1958) version of the same song from that show to your listening at *Stephen Sondheim's Passion Loving You (Live).

The next month *The Lion King* (June 15, 1994; November 13, 1997, on Broadway), Disney's animated paean to self-discovery and responsibility, opened on the big screen. Compare the film version of composer Elton John and lyricist Tim Rice's uber-optimistic, Zulu-inflected "Circle of Life" at *The Lion King—Circle of Life, with the Broadway version as presented in 2014 at the Capitol Theatre in Sydney, Australia, during the Helpmann Awards (est. 2001; named after choreographer-dancer-theatre director Robert Helpmann, 1909–1986), at *The Lion King—Circle of Life—Helpmann Awards.

Opening on Broadway four days after *Lion King* on November 17, 1994, composer Andrew Lloyd Webber and lyricists Don Black and Christopher

Hampton's tragic story *Sunset Boulevard*, based on the August 1950 Billy Wilder film, boasts the climactic "As If We Never Said Goodbye." As fictional silent screen star Norma Desmond, Glenn Close (b. 1947) intensely puts the surging tune over during Webber's 50th birthday celebration at London's Royal Albert Hall in 1998, at *As If We Never Said Goodbye Royal Albert Hall.

Smoky Joe's Café (March 2, 1995) was a jukebox, Revue-type musical showcasing nearly forty songs in the rock and roll, rhythm and blues catalogue of hit-makers Jerry Leiber (1933–2011) and Mike Stoller (b. 1933). Classics such as the 1952 "Hound Dog," at *Big Mama Thornton Hound Dog, made Big Mama Thornton (née Willie Mae Thornton; 1926–1984) a star; the 1956 "Ruby Baby" a hit for the Drifters (formed 1953) the same year, at *The Drifters Ruby Baby; 1957's "Jailhouse Rock" for Elvis Presley (1935–1977); and 1959's "Love Potion No. 9" a hit for the Clovers (formed 1946) at *Love Potion No. 9 Clovers. The 1963 Drifters tune, "On Broadway," became a huge hit for George Benson (b. 1943) in 1978, memorialized during the opening audition scene of Bob Fosse's semi-autobiographical 1979 film *All That Jazz*, at *On Broadway All That Jazz.

With Alan Menken music and Stephen Schwartz lyrics, Disney's 33rd animated film, *Pocahontas* (June 23, 1995), tells the highly romanticized story—partly historical, mostly dramatic—of the famed Native American (née Matoaka; c. 1596–1617), a member of the Powhatan tribe in the area now known as Virginia, who experiences several adventures with English settlers, especially John Smith (1580–1631). A plea for ecological responsibility and respect for Indigenous Peoples' land rights, the synesthetic "Colors of the Wind," tremulously sung by Judy Kuhn at *Pocahontas Colors of the Wind, was inspired by an alleged letter to the U.S. Congress written (or spoken) by Chief Seattle (c. 1786–1866). It became the heart and soul of the film.

Broadway's *Swinging on a Star* (October 22, 1995) was another jukebox musical, this time featuring the lyrics (and occasionally, music) of Johnny Burke (1908–1964), one of the "greats" from the American Songbook pantheon. Burke became well-known for his lyrics in 25 Bing Crosby films; in 1940, he started work with composer Jimmy Van Heusen (né Edward Chester Babcock; 1913–1990), his most frequent collaborator. Written for Crosby's 1944 film, *Going My Way*, Bing croons "Swinging" at *Bing Crosby Swinging on a Star, which is worth comparing to the even more swinging 1962 version by Frank Sinatra (1915–1998) at *Frank Sinatra Swinging on a Star.

Burke's lyrics for "Pennies from Heaven," written for the 1936 film of the same name with music by Arthur Johnston (1898–1954), helped make vocalist Arthur Tracy (né Abba Avrom Tracovutsky; 1899–1997) a household name in the 1930s. His version even brought him out of retirement when, out of hundreds of covers, his was chosen for the 1981 Steve Martin (b. 1945) film

Pennies from Heaven, lip-synched and danced to by avant-garde playwright, dancer, actor, and director Vernal Martin Bagneris (b. 1949; *One Mo' Time, Bubbling Brown Sugar*) at *Pennies from Heaven (1981).

After a 35-year absence, Julie Andrews (née Julia Elizabeth Wells; b. 1935) returned to Broadway—her last role had been in Lerner and Lowe's 1960 *Camelot*—by reprising her 1982 *Victor/Victoria* film role with the stage version on October 25, 1995. Composer Henry Mancini and lyricist Leslie Bricusse's (b. 1931) "Le Jazz Hot" featured the nearly 60-year-old's fabulous chops and gams on display as choreographed by a young Rob Marshall at *Julie Andrews Le Jazz Hot (1982).

On April 25, 1996, tap star Savion Glover's (b. 1973) black history dance musical *Bring in 'da Noise, Bring in 'da Funk* left its 1995 Off broadway home for the Great White Way. Trying to hail a cab in New York was never so frustratingly syncopated as in the number "Taxi," re-created for the Tony Awards that June at *Bring in 'da Noise, Bring in 'da Funk 1996 Tony Awards.

Based on the Tom Hanks (b. 1956) movie of the same name from 1988, with music by David Shire (b. 1937), lyrics by Richard Maltby, Jr. (b. 1937), and choreography by Susan Stroman (b. 1954; *Contact, The Producers*), all were featured in Broadway's *Big: The Musical* (April 28, 1996). Due to a wish come true from a fortune-telling machine called Zoltar Speaks, "This Isn't Me" (at *Big This Isn't Me), as sung by Daniel H. Jenkins (b. 1963; *Big River, Billy Elliot*) and cast, finds Josh marveling over his transformation from a 12-year-old boy into a 30-year-old man. The musical recapitulates the childlike "Playing the Piano" scene from the film, and it's the original at *Big (1988) Playing the Piano Scene, starring Hanks and Robert Loggia (1930–2015), that remains as charming today as then.

The following day and, sadly, posthumously, on April 29, 1996, playwright, composer, and lyricist Jonathan Larson's (1960–1996) *Rent*, the Pulitzer Prize–winning centennial update of Giacomo Puccini's (1858–1924) opera *La Bohème*, opened eight blocks south. If you've never done the math, "five hundred twenty-five thousand six hundred minutes" compose one full year and are the evocative lyrics that start the show in "Seasons of Love," which opens the November 2005 Christopher Columbus–helmed film at *Seasons of Love.

Composer Alan Menken and lyricist Stephen Schwartz's *"God Help the Outcasts" was written for the kind Esmeralda (sung by Heidi Mollenhauer) and led the heartfelt tunes of Disney's 34th animated musical, *The Hunchback of Notre Dame* (June 21, 1996). The film was based on French novelist Victor Hugo's (1802–1885) epic 1831 novel of the same name and, while the stage musical version did well in Berlin (1999), Florida (2013) and New Jersey (2014), it has yet to make it to Broadway.

December 8, 1996, saw Woody Allen's (né Allan Stewart Konigsberg; b.

1935) loving paean to musical comedy, *Everyone Says I Love You*, open onscreen. All of the actors—except Goldie Hawn (b. 1945) and Drew Barrymore (b. 1975)—sang their own songs, culminating in Goldie literally flying in and out of Woody's arms in their touching and magical on-location duet along the Seine River set to 1931's "I'm Through with Love," written by Joseph Anthony Livingston (1906–1957), Matty Malneck (1903–1981), and Gus Kahn (1886–1941), at *Everyone Says I Love You I'm Through with Love.

The multiple Tony Award–winning musical *Titanic* (April 23, 1997) had tunes by Maury Yeston (b. 1945; *Nine, Grand Hotel*) and a book by Peter Stone (1930–2003); coincidentally (or not?), James Cameron's multiple Academy Award–winning film of the same name, starring Leonardo DiCaprio (b. 1974) and Kate Winslett (b. 1975), came out in December the same year. Near the beginning of the show, "There She Is," at *Titanic 1997 Tony Awards, gives us just a hint of the vast symphonic sound—titanic, one might say—that the composer was after in this paean to what he calls "humanity's romanticization of progress through technology" ("Titanic (Musical)"; https://en.wikipedia. org/wiki/Titanic_(musical); retrieved December 17, 2017).

Steel Pier (April 24, 1997), with music by John Kander and lyrics by Fred Ebb, was a musical about a wide variety of people struggling to win one particular (fictional) marathon dance, held at the famous Steel Pier Amusement Park (formed 1898) in Atlantic City, New Jersey, during the Depression. Unbeknownst to all the others, one of the many characters in the show has only three weeks to live. Karen Ziémba (b. 1957; *A Chorus Line, Contact*) as Rita evokes the thirties with her signature ballad "Lovebird"—recorded to sound like an old scratchy record—at *Lovebird Steel Pier.

Prior to Disney Disney-fying the Times Square streets in the late 1980s, XXX-rated movie theatres and hustlers of all kinds proliferated the area. *The Life* (April 26, 1997), with music by Cy Coleman (1929–2004; *Little Me, Sweet Charity, City of Angels*) and lyrics by Ira Gasman (*Radiant Baby*), recounts in fairly accurate detail the (s)exploits of many of those denizens, particularly in the upbeat and strutting "Use What You Got" at *The Life Use What You Got.

Moving through a number of demo/concept albums and complete work recordings, the horror-drama musical *Jekyll & Hyde* finally reached Broadway on April 28, 1997. Based on Scottish author Robert Louis Stevenson's (1850–1894) gothic novella *The Strange Case of Dr Jekyll and Mr Hyde* (1886), the story has, apparently, spawned over 120 stage adaptations and films—most notably, the classic 1931 black and white movie starring Fredric March (1897–1975; *The Best Years of Our Lives, Inherit the Wind*). This Broadway show boasts music by Frank Wildhorn (b. 1959; *Camille Claudel, Finding Neverland*) and lyrics by Wildhorn, Leslie Bricusse (b. 1931), and Steve Cuden (b. 1955). Early in the show, on the 1994 recording titled *The Complete Work: Jekyll and*

STRANGE CASE

OF

DR JEKYLL AND MR HYDE

BY

ROBERT LOUIS STEVENSON

LONDON

LONGMANS, GREEN, AND CO.

1886

Scottish author Robert Louis Stevenson's (1850–1894) novella *The Strange Case of Dr Jekyll and Mr Hyde* (1886) was adapted into over 100 stage and film versions, one of which became a 1997 Broadway musical with songs by Frank Wildhorn (b. 1959).

Hyde, The Gothic Musical Thriller, the London townspeople explain how everyone's own good and evil is hypocritically lacquered over by a façade in "Façade" at *Jekyll and Hyde Façade.

Loosely based on the Greek mythological story of Heracles (son of Zeus and Alcmene), *Hercules* (June 27, 1997), Disney's 35th animated feature, starred the voices of Tate Donovan (Hercules), Danny DeVito (Philoctetes, or "Phil") and James Woods (Hades). "Go the Distance" at *Hercules Go the Distance, as sung by Roger Bart (b. 1962; *You're a Good Man, Charlie Brown*), and *Michael Bolton Go the Distance (Music Video), provide two unique takes on the hit song.

Side Show (October 16, 1997), with Henry Krieger (b. 1945; *Dreamgirls*) music and Bill Russell (b. 1949; *Elegies for Angels, Punks and Raging Queens*) lyrics, was loosely based on the lives of conjoined twins Daisy and Violet Hilton (1908–1969) as they tried to create some semblance of normality—marriage for one, fame for the other—while struggling to find work, first in a side show, then Vaudeville, then the Burlesque circuit. Played respectively by Emily Skinner (*Prince of Broadway, Billy Elliot*) and Alice Ripley (b. 1963; *Next to Normal, American Psycho*), their impossibly unfair early 20th-century quandary is all too clearly evident in the heartbreaking duet anthem "Who Will Love Me as I Am?" at *Who Will Love Me as I Am Side Show.

Based on the 1905 novel of the same name by Hungarian-born novelist Baroness Emma Orczy (1865–1947), one of the first stories to boast a spy hero with a secret identity, *The Scarlet Pimpernel* (November 19, 1997) featured music by Frank Wildhorn (b. 1959; *The Civil War, The Count of Monte Cristo*) and lyrics/book by Nan Knighton (*Camille Claudel*). (A pimpernel is a plant in the primrose family whose flowers—either white, purplish, or scarlet—close in cloudy weather, hence the secretive nature of the lead character.) As Marguerite, the Pimpernel's true love, the crystalline sensuality of soprano Christine Andreas (b. 1951; *On Your Toes, Rags*) ripples through "When I Look at You" at *Scarlet Pimpernel When I Look at You.

Based on the 1975 book by novelist and professor E. L. Doctorow (1931–2015), *Ragtime* (January 18, 1998), as represented by the interactions among three different families of distinct class and color and ethnicity, placed front and center the challenge of immigrants at the turn of the 20th century in their efforts to adapt to turbulent societal change. Viewed through the lens of our similar 21st-century struggles, their difficulties appear, unfortunately, timeless. The rich mix of the contemporary and traditional in Stephen Flaherty's (b. 1960) music and Lynn Ahrens's (b. 1948) lyrics—they often work together, as on *Once on This Island, Seussical*, and *Rocky the Musical*—is particularly piercing as the character of Mother (Marin Mazzie [1960–2018], from the original production) sings *"Back to Before," a power ballad about the impossibility of returning to the past.

Broadway's *The Capeman* (January 29, 1998) is the story of Puerto Rico–born, convicted Vampires gang murderer Salvador Agron (1943–1986), and his life before and after jail. With music in the Doo Wop, gospel, and Latin music styles by singer-songwriter-guitarist Paul Simon (b. 1941) and lyrics by Simon and Saint Lucian poet and playwright Derek Walcott (1930–2017), "Time Is an Ocean," a swaying samba song of redemption, features Marc Anthony (né Marco Antonio Muñiz; b. 1968) as young Salvador, Rubén Blades (né Rubén Blades Bellida de Luna; b. 1948) as adult Salvador, and Ednita Nazario (b. 1955) as Esmeralda Agron (Salvador's mother) at *The Capeman Time Is an Ocean.

Disney's 36th animated film, *Mulan* (June 19, 1998), is based on the legendary Chinese woman warrior Hua Mulan, who takes the place of her aging father in the army via disguise, fights for 12 years, and then returns home without asking for any reward. The film designers merged German Expressionism, Chinese painting and watercolor, spaghetti westerns, and 1950s/1960s epics to achieve its unique look, evident in the pensive song "Reflection," at *Mulan Reflection, with music by Matthew Wilder (né Matthew Weiner; b. 1953), words by David Zippel (b. 1954), and vocal by Lea Salonga.

Following the life of Moses as adapted from the Book of Exodus—and, for accuracy, incorporating suggestions from Christian, Jewish, and Muslim scholars—*The Prince of Egypt* (December 16, 1998; DreamWorks Pictures) developed a realistic feel for its look via a mix of traditional and computer-generated animation. When Moses's people break free from the chains of slavery, Sally Dworsky (b. 1964; *The Lion King, Shrek*) and Michelle Pfeiffer (b. 1958; *The Fabulous Baker Boys, Hairspray*), accompanied by a children's choir, sing the inspirational, even celestial, "When You Believe" at *The Prince of Egypt When You Believe. The score was written by Stephen Schwartz.

Jason Robert Brown (b. 1970; *Honeymoon in Vegas*) wrote the songs for *Parade* (December 17, 1998), a true-life story of the 1913 Georgia lynching of Jewish factory worker Leo Frank (1884–1915), convicted of raping and murdering a 13-year-old girl (posthumously pardoned), the subsequent emergence of the Anti-Defamation League (formed 1913), and the re-emergence of the Ku Klux Klan (second Klan formed 1915). The repetitious, overlapping voices in "The Factory Girls/Come Up to My Office" accumulate into accusations of Frank as they stir the fear and hatred of average folk looking for a scapegoat at *The Factory Girls/Come Up to My Office.

The inimitable body isolations, asymmetries, syncopations, and turned-in quirks of Bob Fosse are on display throughout the Broadway Revue *Fosse* (January 14, 1999). Compiled, re-created and lovingly staged by Fosse alums Chet Walker, Ann Reinking (b. 1949), Gwen Verdon, and Lainie Sakakura, the number "I Wanna Be a Dancin' Man" (originally from the 1978 Fosse revue *Dancin'*) at *I Wanna Be a Dancin' Man Fosse—music by Harry Warren (1893–1981) and lyrics by Johnny Mercer (1909–1976)—brings what seems as if every step created by him into one dance.

Frank Wildhorn wrote the music and Jack Murphy the lyrics to the Broadway musical *The Civil War* (April 22, 1999), the songs of which aimed to portray the war through three distinct perspectives: the Union, the Confederacy, and the slaves. On *The Civil War: The Complete* Work recording (January 5, 1999), with Wildhorn music and cast harmonies in the background, speeches by the 16th president of the United States, Abraham Lincoln (1809–1865), African American social reformer, orator, and statesman Frederick Douglass (1818–1895), and women's rights activist Sojourner Truth (née Isabella Baumfree; 1797–1883) were excerpted and interwoven among all the songs. Read by actor James Garner (né James Scott Bumgarner; 1928–2014), Lincoln's first Inaugural Address (March 4, 1861) spoke to the better angels of our nature at *The Civil War Lincoln Better Angels. From 1855, *My Bondage and My Freedom* was Douglass's second of three autobiographies, with excerpts read by Danny Glover (b. 1946) at *The Civil War My Name Is Frederick Douglass. Delivered in December 1851, "Ain't I a Woman?," spoken extemporaneously, can be heard at *The Civil War Sojourner Truth Ain't I a Woman as read by poet Maya Angelou (1928–2014).

Adapted from the 1912 book *Tarzan of the Apes*, written by Edgar Rice Burroughs (1875–1950), *Tarzan* (June 16, 1999) broke ground in the art department, having the first animated character to actually show working muscles in action by using a new process called Deep Canvas to create a sense of three dimensions. With songs by adult contemporary artist Phil Collins (b. 1951), have a listen to Glenn Close as Kala (Tarzan's adoptive mother) introduce the lullaby "You'll Be in My Heart" at *Tarzan You'll Be in My Heart (English). The overt racism of the book was excised completely from the film—Tarzan spends his whole time in Africa with no Africans in sight—nor does Tarzan ever return to London, staying in Africa at the end of the movie. Nearly 75 films have been made about the character, including the 12 most famous ones between 1932 and 1947 starring Olympic swimmer Johnny Weissmuller (1904–1984).

Putting It Together (November 21, 1999), the second of three Stephen Sondheim Revues—as of this 2018 writing—draws together over 30 of the songwriter's tunes from over 40 years of work. Bronson Pinchot (b. 1959) sings "Invocation," at *Invocation and Instructions for the Audience, the introduction to *The Frogs*, Sondheim's 1974 adaptation, which took place in and around the Yale University swimming pool, of ancient Greek comedian Aristophanes's 405 BCE version.

Michael John LaChiusa (b. 1962; *First Daughter Suite, Rain*) wrote the story and songs for the musical *Marie Christine* (December 2, 1999), based on the ancient Greek tragedy of Medea (431 BCE), written by Euripides. The Greek play was the origin of the phrase "Hell hath no fury like a woman scorned." The story follows sorcerer Medea helping Jason retrieve the Golden Fleece, only to be rejected by him upon their return home. In revenge, she kills his new wife, him, their two children, and blinds herself. Updated to 1890s New Orleans and Chicago, Audra McDonald (b. 1970; *Lady Day at Emerson's Bar and Grill, Shuffle Along*) as the lead blasts out "Tell Me," at *Marie Christine Tell Me, a warning to her lover Dante (actor Anthony Crivello; b. 1955) what she's capable of. Modern dance choreographer Martha Graham created her own version of the story, *Cave of the Heart*, at *Martha Graham Cave of the Heart, an equally harrowing account set to Samuel Barber's (1910–1981) composition "Medea's Meditation and Dance of Vengeance," commissioned for her 1946 ballet.

TEN

The 2000s

The Wild Party, based on the 1928 Joseph Moncure March (1899–1977) risqué narrative poem of the same name, with a book, music and lyrics by Andrew Lippa (b. 1964; *The Addams Family*, *Big Fish*), opened Off broadway on February 24, 2000. Coincidentally, Michael John LaChiusa's (b. 1962; *Little Fish*, *See What I Wanna See*) own version of the same poem opened on Broadway two months later, on April 13, 2000. It's fun to compare jazz influences on the two shows, particularly in the respective songs that introduce the diverse range of arriving guests. In Lippa's, the tune is the delirious "What a Party," sung by the entire cast at *The Wild Party Off Broadway What a Party; in LaChiusa's, it's the more period "Welcome to My Party," as led by Australian Toni Collette (b. 1972) at *Welcome to My Party Original Broadway Cast.

The 21st-century *Aida* (March 23, 2000), based on the 1871 opera of the same name by Giuseppe Verdi (1813–1901), has music by Elton John (né Reginald Kenneth Dwight; b. 1947; *The Lion King*) and lyrics by Tim Rice (b. 1944; *Jesus Christ Superstar*, *Evita*). "Dance of the Robe," at *Aida the Dance of the Robe, as sung by Trinidad-born Heather Headley (b. 1974; *The Lion King*), Nehebka (director and actress Schele Williams; *Motown the Musical*), and the Nubian slaves, captures Aida's conundrum at serving as princess.

Contact (March 30, 2000), a "dance play" for 18 dancers set to pre-recorded Edvard Grieg (1843–1907), Squirrel Nut Zippers (formed 1993), and Beach Boys (formed 1961) music, among others, tells three stories of people seeking and sometimes making contact in life. Susan Stroman (b. 1954; *Steel Pier*, *Young Frankenstein*) directed and choreographed to a "book" by John Weidman (b. 1946), and she recounts the history of the unlikely development of the show, with excerpts, at *Susan Stroman, Part I.

The American musical *The Full Monty* (October 26, 2000), based on the 1997 British movie of the same name, is a realistic story of six unemployed steel workers from Buffalo, New York, who decide to start a strip act that outdoes even the Chippendales (formed 1979). They do "the full monty,"

British slang (of unknown origin) that literally means doing "everything which is necessary, appropriate or possible"; in this case, taking off all their clothes. With a "manly, industrial-pop score" (Green and Ginell, 2014, p. 6) by David Yazbek (*Dirty Rotten Scoundrels*, *The Band's Visit*)—including songs like "Scrap," "Big-Ass Rock," and "The Goods"—the show culminates in the big moment, "Let It Go," as presented live during the 2001 Tony Awards, at *Patrick Wilson Does the Full Monty. The tune "Man," at *Man Full Monty (with reference to "The Marlboro Man" commercial), about what it's like to be a man, is intriguingly reminiscent of English songwriter Joe Jackson's (b. 1954; "Is She Really Going Out with Him?" "Steppin' Out") own take on the topic, "Real Men," from his 1982 *Night and Day* album, at *Joe Jackson Real Men.

Drawn from over a dozen Dr. Seuss (né Theodore Seuss Geisel; 1904–1991) stories—some of the most accessible, richly imaginative, purely fun anapestic tetrameter verse in the world—*Seussical* (November 30, 2000) has lyrics by Lynn Ahrens (b. 1948; ABC's *Schoolhouse Rock*) and music by Stephen Flaherty (b. 1960; *Lucky Stiff*, *Ragtime*). Kevin Chamberlin (b. 1963; *The Addams Family*) and Anthony Blair Hall (b. 1987; *Ragtime*), as Horton the Elephant and JoJo, a Who that lives in Whoville, respectively, sing the existential, magical duet "Alone in the Universe" at *Seussical Alone in the Universe. Dr. Seuss adaptations worth a look in other media include the 1942 Warner Bros. Merrie Melodies cartoon "Horton Hatches the Egg" (based on the 1940 story of the same name), an excerpt of which can be seen at *Horton Hatches the Egg 1942, and the one feature film written entirely by Geisel, the extraordinarily surreal *The 5,000 Fingers of Dr. T* (1953), reveals Seuss's typically wacky, off-kilter visuals in an excerpt at *#195 5000 Fingers. The film is really a subversive treatise against world domination and oppression!

Begun as a film in March 1968, writer-composer-actor-comedian-producer Mel Brooks's (né Melvin Kaminsky; b. 1926) *The Producers* opened on Broadway on April 19, 2001, and ran almost six years to the day. Starring Nathan Lane (né Joseph Lane; b. 1956) and Matthew Broderick (b. 1962), it was choreographed and directed by Susan Stroman, who also choreographed and directed the second version of the film in December 2005, which also starred Lane and Broderick. A goofball duets number starring old ladies and their walkers, "Along Came Bialy" can be seen at *The Old Ladies Musical.

Owing to a 20-year drought in the near future of a city near you, a megacorporation called Urine Good Company regulates the cost to urinate in numbered public amenities. In the satirical musical *Urinetown* (September 20, 2001), with music by Mark Hollmann (b. 1963) and lyrics by Hollmann and Greg Kotis, you're sent to Urinetown if you can't afford to pee (translation: you're thrown off a roof). It is easy to hear echoes of the socially relevant *The Cradle Will Rock* (1937) and *The Threepenny Opera* (1928) in the show, especially in "It's a Privilege to Pee" at *Urinetown It's a Privilege to Pee, sung by the company and Nancy Opel (b. 1957; *The Toxic Avenger*), as Penelope Pennywise.

After 9/11, people wanted more of an escape than ever (just as during the Depression and World War II), and Broadway's *Mamma Mia!* (October 18, 2001) fit the bill perfectly. With music and lyrics by Swedish pop group ABBA's (1972–1982) alumni Benny Andersson (b. 1946) and Björn Ulvaeus (b. 1945), the hits outweighed the charming story of a young woman unsure which of the three men in her mother's life is her father. "Dancing Queen" (August 1976; number one on Billboard's Top 100), the group's biggest number, can be seen in the July 2008 film version with Meryl Streep, at nearly 60 years old, leading the pack at *Dancing Queen—Mamma Mia.

Screenwriter-director-comedian-author-polymath John Waters's (b. 1946) 1988 film of *Hairspray* was turned into a Broadway show that opened on August 15, 2002 (with a film version of *that* show opening in July 2007). The latter two productions boast tunes by Marc Shaiman (b. 1959) and Scott Wittman (1955), non-stop songs and dances that are the sweetest, perkiest, most infectious and terminally peppy, high-octane performances ever presented in a musical (and that's saying something). The story deals with everything from family values to all kinds of bigotry (weigh-ism, racism, classism, segregation), agoraphobia, plastic surgery, the need for heroes and heroines, the American Dream, the celebration of difference, and the belief that any outsider can triumph.

In a nod to the precedents of farce and commedia dell'arte, Waters used alliterative names for his characters (Link Larkin, Motormouth Maybelle, etc.) and dressed a man *en travestie* for Edna Turnblad's role. In the first film, Edna was played by Divine (né Harris Glenn Milstead; 1945–1988), and in the second, John Travolta (b. 1954). Always played by a newcomer, Tracy Turnblad was played in the first by Ricki Lake (b. 1968), and in the second, Nikki Blonsky (b. 1988). Helping to break the color barrier in 1962 Baltimore (Waters's home town), the song "Without Love," at *Without Love, is wonderfully subversive as sung by the young African American and Caucasian lovers played by Elijah Kelly (b. 1986) and Amanda Bynes (b. 1986), respectively.

Twyla Tharp outdid even her own eclectic, multi-perspectival choreography from her 1982 modern dance "The Golden Section," to David Byrne music, in the Broadway jukebox musical of Billy Joel hits, *Movin' Out* (October 24, 2002). Have a look at the medley "River of Dreams/Keeping the Faith/Only the Good Die Young" at *Movin' Out, performed during the 57th Tony Awards in 2003, and compare it to the 2006 performance of "The Golden Section" by the Alvin Ailey American Dance Theater at *The Golden Section by Twyla Tharp, to see if I'm right.

Boasting tunes like "It Sucks to Be Me," "If You Were Gay," "Everyone's a Little Bit Racist," and "The Internet Is for Porn," composer-lyricists Robert Lopez (b. 1975) and Jeff Marx's (b. 1970) *Avenue Q* (July 31, 2003) barely took second place to 1968's *Hair* for most outrageous song titles. With handheld puppet characters named Princeton (fresh out of college), Christmas Eve (a Japanese American therapist who can't find a client because she's too honest), and Lucy T. Slut (a contemporary Mae West with blonde hair, round head, and wide mouth full of Burlesque innuendos), the show was a Sesame-Street-and-South-Park version of *Real World* meets *Friends*. The tune "Schaden-freude," German for "taking pleasure in others' misfortunes and pain," is an expletive-filled hoot from the soundtrack at *Schadenfreude, while the last song of the show, the lovely and plaintive "For Now," contrasts nicely to the rest of the mayhem, at *For Now.

The Boy from Oz (October 16, 2003), starring Aussie Hugh Jackman (b. 1968), was a jukebox musical based on the life of flamboyant Australian singer-songwriter and hit-maker Peter Allen (né Peter Richard Woolnough; 1944–1992). One of Allen's most heartfelt songs, "Don't Cry Out Loud" (co-written with Carole Bayer Sager; b. 1947), became a 1979 hit for pop singer Melissa Manchester (b. 1951), at *Don't Cry Out Loud Melissa Manchester. Allen's own version, at *Peter Allen Don't Cry Out Loud, is also quite affect-ing—apparently it was written for his mother in an effort to tell her about his AIDS-related illness. Rita Coolidge (b. 1945) had one of her biggest hits the same year to another Allen tune, "I'd Rather Leave While I'm in Love," at *Rita Coolidge I'd Rather Leave While I'm in Love (also co-written with Sager). Allen's own straightforward version is equally touching at *Peter Allen I'd Rather Leave While I'm in Love.

Composer/lyricist Stephen Schwartz, flying under the radar for decades with his work on animated Disney musicals (especially in the 1990s), came back with a wicked vengeance when *Wicked* opened on Broadway on October 30, 2003. The original Glinda the Good Witch (Kristin Chenoweth; b. 1968), Elphaba (Idina Menzel; b. 1971), and the Wiz (Joel Grey; b. 1932) each sing their signature tunes "Popular," "Defying Gravity," and "A Sentimental Man" at *Popular, *Wicked—Defying Gravity, and *A Sentimental Man, respec-tively.

Begun Off broadway in December 1990, John Weidman's (b. 1946; *Pacific Overtures*) book and Stephen Sondheim's (b. 1930) songs of the musical Revue *Assassins* finally arrived on Broadway on April 22, 2004. Starring historical characters such as John Wilkes Booth, Charles Guiteau, Leon Czolgosz, Giuseppe Zangara, and Lee Harvey Oswald, all of whom tried to or succeeded in killing U.S. presidents, the show explores the motivations of each by expanding upon what little information there is on these troubled individuals. As the Balladeer, Neil Patrick Harris (b. 1973) presents many of these stories as American myths, particularly when he sings "The Ballad of Booth" at *Assassins Ballad of Booth. At *Assassins Gun Song, "The Gun Song" explains how easy it is to change the world with just one little gun.

With music and lyrics by David Yazbek, the musical *Dirty Rotten Scoundrels* (March 3, 2005), about the hijinks of two con men who are ultimately conned themselves, was based on the Michael Caine (b. 1933), Steve Martin (b. 1945), and Glenne Headly (1955–2017) 1988 film of the same name (directed by Frank Oz). The funniest scene (out of a bunch) in the film, Ruprecht's intro around the dinner table, at *Steve Martin Is Ruprecht, is represented in "All About Ruprecht" as sung by the songwriter himself at *All About Ruprecht (Original Demo).

Eric Idle (b. 1943), one of the five members of the British television comedy team Monty Python (at its heyday from 1969 to 1983), wrote the libretto for the March 17, 2005, Broadway show *Monty Python's Spamalot*, itself based on the entire team's screenplay for the 1975 film *Monty Python and the Holy Grail*. How does one choose a favorite scene, between, say, the "I'm Not Yet Dead" number from the show's soundtrack at *I'm Not Yet Dead and the film version at *Monty Python Not Dead Yet Scene; the "Always Look on the Bright Side of Life" number at *Spamalot Part 10 and the original in the Jesus Christ spoof film *The Life of Brian* (August 1979) at *Always Look at the Bright Side of Life of Brian, with the whole company and extras singing away as they hang on crucifixes? If one likes satire, I'm not sure one can choose.

With music and lyrics by William Finn (b. 1952), *The 25th Annual Putnam County Spelling Bee* (April 15, 2005) grew out of group improvisation, a little like *A Chorus Line*, and involved breaking the fourth wall at times when the performers brought four different audience members up to spell, many of whom relived their embarrassing preadolescence by tripping over various and sundry words. The show is a kind of "Survivor for Nerds" story about kids who are looking for alternatives to gym. It stars, among other characters, Logainne Schwartzandgrubenierre, a lisping, hyper-pigtailed daughter of gay fathers who melded their last names together. Apparently, Julie Andrews, who played Mary Poppins in the 1964 film of the same name, misspelled "supercalifragilisticexpialidocious" during a guest speller stint on a 2007 KIDS night on Broadway.

Based on the 1936 exploitation film of the same name, the musical comedy *Reefer Madness* made it to Off broadway in 1998 before becoming a made-for-TV film on April 16, 2005. With songs by Dan Studney (*Jack, the Giant Slayer*), David Manning (b. 1973; *Romeo and Juliet vs. The Living Dead*), and Nathan Wang (b. 1956; *Sleeping Dogs*), tunes like "Jimmy Takes a Hit/The Orgy," "The Stuff," and "The Brownie Song" satirically warn the world about the addictive properties of marijuana use. Robert Torti (b. 1961; *That Thing*

That You Do!) as Jesus entreats Christian Campbell (b. 1972; *Big Love, True Detective*) as Jimmy to repent his ways—with his dancing and singing back-up angels—in the song "Listen to Jesus, Jimmy" (at *Listen to Jesus Jimmy), at one point sliding through the open legs of a bevy of beauties—reminiscent of similar technical moves in Busby Berkeley's (1895–1976) "Young and Healthy" number (from 1933's *42nd Street*) at *Young and Healthy Busby Berkeley and Joel (b. 1954) and Ethan Coen's (b. 1957) musical homage "Gutterballs," at *Gutterballs the Big Lebowski, in their 1998 film *The Big Lebowski*.

Richard and Mary Rodgers' grandson Adam Guettel (b. 1964) wrote the complex tunes for Broadway's *The Light in the Piazza* (April 18, 2005). Its operatic "Statues and Stories," at *Light in the Piazza Tony's Performance, is clearly reminiscent of the work of the composer/lyricist's grandfather as well as Guettel's mentor, Stephen Sondheim.

Jersey Boys, the story of the rise and fall and rise of the Four Seasons (formed 1960) pop group, opened on Broadway on November 6, 2005, and was followed nine years later in June 2014 by the film version directed by Clint Eastwood (b. 1930). Among the dozens of hits by the group, have a listen to the original number 13 on the Billboard Charts May 1966 Sandy Linzer/Denny Randell–penned, five-key modulated "Opus 17 (Don't You Worry 'Bout Me)," and the number 1 hit, the Bob Gaudio/Bob Crewe–penned June 1964 "Rag Doll," at *Opus 17 (Don't You Worry 'Bout Me) and *Rag Doll, respectively.

The Woman in White opened on Broadway on November 15, 2005. It was based on Wilkie Collins's (1824–1889) 1859 detective novel/Victorian melodrama of the same name, which addressed the unequal position of married women. William Dudley's (b. 1947) set designs, all video projections coordinated with a rotating stage (see *The Woman in White London), made for a stunning sight alongside Andrew Lloyd Webber's (b. 1948) music, David Zippel's (b. 1954) lyrics, and the full makeup of Count Fosco (who loves his mice), the latter seen in process at *Michael Ball Interview Richard and Judy.

Actress-singer-dancer LaChanze (née Rhonda LaChanze Sapp; b. 1961) inhabits the role of Celie, singing "I'm Here" from *The Color Purple* musical (December 1, 2005), adapted from Alice Walker's 1982 Pulitzer Prize–winning novel set in rural 1909 Georgia. With music and lyrics by Brenda Russell (b. 1949), Allee Willis (b. 1947), and Stephen Bray (b. 1956), compare LaChanze's soundtrack version at *I'm Here from The Color Purple to Jennifer Hudson's transcendent December 2010 Kennedy Center Honors version (for Oprah Winfrey, the original Celie in the December 1985 film) at *Jennifer Hudson—I'm Here—Kennedy Center Honors.

A ten-minute mini-documentary of behind-the-scenes work creating *The Wedding Singer* (April 27, 2006) musical—which was based on the 1998 Adam Sandler film of the same name, about a wedding singer struggling with his past and present relationships and his inability to speak his feelings—can be seen at *Backstage Wedding Singer Broadway. It includes not only insightful interviews with typically visible on-stage folk such as the actors and singers and dancers, but one interview each with choreographer Rob Ashford (b. 1959; 2002 *Thoroughly Modern Millie* revival, *Curtains*), costume designer Gregory Gale (*Urinetown, Rock of Ages*), set designer Scott Pask (*Nine, The Book of Mormon*), and lighting designer Brian MacDevitt (b. 1956; 2002 *The Coast of Utopia*). *The Wedding Singer* was directed by John Rando (*Urinetown*) with an eighties-esque score by the team of composer Matthew Sklar (b. 1973; *Elf* [the musical]) and playwright-lyricist Chad Beguelin (b. 1969; *Aladdin*).

The Drowsy Chaperone (May 1, 2006), a Roaring Twenties spoof based on a fake musical called "The Drowsy Chaperone," has music and lyrics by Lisa Lambert (b. 1962) and Greg Morrison (b. 1965). With characters like Broadway impresario Feldzieg—who puts on an annual *Feldzieg Follies*—gangsters, an aviatrix named Trix, and a Latin lover named Adolpho, the grand anthem to drinking "As We Stumble Along," at *As We Stumble Along, is sung by the drowsy (translation: alcoholic) chaperone herself, actress Beth Leavel (b. 1955).

Have a look at Bob Dylan (né Robert Zimmerman; b. 1941) himself, singing the original song of the following musical at *Bob Dylan the Times They Are a Changin' 1964. Twyla Tharp's twisty and quirky choreography for *The Times They Are a-Changing* (October 26, 2006) was its second major draw, as noted on TV's *The View* at *Bob Dylan The View, set to a contemporary version of Dylan's "Like a Rolling Stone" (1965). Out of his still expanding output of over 360 songs and 35 albums (as of 2017), a couple of classic tunes—"You're Gonna Make Me Lonesome When You Go" (*Blood on the Tracks*, 1974) and "You Ain't Going Nowhere" (1967), on Vimeo (at https://vimeo.com/968977) and at *The Byrds You Ain't Going Nowhere, from 1968, are just two tunes of his worth at least one listen (or repeat, if you're a Dylan lover).

Grey Gardens (November 2, 2006), a musical based on brothers Albert and David Maysles' 1975 documentary film about the dysfunctional relationship of the Beales sisters, Big and Little Edie (Jackie Kennedy's real aunt and cousin), presents a fictionalized account of their younger lives in act 1 and a fairly accurate version of their later ones in act 2. The actress who plays Big Edie in act 1 also plays Little Edie in act 2, a fun and challenging conceit. Tony Award–winner Christine Ebersole (b. 1953) as Little Edie sings "Around the World" with the musical's composer, Scott Frankel (b. 1963), accompanying her on piano at *Christine Ebersole—"Around the World" (lyrics by Michael Korie; b. 1955).

Composer Duncan Sheik (b. 1969) and lyricist Steven Sater's (birthdate unknown) Broadway show *Spring Awakening* (December 10, 2006) was based on the pre–German Expressionist writer Frank Wedekind's (1864–1918) 1891 play, both of which dealt with "burgeoning adolescent sexuality, homosexuality, peer pressure, teen suicide, abortion, masturbation, and adult hypocrisy" (Green and Ginell, 2014, p. 345). With in-your-face songs like "Totally Fucked," "Touch Me," "My Junk," "The Word of Your Body," and "The Bitch of Living," the high-intensity anarchic medley "Mama Who Bore Me/The Bitch of Living/Totally Fucked" (with Lea Michele) from the 2007 Tony Awards (the "fuck" is bleeped out) can be seen at *Spring Awakening Tony Performance.

Curtains (March 22, 2007), a charming and sardonic homage to backstage murder mysteries that takes place in 1959 Boston, was intended to be composer John Kander and lyricist Fred Ebb's next Broadway show after the 1997 *Steel Pier*, but it needed the help of composer/lyricist Rupert Holmes (b. 1947; "Escape (the Pina Colada Song)," *Drood*) to reach completion after both Ebb and book writer Peter Stone (*1776*, *Titanic*) died. Typical of Kander and Ebb's satirical jabs at whatever's on display, *"It's a Business" tells 'em to forget onstage art and just crank it out for the bucks. "Show People" is a more straightforward valentine to performers, rousingly put over by lead David Hyde Pierce (b. 1959; Dr. Niles Crane on TV's *Frasier*) and the rest of the cast during the 2007 Tony Awards at *The Cast of Curtains Performs at the 2007 Awards.

Director Julie Taymor (b. 1952; *Titus*, *Frida*) and choreographer Daniel Ezralow (b. 1956; *Love*, *Spider-Man: Turn Off the Dark*) created a quirky sixties counterculture story out of over 30 tunes (and dozens of song characters) by the Beatles in the *Across the Universe* (October 12, 2007) jukebox musical/romantic drama film. At one point, when Max is drafted into the army during "I Want You (She's So Heavy)," at *Across the Universe I Want You She's So Heavy—performed by Joe Anderson (b. 1982), Dana Fuchs (b. 1976), and T. V. Carpio (née Teresa Victoria Carpio; b. 1981)—we see a unique application of 19th-century Diorama when characters dance and lie upon and jump over and around several floor treadmills. Unlike in the 1969 Beatle version of the song, Taymor and Ezralow refer not to a woman as being heavy but, both literally and metaphorically, the Statue of Liberty.

Its title a phrase from Shakespeare's 1603 *Othello*, the comedy-drama rock musical *Passing Strange* (February 28, 2008), with lyrics and story by Stew (né Mark Stewart; b. 1961), could refer to travel, passing as white, the passage of time—or all three.

> *Passing Strange* is a brilliant work about migration—a geographical migration but also its hero's migration beyond the tenets of "blackness" and toward selfhood.... His story centers on a young black man who discovers his own Americanness while growing up, first, in Los Angeles and, later, in Europe. The Youth (Daniel Breaker) is a rock-and-roll Candide—a wanderer whose innocence is never entirely corrupted [Hilton Als; "Young American"; *New Yorker*; June 11, 2007].

German author Frank Wedekind's (1864–1918) *Spring Awakening* (1891), a play critical of the sexually oppressive culture of his 19th-century homeland, was made into a Broadway musical of the same name in 2006.

The poetic and dreamlike "Come Down Now" (especially the first part), at *Great Performances Passing Strange Come Down Now—sung by Rebecca Naomi Jones (b. 1981; *American Idiot, Hedwig and the Angry Inch*) and Stew himself—is reminiscent of Elton John's similarly pensive 1971 ballad "Come Down in Time" as performed live in 2003 by the songwriter at *Elton John Come Down in Time (Live 2003).

Before Lin-Manuel Miranda's (b. 1980) fame skyrocketed in August 2015 with his direction, lyrics, music, and lead acting in the impossible-to-get-tickets-to hip hop musical *Hamilton*, he had created, directed, written songs for, and also starred in the genre-breaking musical about life in the Washington Heights section of uptown New York City called *In the Heights* (March 9, 2008). Hear and watch Miranda and cast lead the infectious, foot-stomping mix of rap, Spanish, and four-part harmony (listen carefully for homages to Cole Porter and Glenn Miller's "Take the A Train," too) in the title song at *In the Heights 2008 Tony Awards Performance Musical.

Eight years before a high school senior named "Evan" became a household name in *Dear Evan Hansen*, October 5, 2008, saw the twelve-and-a-half-year-old character Evan Goldman, along with Jason Robert Brown's (b. 1970) songs, arrive on Broadway via *13*, the only show ever starring only teenage actors, singers and musicians; no doubt, an all *pre-teen* musical is just around the corner. Sung by the original cast at *13 the Musical Recording A Little More Homework, growing up into teen-hood was never so tough—and clearly presented—than in this production. Epitomized by "A Little More Homework," busy actor-singer Graham Phillips (b. 1993) nails a summary of life just prior to turning 13 (with the rest of the cast members) at *13/Becoming a Man.

Based on the September 2000 film *Billy Elliot,* the Broadway show *Billy Elliot: The Musical* opened in November 13, 2008 (followed by a November 2014 release of a film of the Broadway musical called *Billy Elliot the Musical Live*). With music and lyrics by Sir Elton John and Lee Hall (b. 1966), respectively, as in the opening number "The Stars Look Down" at *Billy Elliot—Stars Look Down, two parallel stories take place simultaneously: the actual coal miner strike of 1984–1985 in County Durham of northeast England and the life of 11-year-old Billy Elliot, who prefers studying ballet to mining for coal. The show ends with Billy's performance during *Matthew Bourne's Swan Lake* (1996), a contemporary take on the original classical ballet (1895) that can be seen at *Matthew Bourne's Ballet Clips Swan Lake. *Billy Elliot: The Musical* boasted the only time three people shared a Tony for Leading Actor—boys named David Alvarez (b. 1994), Trent Kowalik (b. 1995), and Kiril Kulish (b. 1994)—who all rotated in the lead.

The next month—December 14, 2008—found *Shrek the Musical* taking to the Broadway boards. The show was based on the American cartoonist

William Steig's 1990 picture book *Shrek!* and the May 2001 computer-animated film *Shrek*—itself followed by its three-and-counting sequels: *Shrek 2* (2004), *Shrek the Third* (2007), and *Shrek Forever After* (2010). "I Think I Got You Beat," as sung by Brian d'Arcy James and Sutton Foster, playing Shrek and Fiona, respectively, at *Shrek the Musical—I Think I Got You Beat, is a 21st-century version of Irving Berlin's "Anything You Can Do" from *Annie Get Your Gun* (1946), complete with burps and farts in their efforts to outdo each other. "Travel Song," at *Shrek the Musical Travel Song, showcases playwright-screenwriter-lyricist David Lindsay-Abaire's (b. 1969) clever lyrics wedded to female composer Jeanine Tesori's (b. 1961) pop-inflected, upbeat tune—a charming duo ditty for Shrek and Donkey (Daniel Breaker; b. 1980).

The jukebox musical *Rock of Ages* (April 7, 2009)—and the 2012 film of the same name, starring Tom Cruise (b. 1962)—showcases glam rock anthem hits of 1980s groups such as Twisted Sister, Journey, Poison, and Styx. Two songs from the first two groups, "I Wanna Rock" (1984) and "Don't Stop Believin'" (1981)—with a brief pause to flirt with Liza Minnelli (b. 1946) in the front row—feature Constantine Maroulis (b. 1975; *American Idol*), Amy Spanger (b. 1971; *Tick, Tick … BOOM!*), and James Carpinello (b. 1975; *Saturday Night Fever, Xanadu*), plus a few nostalgic cameos, at *Rock of Ages Broadway Medley Live @ 2009 Tony Awards.

By the 21st century, the complicated relationship struggles surrounding bachelor Bobby in Stephen Sondheim's 1970 *Company* had morphed into the harrowing family dynamics of composer Tom Kitt (b. 1974) and lyricist Brian Yorkey's (b. 1970) Broadway musical *Next to Normal* (April 15, 2009), exemplified by the song *"Who's Crazy/My Psychopharmacologist and I." Rendered by Best Actress Alice Ripley (b. 1963) as she deals with her character's bipolar disorders, listen for the ironic homage to "My Favorite Things" from 1959's *The Sound of Music*. Roll over, Rodgers and Hammerstein.

Based on the 1980 film of the same name with music and lyrics by Dolly Parton (b. 1946), *9 to 5* (April 30, 2009) is the story of three women who work for the domineering and lecherous Franklin Hart, Jr. Needless to say, he gets his comeuppance while they more than improve business. The country twang that builds to a rock anthem in "Change It" says it all at *9 to 5 Change It—ain't nothin' gonna happen unless *you* get it done yourself.

Inspired by the real-life story of pioneering radio DJ Dewey Phillips (1926–1968) and his love for black and white rhythm and blues and rock and roll, *Memphis* (October 19, 2009) zeroes in on the post–World War II challenges of integration in the title town. At the *Memphis Tony Awards Performance 2010, the hyper-kinetic singing and dancing of "Music of My Soul"—choreography by Columbian Serjio Trujillo (*On Your Feet!, The Addams Family*) and songs by David Bryan (b. 1962; keyboardist for Bon Jovi, *The Toxic Avenger*)—as led by Chad Kimball (b. 1976) and Montego Glover

(b. 1974), plus company, knocks the socks off the cheering crowd. Backed by a bevy of gospel singers, "Make Me Stronger" (at *Make Me Stronger Memphis) powers Dewey into urging his mother and the white folk to get themselves down to a black church.

The Broadway show *Fela!* (November 23, 2009) explores Nigerian-born Fela Anikulapo ("He who carries death in his pouch") Kuti's (1938–1997) controversial life as an artist, political activist and revolutionary musician, as well as his pioneering blend of jazz, funk, traditional African rhythms and Pidgin English lyrics that launched the Afrobeat community. Directed and choreographed by famed modern dancer/choreographer Bill T. Jones (b. 1952), the foot-stomping 1977 "Zombie," from the album *Zombie: Fela and Afrika 70*, highlights the performer's high-octane energy as singer and saxophonist in American-born (with Sierra Leone ancestry) Sahr Ngaujah's (birthdate unknown) version at *FELA! On Broadway Sneak Peak: "Zombie."

ELEVEN

The 2010s

April was quite the month in 2010: not one but five musicals opened on Broadway. A tune-filled version of the imaginary lives of the humorously ghoulish Addams family, *The Addams Family* opened on April 8, 2010, and was based on cartoonist Charles Addams's (1912–1988) fifty years of macabre cartoons for *New Yorker* magazine (plus the 1964–1966 TV series and two Hollywood films, in 1991 and 1993). Early in the show, ubiquitous-at-the-time Nathan Lane as Gomez and Bebe Neuwirth (b. 1958) as Morticia bemoan daughter Wednesday's falling in love with a normal boy in *"Where Did We Go Wrong?" To glean a sense of the myriad variety of the musical arts, two very different versions of a song titled "What If?" are worth comparing—a mere four years apart and in two vastly different shows—here in *The Addams Family* and *If/Then* (see below, from 2014), at *The Addams Family—What If and *What If?—If/Then, respectively.

The Million Dollar Quartet, composed of Johnny Cash (1932–2003), Elvis Presley (1935–1977), Carl Perkins (1932–1998), and Jerry Lee Lewis (b. 1935), played just one gig together—a scrappy, impromptu jam that happened by chance—on the afternoon of December 4, 1956, at record producer Sam Phillips's (1923–2003) fabled Sun Records studio in Memphis, Tennessee. Opening on April 11, 2010, at the Nederlander Theatre, the stage musical of the same name dramatized it. But there is no substitute for the original four roughly but assuredly coming together as they perform a handful of the 23 tunes on a scratchy recording of that event at *The Million Dollar Quartet.

Starting on April 20, 2010, with songs like "Before the Lobotomy," "Jesus of Suburbia," "Give Me Novocaine," and the title song—at *AI Cast—American Idiot on the Tony Awards—punk band Green Day's (formed 1987) Broadway show *American Idiot*, based on the group's August 2004 concept album, anarchically assaulted its audience's senses. Occasionally the show softened its tone with songs like the existential "Boulevard of Broken Dreams" (at *American Idiot Cast Boulevard of Broken Dreams) and the plaintive

195

"Wake Me Up When September Ends" (at *Wake Me Up When September Ends), the latter of which is reminiscent of Rod Stewart's (b. 1945) classic ode to avoiding a return to college, "Maggie May," at *Maggie May, from his 1971 album *Every Picture Tells a Story*.

April 22, 2010, saw the third (of three and counting) musical Revues open of Stephen Sondheim's (b. 1930) work, this one entitled *Sondheim on Sondheim*. In addition to a delicious reworking of hits and rarities from the composer-lyricist's vast catalogue, the show interspersed contextualized videos of Sondheim interviews as he discusses his work and inspirations—what longtime collaborator and librettist James Lapine called "a collage of his life"—as displayed on 64 plasma screens spread throughout the theatre. Watch versatile lyric sopranos Vanessa Williams (b. 1963) and Barbara Cook (1927–2017), both in the original cast, solo and then gorgeously overlap on "Not a Day Goes By" (from 1981's *Merrily We Roll Along*) and "Losing My Mind" (*Follies*, 1971) on TV's *The View* at *Losing My Mind/Not a Day Goes By. A tasty and teasing overview of the show can be seen at *Highlights from Broadway's Sondheim on Sondheim.

Torn between her love for Jesus and Judy (Garland), Kansas-grown half-Mennonite Sherie Rene Scott (b. 1967; *Dirty Rotten Scoundrels*, *The Little Mermaid*) created and performed solo the loosely autobiographical *Everyday Rapture* (April 29, 2010) musical. Harry Nilsson's (1941–1994) original version of "I Guess the Lord Must Be in New York City" (*Harry* album, 1969) at *Harry Nilsson I Guess the Lord Must Be in New York City, contrasts nicely to Scott's humble, awestruck version, encapsulating her arrival in the city, at *Everyday Rapture I Guess the Lord Must Be in New York City. And watching her contextualize Garland's 1950 *Summer Stock* hit "Get Happy" with her first time "singing outside church" in front of all sorts of New Yorkers, at *Everyday Rapture Get Happy, has to be seen to be believed. I like to think Judy would happily laugh and cry.

Composer-lyricist Michael Friedman's (1975–2017; *The Fortress of Solitude*) songs scream their story about the controversial populism (and personal life) of our seventh president, soldier and statesman Andrew Jackson (1767–1845), in the Broadway musical *Bloody, Bloody Andrew Jackson* (October 13, 2910). Contrasting with the hard and loud rock sound of most of its score, the musical's final song, "Second Nature," takes a step back—via simple acoustic guitar and vocal—from the maelstrom of Jackson's life to provide a macrocosm of Jackson's unpleasant legacy at *Second Nature Andrew Jackson. The tune brings to mind the richly ironic Talking Heads song "(Nothing but) Flowers," from their 1988 album, *Naked*, at *Nothing but Flowers, Talking Heads.

On Halloween, 2010, a musical based on the false accusation by two white girls of rape by nine black men, apprehended in 1931 Scottsboro, Alabama, opened. Presented in typically sly, knowing fashion by composer and lyricist John Kander and Fred Ebb (the latter having died in September 2004 during its creation) via the unique (and questionable) Minstrel Show format, here are excerpts from *The Scottsboro Boys* at *Scenes from The Scottsboro Boys with pieces of songs such as "Commencing in Chattanooga" and the yearning ballad "Go Back Home."

Based on the 1988 Pedro Almodóvar (b. 1949) film of the same name, November 4, 2010, saw *Women on the Verge of a Nervous Breakdown* open on Broadway. With music and lyrics by David Yazbek (b. 1961; *The Full Monty*, *Dirty Rotten Scoundrels*, *The Band's Visit*), soprano Laura Benanti (b. 1979; *She Loves Me*, *Meteor Shower*) as Candela peppers the patter song "Model Behavior," at *Model Behavior Women on the Verge, with some of the manic fervor of Almodóvar's story.

Based on the 1994 Australian film *The Adventures of Priscilla, Queen of the Desert*, the musical *Priscilla, Queen of the Desert* opened on Broadway on March 20, 2011. The show used well-known pre-recorded pop songs as its score, which were lip-synched by the performers—Tina Turner's 1984 "What's Love Got to Do with It?," Dionne Warwick's 1967 "I Say a Little Prayer," John Denver's 1974 "Thank God I'm a Country Boy," and many others. The show

> tells the story of two drag queens and a transgender woman, who contract to perform a drag show at a resort in Alice Springs, a resort town in the remote Australian desert. As they head west from Sydney aboard their lavender bus, Priscilla, the three friends come to the forefront of a comedy of errors, encountering a number of strange characters, as well as incidents of homophobia, while widening comfort zones and finding new horizons ["Priscilla, Queen of the Desert (Musical)"; https://en.wikipedia.org/wiki/ Priscilla,_Queen_of_the_Desert_(musical); retrieved December 3, 2017].

Winning Best Costume Design Tony, the outfits themselves are more than on display—oh yes, the singers and dancers are also visible, led by one of the original Weather Girls, Martha Wash (b. 1953)—at *Priscilla Queen of the Desert Tony Award Performance as they sing "It's Raining Men," the Weather Girls' 1982 hit.

Opening on March 24, 2011, *South Park* creators Trey Parker and Matt Stone devised, along with *Avenue Q* and *Frozen* co-composer Robert Lopez, the "atheist's love letter to religion" musical *The Book of Mormon*, a multi–Tony Award winning show that was topped by Best Musical. Catchy tunes include

- The up-tempo introduction to the Church of the Latter Day Saints, "Hello";
- The egotistical power ballad "You and Me (but Mostly Me)";
- The way-more-than-irreverent double entendres of "Turn It Off";
- The JC Superstar–like "All-American Prophet";

- The origin of all political liars, "Making Things Up Again";
- The sexualizing of religion, "Baptize Me";
- The eroticization of culture via stereotypical appropriations, "I Am Africa";
- The full-of-scatological BS, "Joseph Smith American Moses";
- The X-rated spoof of *The Lion King*'s "Hakuna Matata" via "Hasa Diga Eebowai," which should not be translated here;
- And the relatively mild hit song "I Believe," as sung by Elder Price (performer Andrew Rannells) on the 65th Annual Tony Awards ceremony at *I Believe from the Book of Mormon.

Somehow, the show simultaneously offended, lampooned, and praised religion, Africans, self-righteousness, and a host of other human frailties ... all the way to the box office. If you want to better understand the difference in tone between *Mormon* and *Lion King*, compare *The Book of Mormon Hasa Diga Eebowai with *The Lion King on Broadway Hakuna Matata (Kenyan Swahili meaning "no worries")—if you dare.

Based on the 2002 film of the same name—a story about real-life con artist Frank Abagnale, Jr. (b. 1948), who is currently (and ironically) an American security consultant—famed dramatist Terrence McNally's (b. 1938) libretto and Marc Shaiman and Scott Wittman's score (*Hairspray, Charlie and the Chocolate Factory*) are featured in the Broadway show version (April 10, 2011) of *Catch Me If You Can*. Groove on down to "Live in Living Color" as performed by the cast and the original stage Abagnale, Aaron Tveit (b. 1983), at *Live in Living Color—Aaron Tveit.

Cuban American Janet Dacal (*In the Heights, Prince of Broadway*) takes the lead role of Alice in *Wonderland* (April 17, 2011), composed by Frank Wildhorn (b. 1959). With lyrics by co-book writer Jack Murphy (*The Civil War, Swing!*), the show is a contemporary take on the Lewis Carroll (1832–1898) stories set in Queens, New York, behind the looking glass and down a rabbit hole. All sorts of travels and travails help remind Alice what really matters as she sings "Once More I Can See" at *Once More I Can See Wonderland.

The jukebox musical *Baby It's You!* (April 27, 2011) loosely tells the story of record producer/music executive Florence Greenberg (1913–1995) and her founding of Scepter Records (formed 1959). She was responsible for the career starts of the Isley Brothers (see 1961's "Twist and Shout," at *Isley Brothers Twist and Shout), Dionne Warwick (see 1964's "Walk On By," at *Dionne Warwick Walk On By), and the Shirelles (see 1959's "Dedicated to the One I Love," at *The Shirelles Dedicated to the One), among many others. Ripe for sing-alongs, over 40 hits blast their way onto the stage in rapid succession. It is fun to compare the original hits of the first and third songs above to follow-up covers by the Beatles in 1963 at *The Beatles Twist and Shout and the Mamas and the Papas in their 1967 *Dedicated to the One I Love.

Because of injuries and its hyper-expensive technical challenges, the visual-effects-laden *Spider-Man: Turn Off the Dark* had the longest preview period in history—182 performances—before finally opening at a retrofitted Foxwoods Theater on June 14, 2011. With a book co-written by Julie Taymor (of *Lion King* and *Across the Universe* fame), mask design by and direction credited to Taymor, choreography both onstage and above the audience by the viscerally imaginative Daniel Ezralow (Cirque de Soleil's *Love*), and songs by U2 members Bono and the Edge, its extravagant nature (if not high geek quotient tie-in to Marvel Comic origins) could not be denied, as witnessed in this fan-made preview at *Spider-Man Turn Off the Dark Extended Preview.

With Frank Wildhorn (*Jekyll & Hyde, Wonderland*) music and Don Black (b. 1938) lyrics creating a score filled with rockabilly, blues and gospel, the Broadway musical *Bonnie & Clyde* (December 1, 2011) was based on the true exploits of outlaws Bonnie Parker (1910–1934) and Clyde Barrow (1909–1934), young lovers on the run in the Midwest during the Great Depression. "You Can Do Better than Him," at *You Can Do Better Than Him Bonnie and Clyde, is a warning about Clyde sung in heartbreaking country style by actor Louis Hobson playing Deputy Sherriff Ted Hinton—who had a real-life crush on Bonnie—that is then countered by Clyde, played by Jeremy Jordan (b. 1984). The duo's tragic story was popularized by director Arthur Penn's (1922–2010) 1967 hit film *Bonnie and Clyde*, starring Faye Dunaway (b. 1941) and Warren Beatty (b. 1937). Georgie Fame (né Clive Powell; b. 1943) came out with a number one hit in January 1968, titled "The Ballad of Bonnie and Clyde," at *Ballad of Bonnie Clyde Georgie Fame.

Based on the 2007 film of the same name about a guy and girl who meet, fall in love, but then separate (among other complications), *Once* (March 18, 2012) opened on Broadway with music and lyrics by singer-songwriters (Irish) Glen Hansard (b. 1970) and (Czech) Markéta Irglová (b. 1988). Compare the spare accompaniment (guitar, piano, vocals) of the lovely Academy Award–winning song "Falling Slowly" from the film version as performed by its originators at *Glen Hansard, Marketa Irglova—Falling Slowly with its just-barely-less-spare accompaniment from the show starring Steve Kazee (b. 1975) and Cristin Milioti (b. 1985) at *Cristin Milioti, Steve Kazee—Falling Slowly.

Based on the 1990 Patrick Swayze and Demi Moore posthumous love story film *Ghost*, which blew the 1965 Righteous Brothers' hit song "Unchained Melody" out of the stratosphere, the now iconic scene from the film can be seen at *Ghost Soundtrack Unchained Melody—*Ghost: The Musical* (April 23, 2012). It took the onstage magic of human/ectoplasm relationships to heart as discussed and exemplified by illusion consultant Paul Kieve (b. 1967; *Harry Potter and the Prisoner of Azkaban, Matilda the Musical*) at *The Illusions of Ghost the Musical—Featuring Master Illusionist Paul Kieve.

Very loosely based on *Oh, Kay!*, the 1926 Gershwin musical, *Nice Work If You Can Get It*, starring Matthew Broderick (b. 1962) and Kelli O'Hara (b. 1976), opened on Broadway on April 24, 2012. Following in a burgeoning tradition of pastiche Gershwin Revues like *My One and Only* (1983) and *Crazy for You* (1992), *Nice Work* was once again a cornucopia of George and Ira Gershwin hits such as the title song, "Someone to Watch over Me," "Let's Call the Whole Thing Off," and the bittersweet "But Not for Me," originally written for the brothers' 1930 show *Girl Crazy*. Compare Kelli O'Hara's version of the song in this show, at *But Not for Me Nice Work, with a 1978 recording—complete with record scratches—of the original singer of the song, Ginger Rogers (1911–1995), crooning it in her late sixties at *Ginger Rogers But Not for Me (Rare 1978 Recording).

All about the world of competitive cheerleading, *Bring It On: The Musical*, with music by Tom Kitt and Lin-Manuel Miranda and lyrics by Miranda and Amanda Green, was loosely based on the 2000 hit film of the same name (starring Kirsten Dunst, which spawned numerous sequels). Opening on Broadway on July 12, 2012, the show was a mix of hip hop, song, and cheerleading routines. "It's All Happening" rocked the stage with award-winning choreography by Andy Blankenbuehler (b. 1970; *Hamilton, Bandstand*) at *It's All Happening Live @ The 2013 Tony Awards.

Originally based on American storyteller Jean Shepherd's (1921–1999) book *In God We Trust: All Others Pay Cash* (1966), *A Christmas Story: The Musical* (November 19, 2012) grew out of the producers' love of the nostalgic 1983 hit film of the same name. In a song by Pasek and Paul—composer/lyricists Benj Pasek (b. 1985) and Justin Paul (b. 1985), of *Dear Evan Hansen* and *La La Land* fame—and choreography by Warren Carlyle (*After Midnight*), a bevy of hot tapping nine-year-olds steal the show from Miss Shields (Anglo-Australian actress Caroline O'Connor; b. 1962) at the 2013 Tony Awards during the "Red Ryder Carbine Action BB Gun/You'll Shoot Your Eye Out" medley at *A Christmas Story Live @ 2013 Tony Awards.

As tempting as it might be in hearing the title to think it's about sex of a kinky kind, *Hands on a Hardbody* (March 21, 2013) is a musical based on the 1997 film *Hands on a Hard Body: The Documentary*, the story of a yearly competition (formed 1992) held in Longview, Texas, for the ownership of a Nissan Hardbody truck, in which contestants must keep just their hands on the truck for however long it takes to outlast all the others. (The 1995 competition on which the movie and show is based lasted 77 hours.) Insights into the Doug Wright (b. 1962; *The Little Mermaid, War Paint*) book, Amanda Green's (b. 1963; daughter of lyricist Adolph Green; *Bring It On*) lyrics, and Trey Anastasio's (b. 1964; the band Phish) richly harmonic, straight ahead rock music infuse the seven minutes of the studio album recording at *Exclusive Video Sing Along Hands on a Hardbody Recording Studio, with songs such as "Used to Be" (Keith Carradine [b. 1949], as J. D. Drew), "If I Had This Truck" (cast), and "Stronger" (David Larson [b. 1980], as Chris Alvaro).

A show about father-son relations, acceptance, and a shoe factory that goes *très moderne*, *Kinky Boots* opened on April 4, 2013, with a book by Harvey Fierstein (b. 1954; *La Cage aux Folles, Torch Song Trilogy, Hairspray*) and music and lyrics by Tony Award–winning Cyndi Lauper (b. 1953), the first time one woman alone won this honor. An innovative use of four portable conveyor belts—a collaborative design (and innovative version of Diorama) created by director-choreographer Jerry Mitchell (b. 1960; *The Full Monty, Legally Blonde, Catch Me If You Can*) and scenic designer/architect David Rockwell (b. 1956)—is on display in "Everybody Say Yeah" at *Kinky Boots, Everybody Say Yeah, Live 2013 Tony Awards. But the soul of the show may very well be in the songs "Soul of a Man" (sung by Stark Sands [b. 1978], as Charlie) and "Not My Father's Son" (sung by Sands and Billy Porter [b. 1969], as Lola) at *Stark Sands—Soul of a Man and *Billy Porter, Stark Sands—Not My Father's Son (Acoustic Version), respectively.

Matilda the Musical, based on the 1988 Roald Dahl novel with music and lyrics by Tim Minchin (b. 1975; *Groundhog Day*), opened on April 11, 2013. Exploiting the author's penchant for both grotesquerie and pathos through many of the songs—such as "Naughty," "Bruce," and "Revolting Children"—"When I Grow Up," apparently the first tune Minchin wrote for the show, encapsulates that magical mix of yearning and escape all children have (including grown-ups) as they fly high over the audience on rope swings. Have a look at the touching, dreamlike British version at *When I Grow Up Matilda the Musical.

Three days later, *Motown: The Musical* opened (April 14, 2013) and showcased over 60 of Motown's greatest hits as originally performed by Diana Ross and the Supremes, Smokey Robinson and the Miracles, Marvin Gaye, the Jackson Five, Stevie Wonder, and more—albeit in truncated form, mostly—in a jukebox musical loosely based on founder Berry Gordy's (b. 1929) life story. Valisia LeKae (b. 1979) is particularly uncanny as Diana Ross, as are the portrayals of the Jackson Five and Stevie Wonder in the London tour version, at *Motown the Musical Performance on Tonight at the Palladium.

First Date (August 8, 2013), a musical about a blind date that unfolds in real time, kicks off with five New Yorkers sharing disaster stories in "The One" at *First Date the Musical—The One. With music and lyrics by Alan Zachary and Michael Weiner, "First Impression," "Awkward Pause," and a trio of "Bailout Songs" exemplify the based-on-experience book by Austin Winsberg. The show lasted but five months on Broadway, but has been a big hit touring the planet in such places as Argentina, Australia, and Japan.

Based on the Tim Burton–directed comedy-drama 2003 film *Big Fish*, the October 6, 2013, Broadway musical of the same name featured direction and choreography by Susan Stroman (b. 1954; *Contact, The Producers, The Scottsboro Boys*). A double story with fantasy flashbacks of a son struggling to understand his father—see 1984's *Sunday in the Park with George* and 2014's *If/Then* for variants on this format—the show starred Norbert Leo Butz (b. 1967; *Dirty Rotten Scoundrels, Catch Me If You Can*) as Edward Bloom and Kate Baldwin (b. 1975; *Finian's Rainbow, Hello, Dolly!*) as Sandra Bloom. The lovely duet with the leads falling in love, "Time Stops," showcases the music and lyrics of Andrew Lippa (b. 1964; *The Wild Party, The Addams Family*) at *Time Stops from Big Fish.

Steven Lutvak's (b. circa 1960) music and lyrics wittily suffuse *A Gentleman's Guide to Love & Murder* (November 17, 2013), a musical comedy loosely based on the 1949 British black comedy film *Kind Hearts and Coronets*. Introduced by the versatile Jefferson Mays (b. 1965), who plays all nine D'Ysquith characters in often rapid succession, the triple counterpoint harmonies by Monty, Phoebe, and Sibella—performed by Bryce Pinkham (b. 1982), Lauren Worsham (b. 1982), and Lisa O'Hare respectively—in "I've Decided to Marry You," at *2014 Tony Awards, Gentleman's Guide to Love, give the best Gilbert and Sullivan patter song a proverbial run for the money.

With songs as diverse as "Pleasant Valley Sunday" (hear the Monkees' 1967 hit version at *The Monkees Pleasant Valley Sunday), "(You Make Me Feel Like) A Natural Woman" (Aretha Franklin's 1967 megahit at *You Make Me Feel Like a Natural Woman), and Carole King's (b. 1942) own performance of "You've Got a Friend" at *Carole King You've Got a Friend," from her groundbreaking 1971 *Tapestry* album, *Beautiful: The Carole King Musical*, opened on January 12, 2014. Starring Jessie Mueller (b. 1983; *Waitress*) in an eerily accurate incarnation of the artist, watch them trade riffs when Carole herself visits the cast after a performance at *Carole King Performs with the Cast.

The Bridges of Madison County (February 20, 2014), based on Robert James Waller's 1992 novel of the same name (the film, starring Clint Eastwood and Meryl Streep, opened in June 1995), has music and lyrics by Jason Robert Brown (*Parade, Honeymoon in Vegas*). Sung by actor-singer Steven Pasquale (b. 1976), "It All Fades Away," at *Steven Pasquale Sings It All Fades Away, is *National Geographic* photographer Robert Kincaid's reminiscence about his (ultimately doomed) four-day love affair with Italian war bride Francesca Johnson.

Based on the Academy Award–winning 1976 film *Rocky*, written by and starring Sylvester Stallone (b. 1946), Broadway's *Rocky the Musical* opened on March 13, 2014, with lyrics by Lynn Ahrens and music by Stephen Flaherty. Nominated for four Tony Awards, it won for Best Scenic Design by Chris

Barreca, which included multiple screen projections and even a Jumbotron around the stage (as in the film); the ring extended out into the audience for the climactic fight. A brief but fascinating analysis of that intensely collaborative finale, complete with Brit Steven Hoggett's (b. 1971) visceral choreography, can be seen at *Rocky Broadway—The Anatomy of a Knockout.

"Friend Like Me," one of the last songs lyricist Howard Ashman wrote before his death in 1991, became one of the big hits (along with "Whole New World") of the November 1992 animated film *Aladdin* (as sung by the Genie, voiced by Robin Williams), as well as the March 20, 2014, Broadway show (with the Genie played by James Monroe Iglehart). Compare and enjoy both energetic versions twenty-two years apart at *Aladdin Friend Like Me (English) and *Tony Awards 2014 Scene 2 Aladdin.

Idina Menzel (b. 1971; *Rent, Wicked, Frozen*) stars in *If/Then* (March 30, 2014), with words and music by Brian Yorkey and Tom Kitt, respectively. In parallel stories of a woman named Elizabeth who takes two different paths in life—as Liz and Beth Menzel belts out several power ballads, including the expletive-filled, heartbreaking "I Hate You," at *I Hate You—If/Then. The tune is interspersed with some dialogue and song by James Snyder (b. 1981), whose character Josh has just died on his last overseas tour of duty. Without fully answering them, the show poses the questions: Does happily-ever-after even exist? If not, can what remains be at least partially fulfilling? The finale, centered on the song "What If?" adds to the questions with more questions— and few answers—at *What If?—If/Then.

Based on his own October 1994 black comedy crime film *Bullets over Broadway*, Woody Allen's musical of the same name (co-produced by his sister, Letty Aronson; b. 1943) opened on Broadway on April 10, 2014. Replete with preexisting popular songs from the 1920s, "Tain't Nobody's Biz-ness If I Do" (1922; Porter Grainger and Everett Robbins), at *68th Tony Awards Performance Bullets over Broadway, showcases Canadian Nick Cordero (as Cheech; *Waitress, A Bronx Tale*) singing and dancing with the cool gangster cast in Susan Stroman's (*Crazy for You, Contact, The Scottsboro Boys*) high-voltage tap choreography.

Based on the 1969 short story "The Ugliest Pilgrim," by Doris Betts (1932–2012), *Violet* (April 20, 2014) tells the tale of a disfigured girl (played by Sutton Foster; b. 1975) in the segregated south of the 1960s who takes a bus from North Carolina to Oklahoma in order to be healed by a televangelist. On the way, she meets Flick and Monty, two poker-playing soldiers played by Joshua Henry (b. 1984; *The Scottsboro Boys*, 2018 *Carousel* revival) and Colin Donnell (b. 1982; *Jersey Boys*, 2011 *Anything Goes* revival), respectively, who listen to and join her as she sings about all the movie star body parts she'd replace her own with in "All to Pieces," at *Violet Tony Nominated Musical.

Starting Off broadway in 1998, *Hedwig and the Angry Inch* wound its way across the United States and London for 16 years until finally making it to Broadway on April 22, 2014. *Hedwig* is

> a rock musical about a fictional rock and roll band fronted by a genderqueer East German singer, Hedwig Robinson. The book is by John Cameron Mitchell [b. 1963; *Rabbit Hole, How to Talk to Girls at Parties*], and the music and lyrics are by Stephen Trask [né Stephen R. Schwartz; b. 1966; *In Good Company, Little Fockers*]. The story draws on Mitchell's life as the son of a U.S. Army Major General who once commanded the U.S. sector of occupied West Berlin. The character of Hedwig was inspired by a German divorced U.S. Army wife who was a Mitchell family babysitter and moonlighted as a prostitute at her Junction City, Kansas, trailer park home ["Hedwig and the Angry Inch (Musical)"; https://en.wikipedia.org/wiki/Hedwig_and_the_Angry_Inch_(musical); retrieved December 30, 2017].

Mostly filled with hard-, punk-, and androgynous-seventies glam-rock tunes, the contrasting narrative "Origin of Love"—seen in the 2001 film starring Mitchell himself, at *Origin of Love Hedwig (2001)—is based on Plato's description of the three distinct sexes of humans in his *Symposium* (c. 385–370 BCE). And the true love ballad, "Wicked Little Town," at *Wicked Little Town Hedwig (2001), has Hedwig singing to Christian teenager Tommy Speck.

Based on his childhood in the far northern England shipbuilding town of Wallsend, on the Tyne River, Sting's (né Gordon Matthew Thomas Sumner; b. 1951) musical *The Last Ship* (October 26, 2014) is thick with Tyneside accents and the fierce physicality of Steven Hoggett choreography. Embedded alongside songs about ships and August winds and sailing away and a dead man's boots is the lovely ballad "The Night the Pugilist Learned How to Dance" at *The Night the Pugilist 2015 Drama Desk Awards. It is sung by Michael Esper (b. 1976; *American Idiot*) and Collin Kelly-Sordelet, as Gideon Fletcher and Tom Dawson, respectively.

Composer and lyricist Dave Malloy's (b. 1976; *Ghost Quartet*) sung-through musical *Natasha, Pierre & the Great Comet of 1812* (November 14, 2014), is based on section 8 of Russian author Leo Tolstoy's (1828–1910) epic novel *War and Peace* (1869). As with many of John Doyle's spare productions of Sondheim, *The Band's Visit*, and other similar shows, the singers and actors in this musical play their own instruments onstage. Malloy's pastiche of song styles hint at the novel's scope: two highlights are the celestial "No One Else" at *No One Else, sung by Denée Benton (b. 1992; TV's *UnREAL*), and "The Great Comet of 1812" finale at *The Great Comet of 1812, with singer-songwriter Josh Groban (b. 1981) as Pierre (plus company).

Interestingly, the comet referred to in the title (and mentioned in Tolstoy's book) was discovered in March of 1811, reaching its brightest peak in October of that year—its tail is reported to have been a length one and a half times as wide as the sun—but it had waned by January of 1812. Sometimes

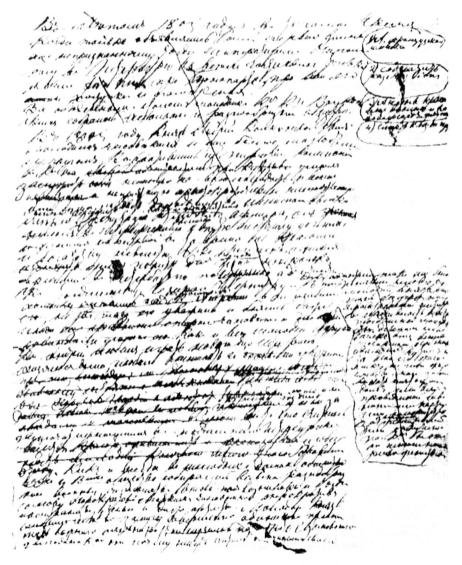

Russian author Leo Tolstoy's (1828–1910) notes from the ninth draft of his epic 1869 novel *War and Peace,* **parts of which were inspiration for the 2014 musical** *Natasha, Pierre & the Great Comet of 1812.*

referred to as Napoleon's Comet, it was claimed to portend the ruler's invasion of Russia and the War of 1812.

Tony Awards were well earned by New York City Ballet principal Robert Fairchild (b. 1987) as Outstanding Actor and British-born Christopher Wheeldon (b. 1973) for Direction and Choreography of the Broadway show *An*

American in Paris (April 12, 2015). With songs written by George and Ira Gershwin, it was named after George's 1928 orchestral piece and based on the Academy Award–winning 1951 Gene Kelly film. The tune "Liza," written for the 1929 Florenz Ziegfeld show *Show Girl*, is sung and danced with a stylistic nod to Kelly by Fairchild and British ballerina Leanne Cope (b. 1983) on TV's *Live with Kelly and Michael* at *Robert Fairchild and Leanne Cope Liza.

The 1998 Allan Knee play *The Man Who Was Peter Pan*, a story about Sir James Matthew Barrie, first baronet—more famously known as J. M. Barrie (1860–1937), the author of the universally loved *Peter Pan, or the Boy Who Wouldn't Grow Up* (1904 play, 1911 novel)—was made into the 2004 film *Finding Neverland* (starring Johnny Depp, Kate Winslet, Julie Christie, and Dustin Hoffman) and in turn evolved into the musical *Finding Neverland* (April 15, 2015), with music and lyrics by English singer-songwriters Gary Barlow (b. 1971) and Eliot Kennedy. The wonder-filled song "Believe," as sung and performed by Matthew Morrison (b. 1978; *Glee, Hairspray, The Light in the Piazza*) and cast during a Good Morning America telecast at *Finding Neverland (Broadway) Believe, gracefully captures the simple magic of childhood's imagined dreams as reality.

Based on cartoonist Alison Bechdel's (b. 1960) 2006 graphic novel of the same name—Bechdel is famous for her long-running comic strip, *Dykes to Watch Out For*, which ran from 1983 to 2008—*Fun Home* (April 19, 2015) has music by Jeanine Tesori (*Caroline, or Change, Violet*) and lyrics and book by Lisa Kron (b. 1961; *2.5 Minute Ride*). Its title is both pun and misnomer, the nickname the children of the story gave to the funeral home in which they lived and which their father owned. A show about courage, heartache, tenderness, coming out, joy, and vulnerability, soprano Judy Kuhn's (b. 1958; *Mystery of Edwin Drood, Pocahontas*) rendition of "Days and Days," as the original mother and wife Helen Bechdel at *Fun Home Days and Days, encapsulates all of those emotions and more.

Brothers Karey (b. 1964) and Wayne Kirkpatrick (b. 1961) wrote the music and lyrics to *Something Rotten!* (April 22, 2015), a musical that follows fictional 1595 London theatre owners Nick and Nigel Bottom in their quest for success as they compete with the Bard himself, William Shakespeare. Numerous humorous tunes (with harmonies deftly honoring the rock group Queen's vocal layering) proliferate the score: "Hard to Be the Bard" can be heard and seen at *Something Rotten Performs Hard to Be the Bard at Broadway at the White House, which aired on Thanksgiving, November 26, 2015; "God, I Hate Shakespeare," at *God, I Hate Shakespeare; and "A Musical," at *Musical References in a musical, Something Rotten, simultaneously pays homage and parodies dozens of musicals, a good test for fans.

Inspired by the 2004 Ron Chernow (b. 1949) biography of the same name, *Hamilton* (August 6, 2015) is a sung and rapped-through musical about

Founding Father Alexander Hamilton (c. 1757–1804). With songs and a book by (and originally starring, in the title role) Lin-Manuel Miranda (b. 1980; *In the Heights, Bring It On: The Musical*), the show hews closely, with occasional dramatic license, to the actual historical record. *Time Out New York*'s David Cote had this to say about the show (August 11, 2015):

> I love *Hamilton*. I love it like I love New York, or Broadway when it gets it right. And this is so right…. A sublime conjunction of radio-ready hip-hop (as well as R&B, Britpop and trad showstoppers), under-dramatized American history and Miranda's uniquely personal focus as a first-generation Puerto Rican and inexhaustible word-smith, Hamilton hits multilevel culture buttons, hard…. The work's human drama and novelistic density remain astonishing.

One of the many hits to come out of the show, the title song "Alexander Hamilton," was actually previewed for President Barack Obama more than six years before it made it to Broadway. On May 12, 2009, Miranda was the highlight of the White House Evening of Poetry, Music, and the Spoken Word, and the culturally significant number can be seen and heard at *Lin-Manuel Miranda Performs at the White House Poetry Jam.

Disaster! (March 8, 2016) is a spoof of 1970s disaster movies featuring over three dozen me generation songs such as "Hot Stuff" (1979; Donna Summer), "Without You" (1971; Harry Nilsson), and "I Will Survive" (1978; Gloria Gaynor), compiled by musician, writer, and radio host Seth Rudetsky. To get a sense of the loving mix of homage and parody, have a peek at a host of cast interviews on opening night at *Opening Night Disaster on Broadway.

Primarily taking place just after World War II in the Blue Ridge Mountains of North Carolina, *Bright Star* (March 24, 2016), inspired, written and composed by actor, comedian and musician Steve Martin (b. 1945; *Saturday Night Live, Roxanne, Meteor Shower*) and singer-songwriter Edie Brickell's (b. 1966) album *Love Has Come for You* (2013), is worth comparing to modern dancer-choreographer Martha Graham's "Appalachian Spring" ballet, in collaboration with composer Aaron Copland (1900–1990) from 72 years earlier; see *Martha Graham's Appalachian Spring. As sung by Carmen Cusack, originator of the role of Alice Murphy, "Sun Is Gonna Shine" captures the sweet bluegrass sound of the show at *Sun Is Gonna Shine (Single Version).

With music and lyrics by Duncan Sheik (b. 1969; *Spring Awakening*) and based on the controversial, uber-violent, and misogynistic 1991 novel of the same name by Bret Easton Ellis (b. 1964), *American Psycho* (April 21, 2016) is a story about the narcissistic, objectifying life of serial killer and young, wealthy investment banker Patrick Bateman. "Selling Out," as put over by the cast and shirtless lead Benjamin Walker (b. 1982; *Bloody Bloody Andrew Jackson*), at *American Psycho the Musical on the Late Show with Stephen Colbert, features impersonal, robotic choreography by Lynn Page and eight large-screen video projections filled with consumer imagery and buzzing static violently thrust toward the audience, a set and lighting design created by Finn Ross (*The Curious Incident of the Dog in the Night Time*).

Just before Intermission, the aroma of fresh-baked apple pie wafts in to the audience during Broadway's *Waitress* (April 24, 2016), a musical based on the 2007 film of the same name. (The slices are for sale, too.) The story of a pregnant woman in a loveless marriage who looks to turn her life around by entering a local pie contest, the show's top four creative spots, and many others, are filled by women—still a rarity, but another instance of hopeful change in the male-dominated world of musical theatre. The musical is directed by the influential Diane Paulus (b. 1966; *Finding Neverland, The Gershwin's Porgy and Bess*) and filled with songs by Sara Bareilles (b. 1979). "She Used to Be Mine" is sung in a plaintive bittersweet by the composer herself with alternating first- and third-person lyrics at *Sara Bareilles She Used to Be Mine; it encapsulates lead character Jenna's state of mind after her husband Earl steals her money and vacates the premises.

Tuck Everlasting (April 26, 2016), a Broadway show demonstrating both the appeal and dangers of immortality, is based on the acclaimed 1975 Natalie Babbitt (1932–2016) children's book—also made into popular 1981 and 2002 films—and has words and music by Nathan Tysen (b. 1977) and Chris Miller, respectively. The nature-filled imagery of "The Wheel," as sung by Michael Park (b. 1968; *As the World Turns*) and Sarah Charles Lewis (b. 2004), deftly explains what makes our mortal life worth living at *The Wheel Tuck Everlasting.

Based on the autobiographical 1989 Off broadway one-man show by Chazz Palminteri (né Calogero Lorenzo Palminteri; b. 1952; *Bullets over Broadway*), and the subsequent September 1993 film of the same name, the musical *A Bronx Tale* opened on Broadway on December 1, 2016. Co-directed by Jerry Zaks (b. 1946) and Robert De Niro (b. 1943), the show was about a boy torn between the world of his hard-working father and organized crime. Its opening number, "Belmont Avenue," with music by Alan Menken and lyrics by Glenn Slater (b. 1968; *The Little Mermaid, Sister Act, School of Rock*), introduces the Little Italy scene of the story as seen on NBC's *Today* show at *A Bronx Tale Cast Perform Scene from New Musical.

The Broadway musical *Dear Evan Hansen* (December 4, 2016) starts with a teenager who struggles with severe social anxiety and snowballs from there.

> It helps to suspend the disbelief that sullen, anti-social teenagers can change quickly. Surely that's a process requiring time-released hormonal adjustments. It is hard to accept that a long-admired-from-afar girl can change Evan's outlook on life so rapidly or that Connor's teenage disequilibrium leads him to do what he does. Coming through loud and clear, however, is the fact that what starts as deceit can be blown totally out of proportion by the Internet, where lies are disseminated with lightning speed leaving plenty of victims in their wake [Susan Davidson; "CurtainUP Review: *Dear Evan Hansen*"; *CurtainUP*; July 30, 2015.]

Inspired by the real-life death of a high schooler in Benj Pasek's life, Pasek and Justin Paul's (*The Greatest Showman, La La Land*) tunes capture the angst and hope of many high school seniors uncertain of their place in life, now or in their future. As sung by Ben Platt (b. 1993; *The Book of Mormon*) as Evan and Will Roland (b. 1989) as Jared, "Sincerely, Me" gives truth to the lie about a fake relationship, and how it can blow up in everyone's face, at *Sincerely, Me Evan Hansen.

December 2016 turned out to be quite the month for Pasek and Paul. Five days after *Dear Evan Hansen* premiered, the movie musical *La La Land* (December 9, 2016) opened with their lyrics set to composer Justin Hurwitz's (b. 1985; *First Man*) music. Similar in tone to Jacques Demy's (1931–1990) *The Young Girls of Rochefort* (1967), with dance and song emanating out of simple, everyday life—rather than, say, MGM's big and splashy musicals of the forties—director Damien Chazelle (b. 1985; *Guy and Madeline on a Park Bench, Whiplash*) was inspired by the full-figure dancing of the Fred and Ginger films of the thirties, as well as the widescreen technique of fifties Cinemascope pictures. Also as in real life, the love story between aspiring actress Mia and struggling jazz pianist Sebastian—Emma Stone (b. 1988; *The Amazing Spider-Man, Birdman*) and Ryan Gosling (b. 1980; *Crazy, Stupid, Love; The Big Short*), respectively—does not end happily ever after for the two of them; they move on towards their own hopeful futures, but separately.

Before that denouement, however, Chazelle gives us a lengthy *American in Paris*–style dance fantasy (at *La La Land Epilogue), choreographed by Mandy Moore (b. 1976; *So You Think You Can Dance*) and orchestrated to a Hurwitz tune, replete with references to classic musicals with sailors (*Anchors Aweigh, On the Town, It's Always Fair Weather*), artwork like *American in Paris*, a Seine stroll (see *Our Love Is Here to Stay Gene Kelly), a kind of yellow brick road, a *Funny Face* jazz club (see *Funny Face Bohemian Dance), and a *Broadway Melody of 1940* set (compare to Fred Astaire and Eleanor Powell's dance in that film at *Begin the Beguine Fred Astaire). See if you can catch all the references.

Irene Sankoff and David Hein, the married-couple composer-lyricists for the 2009 Toronto Fringe Festival's production of *My Mother's Lesbian Jewish Wiccan Wedding*, wrote the songs for *Come from Away* (March 12, 2017), a musical based on the harrowing true-story diversion and uncommon welcome of 7000 people on 38 planes from New York City on September 11, 2001, upon their arrival in the small Canadian town of Gander, Newfoundland. Embedded within tunes about waiting on the plane for over a day and uncertain why they were diverted ("28 Hours/Wherever We Are"), how the townspeople will feed and house that many stranded folks ("Blankets and Bedding"), and finding out why they've landed in Canada ("Lead Us out of the Night"), comedian-actress Jenn Colella (b. 1974), who plays real-live female pilot Beverley Bass, sings her heart and mind out about her personal journey in arriving at this time and place at *Come from Away "Me and the Sky," as performed on TV's *The View*.

  Based on the 2001 film of the same name, *Amélie* (April 3, 2017)—a complicated story about a young altruistic Parisian waitress, her family and friends with a host of issues (paranoia, germ phobia, obsessiveness), and her fascination with the magical details of daily life—boasts songs by composer Daniel Messé and lyrics by Messé and Nathan Tysen (b. 1977; *Tuck Everlasting*). A mash-up of "Times Are Hard for Dreamers" and "Tour de France" gives us a sense of Amélie's world at *Phillipa Soo and Broadway Cast Perform Medley as performed by Phillipa Soo (b. 1990; *Hamilton*; *Natasha, Pierre, & the Great Comet of 1812*), David Andino as the Blind Beggar, and the rest of the cast.

  With powerhouse singers Patti LuPone (b. 1949) and Christine Ebersole (b. 1953) as Polish American Helena Rubinstein (née Chaja Rubinstein; 1872–1965) and Canadian-born Elizabeth Arden (née Florence Nightingale Graham; 1878–1966), respectively, self-made multimillionaire women entrepreneurs in a man's world, *War Paint*, the story of a cosmetics rivalry that made makeup respectable, opened on April 6, 2017. Via a sensitively edited cross-cutting of orchestra musicians, black and white photos of Rubinstein and Arden, and excerpts of LuPone and Ebersole singing onstage and recording the soundtrack, *War Paint Medley Forever Beautiful/Pink/Face to Face affords us generous insight into the integrated artistry of three of the show's tunes as created by the team of composer Scott Frankel (b. 1963) and lyricist Michael Korie (b. 1955; *Grey Gardens*).

  Based on the comedic Bill Murray/Andie MacDowell 1993 film *Groundhog Day*, about the annual real-life February 2 will-winter-last-another-six-weeks test with a reluctant groundhog (*Marmota momax*)—in this case, Punxsatawney Phil, from Punxsatawney, Pennsylvania—the Broadway musical of the same name opened on April 17, 2017, with songs by Australian Tim Minchin (b. 1975; *Matilda the Musical*). After facing a mental breakdown ("Stuck"), succumbing to hedonism ("Philandering"), and beginning to learn about himself and inevitability ("Philosopher" and "Night Will Come"), stuck-in-time weatherman Phil Connors chooses philanthropy. Accompanied by a bouncy, upbeat bass in a mostly instrumental jazz riff, Phil finally turns his life around by doing good deeds while traversing the town at *Philanthropy—Groundhog Day.

  With lyrics and music by Lynn Ahrens (*Lucky Stiff*, *My Favorite Year*) and Stephen Flaherty (*Chita Rivera: The Dancer's Life*), respectively, *Anastasia* was based on (and expanded from) the 1997 animated film of the same name. Loosely following the legend of an actual grand duchess, Anastasia Nikolaevna (1901–1918)—both the film and Broadway show were themselves inspired by the original 1952 play of the same name by French author Marcelle

Maurette (1903–1972)—the musical opened on April 24, 2017. "In a Crowd of Thousands," at *In a Crowd of Thousands Music Video, sung by Derek Klena (b. 1991) and Christy Altomare (b. 1986), respectively, recounts the moment Dmitry as a ten-year-old recognizes eight-year-old Anya as the grand duchess—the beginnings of what would have been a happily-ever-after, lifelong love if she hadn't died so young.

Baby Driver (June 28, 2017) is not technically a film musical, but there are so many scenes set to song with the movements of the performers, camera, cars, and edits precisely choreographed as to be fairly called a "kind of a musical" by the director himself. Edgar Wright's (b. 1974; *Shaun of the Dead, Scott Pilgrim vs. the World*) careful eye for detail finds innovative ways of matching music and movement both large (cars screeching at top speeds

Disney's 1997 animated film *Anastasia* and the 2017 Broadway musical of the same name were based on the life of actual Grand Duchess Anastasia Nikolaevna (1901–1918), shown here in a 1914 photograph.

around curves, stopping on dimes) and small (jaws rhythmically chewing gum, mouths slightly sneering) in both his human and his automotive characters. Cinematic flourishes such as multiple camera angles, close-up and long-distance shots, silences and pauses, screams and aural blasts, dollies in and tracking shots out, fast-cut edits and up-under views suffuse nearly every scene with an extremely elevated sense of drama.

This is not an understatement. Take the opening hyperkinetic robbery scene, set to alternative rock band Jon Spencer (b. 1965) Blues Explosion's rowdy "Bellbottoms" (from their 1994 *Orange* album), at *Baby Driver Six Minute Opening Clip. The tune's accelerating speed parallels imagery of patiently waiting getaway driver Baby mimicking melody and lyrics in alternation with rapidly edited shots of the actual robbery, followed by their impossible, only-in-the-movies getaway through the crowded streets itself. Similarly, music video choreographer Ryan Heffington's (b. 1973; King's "Years and Years," Sia's "Rainbow") collaboration with Wright's camerawork is brilliantly set to

1963's R&B jam "Harlem Shuffle" by Bob & Earl (Bobby Byrd and Earl Lee Nelson), at *Baby Driver Coffee Run. The two artists transform a simple coffee run along busy city sidewalks into a surprise-filled pedestrian/camera dance duet that serendipity lovers John Cage (1912–1992) and Merce Cunningham (1919–2009) would have truly loved, I think.

Springsteen on Broadway (October 12, 2017), an autobiographical one-man show performed by Bruce Springsteen (b. 1949), is full of anecdotes and tunes about the daily struggles of Americans. An acoustic version of "The Ghost of Tom Joad," the title track to his 1995 album of the same name at *Bruce Springsteen The Ghost of Tom Joad Live Studio, is based on realist author John Steinbeck's (1907–1968) Depression-era character who is on the run in search of elusive happiness in his 1939 novel *The Grapes of Wrath*.

Based on the 2007 film of the same name but with Middle Eastern–inflected songs by Arab Italian American David Yazbek (b. 1961; *The Full Monty, Dirty Rotten Scoundrels*), *The Band's Visit* (November 9, 2017) tells the story of an evening's tentative intercultural affinities when a touring Egyptian police band gets stuck overnight in the wrong town in Israel. Using an actual onstage musical ensemble that includes indigenous instruments such as the darbuka (goblet drum) and oud (short-necked, pear-shaped lute), this gentle show about hope boasts nearly 20 contemplative tunes performed on a frequently revolving Scott Pask–designed set. The sarcastic "Welcome to Nowhere" is knowingly but humorously sung by multilingual musician/actor Katrina Link at *Welcome to Nowhere The Band's Visit, while "Haled's Song about Love," at *Haled's Song About Love The Band's Visit, is silkily crooned by Middle Eastern/American actor Ari'el Stachel, of Yemeni descent, in a bluesy, Chet Baker-ish manner. With shows like this one, international diversity is increasingly represented in the world of musicals.

As orchestrated by composer Tom Kitt (b. 1974; *Next to Normal, If/Then*), songs written by pop-rock artists such as They Might Be Giants, Cyndi Lauper, Steven Tyler, Jonathan Coulter, and the Flaming Lips bring an uber-optimistic message of hope to the musical adaptation of Nickelodeon's hit animated TV show *SpongeBob SquarePants* (December 4, 2017). Selections from the tunes and insights into the show are sprinkled throughout the recording of the soundtrack at *The Making of SpongeBob SquarePants, the New Musical Original Cast Recording. And yes, as originally conceived by marine biologist and animator Stephen Hillenburg (b. 1961), nerdy but lovable sea sponge SpongeBob—he looks more like a kitchen sponge, actually—still lives in a pineapple with his pet snail, Gary, has fantastic adventures with best starfish friend Patrick, and butts up against octopus neighbor Squidward Tentacles in the underwater city of Bikini Bottom.

Inspired by the life of 19th-century museum and circus impresario Phineas Taylor Barnum (1810–1891), *The Greatest Showman* (December 20,

2017) stars Hugh Jackman (b. 1968; *The Boy from Oz, Logan*) and features music and lyrics by songwriting team Benj Pasek and Justin Paul (*Dear Evan Hansen, La La Land*).

> For Jackman, Barnum's story is distinctly American. He says, "I always think of Barnum as being the birth of modern-day America. Everyone around the world knows of America being the land of opportunity and possibility, and if you work hard and you have talent, you have imagination, you can do anything. But that actually wasn't the case in 1850 in America…. There were barriers drawn by class, by race, by many, many different things. And Barnum kind of broke down many of those walls…. He believed that what makes you different actually makes you special. That message resonates today, particularly with young kids. The theme of this movie is all about empowering people to be themselves. That it's actually cool to be yourself…. It's the only path, ultimately, that brings you true happiness" [Bergstrom, 2017, p. 41].

The day before the first read-through of the show, Hugh told visual effects artist and first-time director Michael Gracey that he had just had a skin cancer cut out of his nose, leaving him with 80 stitches and doctor's orders not to sing. Fortunately, a camera was set up to catch the premiere rehearsal of "From Now On," at *The Greatest Showman From Now On. Its touching sentiment is reminiscent of another closing number about time, "For Now," from *Avenue Q* (2003) at *For Now Avenue Q. Elsewhere, "Come Alive," at *Come Alive The Greatest Showman, gives us a sense of the excitement of transferring rehearsal to screen in the big top.

Inspired by Hans Christian Andersen's fabled 1844 fairy tale *The Snow Queen*, Disney's 53rd film, *Frozen* (2013)—the highest-grossing animated film of all time—was adapted into a Broadway show that opened on March 22, 2018. Writing three times as many songs for Broadway as they did for Hollywood, married songwriters Kristin Anderson-Lopez and Robert Lopez's (b. 1975) uber-hit "Let It Go," as sung by Idina Menzel as Elsa at *Disney's Frozen Let It Go, is charmingly complemented by the relatively low-key "In Summer," as sung by Josh Gad (b. 1981), as the Snowman Olaf, at *Frozen—In Summer.

Based on the 2004 movie of the same name, the musical *Mean Girls* opened on Broadway on April 8, 2018. Directed and choreographed by Casey Nicholaw (b. 1962; *Spamalot, The Drowsy Chaperone*), the show, a story about the travails of popularity in high school, has a book by Tina Fey (née Elizabeth Stamatina Fey; b. 1970; *Saturday Night Live, 30 Rock*), music by Jeff Richmond (b. 1961; *Unbreakable Kimmy Schmidt*), and lyrics by Nell Benjamin (*Legally Blonde*). "Apex Predator," at *Mean Girls Performing Apex Predator (on the *Today Show* on May 3, 2018), sets the stage for the entire story.

Taking five years to come to fruition in 2013 Australia, six months of rehearsal with dozens of animatronic technicians and puppeteers and actors and dancers, and five more years before its scheduled arrival on Broadway in late 2018, the *King Kong* musical went back to the original 1932 novella written by Merian C. Cooper (1893–1973) and Edgar Wallace (1875–1932), which was written for the famous 1933 film. With original music by English composer and producer Marius de Vries (b. 1961; Bjork, *Romeo + Juliet*), and lyrics by Michael Mitnick and Craig Lucas, a sense of the magnitude of this creation can be glimpsed at *Sneak Peek King Kong the Musical.

As of this writing (October 2018), some of the dozens of musicals on the way to Broadway include *Beetlejuice* (based on the 1988 film), *The Honeymooners* (based on the 1950s Jackie Gleason television show), and *The Cher Show* (based on Cher's 1960s television show). Musicals bound for Hollywood include *Bohemian Rhapsody*, a biography of the rock group Queen, *Wicked* (based on the 2003 Broadway musical), and *Hamilton*.

Conclusion

After 200-plus pages and nearly 1000 video examples from hundreds of Broadway and Hollywood musicals, let us finally ask the question What *is* a musical? Or better, What makes a *good* musical?

It can seem like all too many shows are about someone called "me, me, me," and you would be right, in a way: their focus *is* on people and their feelings, their emotions. Musicals are indeed a kind of scientific, often exhaustive examination and uncovering of our emotions. We go to a musical and find out about ourselves. Our foibles, our failings, and our noble qualities, too. Because a musical is a fiction—an art created out of reality, carved into reality—we can celebrate vanity, for example, as in "Guido's Song," from *Nine*—not only can we enjoy the show but we can learn from it, too.

Pick a feeling, any feeling, and you'll find its reveal in a musical. Cruelty? "Easy to Be Hard," from *Hair* (1968). Agony? "Agony," from *Into the Woods* (1987). Love? With which show shall we start? "True Love," from *High Society* (1955), is certainly one place love is found. Prejudice, racism? "Carefully Taught," from *South Pacific* (1949), and "If You Could See Her through My Eyes," from the film version of *Cabaret* (1972). Courage? "If I Were King of the Forest," from *The Wizard of Oz* (1939). Need? "People," from *Funny Girl* (1964). Heartbreak? "A House Is Not a Home," from *Promises, Promises* (1968). The list goes on and on and on.

One answer to the question What is a good musical? could be A good musical is an in-depth exploration of the wide range of human emotions, putting on display those qualities that make us human, give us character, and reflect who we are and how we live—through song, narrative, dance, direction, acting, lighting and sound and set and costume design, and a host of other artful actions in the service of that exploration and display.

The question has been asked. Does that answer satisfy? If not, or even if yes, may you continue to go to musicals on stage and in film and keep asking the question, keep looking for the answer.

Don't forget to enjoy yourselves. And bring a friend. Or two.

Bibliography

Altman, Rick. 1987. *The American Film Musical.* Bloomington: Indiana University Press.

Astaire, Fred. 1959. *Steps in Time: An Autobiography.* New York: Cooper Square.

Barrios, Richard. 1995. *A Song in the Dark: The Birth of the Musical Film.* New York: Oxford University Press.

Berger, Marilyn. 1989. "Irving Berlin, Nation's Songwriter, Dies." *New York Times,* September 23, pp. 1, 48.

Bergstrom, Signe. 2017. *The Art and Making of* The Greatest Showman. San Francisco: Weldon Owen.

Bloom, Ken. 2005. *The American Songbook: The Singers, the Songwriters, and the Songs.* New York: Black Dog & Leventhal.

Bloom, Ken, and Frank Vlastnik. 2008. *Broadway Musicals: The 101 Greatest Shows of All Time.* Revised ed. New York: Black Dog & Leventhal.

Brantley, Ben. 2012. *Broadway Musicals from the Pages of the New York Times.* New York: Abrams.

Cote, David. 2005. *Wicked: The Grimmerie, a Behind-the-Scenes Look at the Hit Broadway Musical.* New York: Hyperion.

Denkert, Darcie. 2005. *A Fine Romance: Hollywood/Broadway.* New York: Watson-Guptill.

DK Publishing. 2015. *Musicals: The Definitive Illustrated Story.* New York: DK/Penguin Random House.

Fordin, Hugh. 1996. *MGM's Greatest Musicals: The Arthur Freed Unit.* Cambridge, MA: Da Capo Press.

Green, Stanley, and Cary Ginell. 2014. *Broadway Musicals, Show by Show.* 8th ed. Milwaukee, WI: Applause Theatre & Cinema Books.

Grode, Eric. 2015. *The Book of Broadway: The 150 Definitive Plays and Musicals.* Minneapolis, MN: Voyageur Press.

Hemming, Roy. 1986. *The Melody Lingers On: The Great Songwriters and Their Movie Musicals.* New York: HarperCollins.

Hirschhorn, Clive. 1981. *The Hollywood Musical.* Portland, OR: Octopus Books.

Holden, Stephen. 1987. "Irving Berlin's American Landscape." *New York Times,* May 10.

Hoppin, Richard H., ed. 1978. *Anthology of Medieval Music.* New York: Norton.

Kantor, Michael, and Laurence Maslon. 2010. *Broadway: The American Musical.* Updated and revised ed. Milwaukee, WI: Applause Theatre & Cinema Books.

Kimball, Robert. 2001. *The Complete Lyrics of Irving Berlin.* New York: Knopf.

Levenson, Steven, Benj Pasek, and Justin Paul. 2017. *Dear Evan Hansen: Through the Window.* New York: Grand Central Publishing.

Miranda, Lin-Manuel, and Jeremy McCarter. 2016. *Hamilton the Revolution*. New York: Grand Central Publishing.

Purdum, Todd S. 2018. *Something Wonderful: Rodgers and Hammerstein's Broadway Revolution*. New York: Henry Holt.

Sennett, Ted. 2001. *Song and Dance: The Musicals of Broadway*. Chicago: Metro Books.

Sondheim, Stephen. 2010. *Finishing the Hat: Collected Lyrics (1954–1981) with Attendant Comments, Principles, Heresies, Grudges, Whines and Anecdotes*. New York: Borzoi Books.

_____. 2011. *Look, I Made a Hat: Collected Lyrics (1981–2011) with Attendant Comments, Amplifications, Dogmas, Harangues, Digressions, Anecdotes and Miscellany*. New York: Borzoi Books.

Stempel, Larry. 2010. *Showtime: A History of the Broadway Musical Theater*. New York: W. W. Norton.

Sutton, Dana Ferrin. 1993. *Ancient Comedy: The War of the Generations*. Woodbridge, CT: Twayne.

Viertel, Jack. 2016. *The Secret Life of the American Musical*. New York: Farrar, Straus & Giroux.

Webb, Clifton, and David L. Smith. 2011. *Sitting Pretty: The Life and Times of Clifton Webb*. Jackson: University Press of Mississippi.

Zimm, Michael. 2018. "If You Want Your Child to Succeed, Don't Sell Liberal Arts Short." *Wall Street Journal*, March 3–4, p. A13.

Index